FROM SCOTLAND TO CANADA:
THE LIFE OF PIONEER MISSIONARY
ALEXANDER STEWART

FROM SCOTLAND TO CANADA

THE LIFE OF PIONEER MISSIONARY
ALEXANDER STEWART

Glenn Tomlinson

FOREWORD BY **DONALD E. MEEK**
AFTERWORD BY **MICHAEL A.G. HAYKIN**

www.joshuapress.com

Published by
Joshua Press Inc., Guelph, Ontario, Canada
Distributed by
Sola Scriptura Ministries International
www.sola-scriptura.ca

First published in 2008.
© 2008 Glenn Tomlinson. All rights reserved. This book may not be reproduced, in whole or in part, without written permission from the publishers.

© 2008 Cover and book design by Janice Van Eck.
Edited and indexed by Janice Van Eck. Proofread by Karen Vanzanden.

About the cover… There are no known engravings, paintings or photographs of Rev. Alexander Stewart, the subject of this book. The cover shows the River Tay winding through Perthshire, with Kinnoull Hill and Tower in the foreground (Photograph © Louise McGilviray). Alexander Stewart's signature is reproduced courtesy of the Baldwin Room, Toronto Reference Library, Toronto, Ontario.

Library and Archives Canada Cataloguing in Publication

Tomlinson, Glenn, 1967-
    From Scotland to Canada: the life of pioneer missionary Alexander Stewart / Glenn Tomlinson.

Includes bibliographical references and index.
ISBN 978-1-894400-29-9

    1. Stewart, Alexander, 1774-1840. 2. Baptists—Ontario—Clergy—Biography. 3. Missionaries—Ontario—Biography. 4. Baptists—Scotland—Clergy—Biography. 5. Jarvis Street Baptist Church (Toronto, Ont.)—History. I. Title.

BV2813.S86T64 2008   286'.1092   C2008-903189-X

To my beloved wife Sonja
...*who always knew that the underlying reason for many of our travels was the pursuit of Alexander Stewart*

Contents

Foreword *by Donald E. Meek*   9
Acknowledgements   13
Introduction   15

FROM BIRTH TO REBIRTH
1 Logierait and Moulin: Alexander's early life   23

THE INFLUENCE OF THE HALDANES
2 Alexander Stewart's call to the ministry   43
3 Missionary to the north of Scotland   57
4 Alexander Stewart the Baptist   63

BAPTIST MISSIONARY: FROM THE HIGHLANDS TO UPPER CANADA
5 A church home in Perth   75
6 Baptist missionary to Canada   87

THE FIRST BAPTIST CHURCH, YORK, UPPER CANADA
7 The mission field at York   101
8 York's first Baptist church   113

ITINERANT PREACHER IN ESQUESING AND ENVIRONS
9 Norval: the church in the woods   123
10 Missionary in "the land of the tall pines"   131

YORK: THE RETURN OF A BAPTIST PRESENCE
11 Participating in the voice of reform   139
12 Alexander Stewart's theology   147
13 Rallying the Baptists of York   161

GROWTH IN THE MIDST OF SADNESS
    14 Building March Street Baptist Church   177

YEARS OF DECLINE
    15 Reasons for dissension   193
    16 Maxwell, Caldicott, and the schism of 1836   205

A PERSEVERING SAINT
    17 Observing Toronto's Baptists   219
    18 The death of a saint   227

Conclusion   235
Afterword *by Michael A.G. Haykin*   239

Appendix A: Roll of members, Perth Baptist church, 1812-1815   243
Appendix B: Roll of members, York Baptist church, 1818-1820   245
Appendix C: Petition of James Smith, Alex Stewart, Thos Smith   247
Appendix D: A sermon on baptism, by Alexander Stewart   259
Appendix E: Hymns written by Alexander Stewart   279
Appendix F: Roll of members, York Baptist church, 1827-1840   283
Appendix G: The York Auxiliary Bible Society   287
Appendix H: Marriage register   291

Biographical glossary   297
Bibliography   317
Credits   325

Index   327

Foreword

As an academic with a deep interest in the itinerant Baptist and Congregational preachers who travelled tirelessly through the Highland glens and out to the islands of the Hebrides (to which I belong), I have been enthralled by Pastor Glenn Tomlinson's splendid account of the life and labours of Alexander Stewart. It was very evident to me at an early stage in my research (beginning in the mid-1980s) that the Moulin awakening of 1797 to 1798 was a defining moment in the spiritual history of Perthshire and the entire Grampian area. It brought a parish minister to a saving knowledge of Christ, and through him gospel power was transmitted to others, including the subject of this biography, whose hearts likewise began to "burn within them". As a result of the training and funding provided by Robert and James Haldane, several of these men were enabled to become itinerant preachers, and their labours had a transforming effect on many parts of the Highlands and Islands, far beyond Perthshire. Through processes of social change that encouraged, and even necessitated, emigration, the new, robustly evangelical impulses that electrified the Highland glens and far-flung Hebrides were carried even further afield — across the Atlantic to North America and as far as Australia. In North America, Highlanders like Alexander Stewart began to gather like-minded men and women around them, and these small gatherings laid the foundations of churches such as Jarvis Street Baptist Church in Toronto.

Such men were often "rough diamonds". Their faith and practice were shaped by rugged terrain and, frequently, by harsh opposition. They knew what faith cost, and it was precious to them. They were often defensive and "difficult", but their work, forged in adversity, had an enduring quality, very different from the spiritual froth of a later day. The roll-call of Highland-born preachers of Baptist persuasion in Canada —all of them "rugged individualists"— includes Dugald Sinclair (who allied himself latterly with the Disciples of Christ), William Fraser and Duncan Cameron (both of whom pastored Breadalbane Baptist Church in Glengarry County, Ontario). It has been my pleasure to discover a little of their lives and to be humbled by their self-effacing achievements.

As I discovered when researching the life and work of Dugald Sinclair, which necessitated an all-night session in the National Library of Canada, it is extremely difficult to locate the raw material which is the essential foundation for a fair-minded biography of this kind. Only painstaking effort, and diligent analysis, will reassemble the fragmented picture. The need to cull material from sources in both Scotland and North America can be a deterrent to the fainthearted. Glenn Tomlinson, however, is not of that number, and like the early itinerant preachers in the Highlands, he has been prepared to go the extra ten miles to find the "wandering sheep." The result is a very precise, very moving and very readable account of "Brother Stewart." Guided by Pastor Tomlinson's penetrating insight, and strengthened by a wealth of judicious detail, we follow Alexander Stewart as a preacher in the northern Highlands, in the Rothiemurchus and Elgin areas, and then in Perth, and finally across the Atlantic. His spiritual pilgrimage, from Congregationalist to Baptist, is as well charted as his Atlantic voyage and his later work in what was then Upper Canada. The town of York, which became Toronto, was the principal scene of his labours.

Like most of his kind, Stewart was an evangelical activist whose ceaseless, God-centred toil influenced not only the souls of men and women but also their perspectives on politics, education, Bible distribution and ecclesiology. In this book, we can see the full orb of Stewart's interests, and, from our twenty-first-century vantage-point, we can but marvel that men like him, plucked as brands from the burning, with little formal instruction, could, and did, operate at so many different levels and to such good effect. Such is the miracle of grace. It is also part of the miracle of grace that a witness is maintained despite the faults and failings of the "earthen vessels" to whom faith is entrusted. Alexander Stewart was irascible, dogged and, at times, seemingly obstinate (as a Scottish Baptist!) to the point of separation. Glenn Tomlinson has written honestly about his subject, and we can all learn our much-needed lessons quietly from the complex canvas of Stewart's life.

This book is a labour of great love and fine scholarship that places before us the achievements of a life, with all its imperfections, well lived in the cause of Christ, on both sides of the Atlantic Ocean. It gives me immense pleasure to note that the earlier sections of this book build substantially on the foundations which I and my very good friend, the Rev. Dr. William D. McNaughton, have attempted to lay in our various books and studies. By focusing so ably on the life of one preacher, Glenn Tomlinson takes the story further, and puts all of us greatly in his debt — but our debt to Alexander Stewart and others like him can never be measured fully or repaid on this side of eternity. Stewart may have been a rough diamond, but the diamond shines in this biography, and will continue to do so "more and more unto the perfect day."

Donald E. Meek
Professor of Scottish and Gaelic Studies, University of Edinburgh

Acknowledgements

To complete a book on a relatively unknown figure like Alexander Stewart necessitates the use of many archival repositories and requires some timely providences. I want to direct my ackowledgments in those two veins. First, to the congregation of Jarvis Street Baptist Church, Toronto, many thanks for giving me the freedom to root through your treasure trove of old documents and for allowing me to transcribe your first book of minutes. To the Canadian Baptist Archives at McMaster University, I am grateful for the preservation of a key letter of John Menzies which contained the first tangible evidence I ever found relating to the beginnings of the Baptist cause in Toronto. To the Baldwin Room, Toronto Reference Library, I am thankful for the conservation of Stewart's business papers and John Eglinton Maxwell's diary, both of which shed much light on Stewart's later ministry in Toronto. And perhaps most importantly, to the Thomas Fisher Rare Book Library at the University of Toronto, I am most grateful for your acceptance of the gift of Louis Melzack, whose collection contained Stewart's journal and sermon register and provided the critical bridge between his ministry in Perth, Scotland, and Toronto, Canada.

Second, to Dr. Donald Meek and to Dr. William McNaughton, I am most appreciative for their relatively recent and respective studies on the Baptist and Congregational itinerant experience in Scotland, without which I would have never understood Stewart's Scottish ministry. And to Dr. Michael A.G. Haykin, my sincerest thanks for discovering Stewart's "second" letter in *The New Evangelical Magazine & Theological Review* that led to a previously published letter of his and solidified the birth date of the Toronto Baptists. And also to Dr. Haykin, my heartfelt thanks for encouraging me to convert my roughly ten years of research into the story of Alexander Stewart.

Finally, to my Lord and Saviour Jesus Christ, goes all my praise. I marvel at his grace in using such men as Stewart — "warts and all" — as it encourages me to serve him all the more in his kingdom, despite my frailties. *Soli Deo Gloria.*

Introduction

I have been asked many times over the course of my research into the life of Alexander Stewart (1774-1840) why I have an interest in such an obscure character in the history of Christ's church? And even more to the point, what relevance does his life have for the reader as the church begins the third millennium?

The challenge of history: reconstructing a life

From a personal point of view I have always been intrigued by mysteries. One such mystery that presented itself to me was in the origin of the church I attended. As I began my research into the beginnings of the Jarvis Street Baptist Church, Toronto, Canada, I became increasingly frustrated with the lack of information available on the subject. However, the really enticing mysteries are the ones that are fraught with difficulties, for then the solution becomes so much more satisfying! I was determined to succeed where others had failed. The following "lost cause" — evident by the following inconsistent and ambiguous statements — made me even more determined in my quest:

> The first meeting of which we have any official record, was held on the 16th of October 1829, when the late Joseph Wenham, Esq., of the Bank of Upper Canada, was appointed to keep a regular account of the transactions of the Church. It would seem from incidental allusions in the minutes that one or more meetings, or consultations, had been held before, but there is no record of what was said or done at these supposed meetings. The old Church records are very meagre, being confined to the dry statement of facts or resolutions. No list of the constituent members has been preserved in the Church books, so that it is doubtful whether any one now knows with certainty who were the real constituent members of the church.[1]

> The germ of the Baptist church in Toronto was planted in 1829, at which time a few people of this faith met in an upper room on Colborne street, although there was no permanency until 1840.[2]

> The origin and first name the church first bore, I could never get clearly. From the best information I could get, it appears James Beaty, sen., Peter Rutherford, Wm. McMaster, and others met with Alex. Stewart, a Scotch Baptist preacher, for some time.[3]

I feel very thankful to several old brethren who have kindly

---

1 Robert Alexander Fyfe, *A forty years survey from the Bond Street Pulpit* (Toronto: Dudley & Burns, 1876), 9-10.

2 John Ross Robertson, *Landmarks of Toronto* (Toronto: Telegram, 1914), Vol. IV, 424.

3 Joseph Ash, "History of the rise and progress of our cause in Canada." *Christian Worker*, Reminiscences No. 7, July 1883.

assisted in giving me information I was not in possession of. I have written very largely from memory, and it would be marvellous if in chronicling events covering a period of 55 years, I should not be somewhat astray in dates and some other matters. I had a great desire to do ample justice to everyone personally, and give a correct statement of every matter touched.[4]

An attempt to write a history of the Jarvis Street Baptist Church is met at the outset with difficulties, principally because of the meagre records of its early days. There is no record of the actual date of its formation.[5]

More and more I began to realize that if I were to solve the mystery of the origins of Jarvis Street Baptist Church, I would have to get to know its first pastor, Alexander Stewart. Further, as my studies continued I found my interests were changing: the desire to discover the birth date of a church was supplanted by the challenge and spiritual benefit of reconstructing a life that was devoted to the cause of Christ.

The benefits of history: an untold story

The story of Alexander Stewart is important for two reasons. First, there has been far too little written about Canadian Baptists and in particular the origin of the Baptist witness in Canada's largest city. To my knowledge Stewart's life and the history of the *first* Baptist cause in Toronto has never been told accurately or in its entirety.[6]

---

4 Ash, "Rise and progress." 21, 1884.

5 *Jarvis Street Baptist Church: directory and historical sketch* (Toronto: Dudley & Burns, 1897), 49.

6 An oft-repeated assertion is that the First Baptist Church of Toronto, founded by runaway slaves in 1826 under Elder Washington Christian (1776-1850), was Toronto's first Baptist church. However, this is incorrect. The seed of the present day Jarvis Street Baptist Church was planted in 1818 thereby making it the first Baptist work in the city.

Regrettably, the church is the poorer for it. As a member of Christ's body facing the opportunities of the twenty-first century it is vital that we call to remembrance the history of the church, its trials and triumphs. Why? King Solomon states it so simply: "There is nothing new under the sun" (Ecclesiastes 1:9, NKJV). We are to learn from our past. In the nineteenth century, Robert Alexander Fyfe (1816-1878) stated this fact eloquently as the congregation of Bond Street Baptist Church prepared to move to their new home on Jarvis Street in 1875. His text was Deuteronomy 8:2: "Thou shalt remember all the way which the Lord thy God led thee" (KJV). Fyfe said:

> A man cannot look upon a noble tree, and call to mind the various instrumentalities, in the hand of God, which contributed to give it strength, beauty and symmetry — the winds which fanned it, the storms which shook it, making it anchor itself more firmly in the soil, the rains and dews which moistened and refreshed it, and the sun which warmed it, making it bud and expand through many years — without feeling his pulses quickened and his interest increased. How much more are all our faculties aroused and stimulated, when we trace the growth and development of an immortal being, so fearfully and wonderfully made![7]

The history unfolded in the following pages is the life of one immortal being God saw fit to use.

Second, a biography of Alexander Stewart is unique because it charts the course of a man's ministry in two contexts: Scotland and Canada. There has been scant research done that duly acknowledges the relationship between the evangelical impetus on both sides of the Atlantic. Hence, a recounting of Stewart's service for God will no doubt add to the reader's understanding of both the Scottish and the Canadian evangelical experience.

---

7 Fyfe, *A forty years survey*, 6.

Alexander Stewart was a "despised Baptist". He was a man of unyielding beliefs — his character and convictions remained little changed by his circumstances and his peers, foes and friends alike. In fact, he was so unpliable at times that he has been described thus: "I believe no denomination in this country is yet wholly free from spiritual stones so peculiarly cut, that no other stone can be laid beside them."[8] However, despite his flaws of character, he was used of God; and perhaps this description of the character of the graduates of Robert Haldane's Theological Seminary, including men like Stewart, puts it best: "They were raised up in mercy to a perishing world; and if they did not succeed in drawing multitudes to their chapels, it must be ascribed, in a great measure, to the unbending principles which they ever maintained."[9]

Half a century ago, in their book *Baptists in Upper Canada before 1820*, Stuart Ivison and Fred Rosser decried the fact that "details of his [Stewart's] service among the churches are lacking."[10] What follows is an attempt to shed some light on Alexander Stewart's life and times: the story of a man devoted to the cause of Christ's kingdom and of the many people who were touched by his influence.

Of course, an account such as this is never restricted to the exploits of just one person. Therefore, a biographical glossary has been included at the end of this book, listing those individuals who impacted the life of Alexander Stewart and vice versa.

If at times I wax devotional and let a "Praise God" or an "Amen" slip onto the pages of this work, the reader will forgive me and know that I am simply celebrating the magnanimity of God's sovereign mercy throughout the course of history with a view to the future triumph of his church. I trust that you will both learn and be encouraged by this look at the life of Alexander Stewart.

---

8 Fyfe, *A forty years survey*, 14.
9 Alexander Haldane, *The lives of Robert Haldane of Airthrey, and of his brother, James Alexander Haldane* (Edinburgh: The Banner of Truth Trust, 1990), 331.
10 Stuart Ivison and Fred Rosser, eds., *The Baptists in Upper and Lower Canada before 1820* (Toronto: University of Toronto Press, 1956), 149.

Section 1

From birth to rebirth

1774-1799

Chapter 1

Logierait and Moulin: Alexander's early life

The parish registers of the Scottish Kirk[1] indicate that Alexander Stewart was born and raised among the heather-laden hills of Perthshire. These early records show that Alexander was the youngest of eight known children born to James Stewart and Margaret Scott who were married in Moulin on April 2, 1752. The birth order and names of their children are as follows:

Donald, baptized 4 February 1753, in Moulin.
Anabil, baptized 24 August 1760, in Moulin.
John, baptized 9 May 1762, in Moulin.
James, baptized 1 July 1764, in Moulin.
Hellen, born 7 July 1765, in Logierait.
Margaret, baptized 20 March 1768, in Logierait.
Janet, baptized 7 April 1771, in Logierait.

---

1 "Kirk" is the Scottish idiom for church.

Alexander, baptized 31 July 1774, in Logierait.²

While this family tree is dry, in and of itself, we are fortunately not left totally to our own musings to wonder what the life and surroundings of the Stewarts was like. In fact, two villages appear in the parish account, the description of which will assist us in visualizing the first twenty-five years of Alexander's life. Further, both places of Highland settlement figure prominently in Stewart's life story: Logierait, the place of his birth, and Moulin, the place of his rebirth.

The place of his birth: Logierait, Perthshire

"The village of Logierait, small in size and unimposing in appearance as it now is, figures as a place of much note in our ancient annals."³ William Marshall penned these words in his *Historic Scenes of Perthshire* in 1879, and no doubt Alexander was aware of the ties his birthplace had to figures of royalty and Scottish patriotism.⁴ His childhood explorations would have taken him to the castle near

---

2   Parish registers of Logierait & Moulin, Perthshire, Scotland.

3   William Marshall, *Historic scenes in Perthshire* (Edinburgh: Wm. Oliphant & Co., 1879), 162.

4   Four years prior to the writing of these words another one of Logierait's sons would return to his native village. That this individual was baptized in the same town as Alexander Stewart and that he would later become a prominent member in the same congregation that Stewart founded in Canada, although two generations later, strikes this writer as a testimony to God's overarching providence in all the affairs of his creation. The Honorable Alexander Mackenzie (1822-1892), born in Logierait, was Canada's second prime minister (1873-1878) and a member of the Jarvis Street Baptist Church, Toronto. He returned to his native Scotland in 1875 and was described thus: "Mr. Mackenzie's replies on all these occasions were worthy of one of nature's nobles, and of the Premier of Canada. They were full of good sense, and of patriotic and philanthropic feeling. They shewed, too, a thorough mastery of political science, and an ardent devotion to the advancement and welfare of humanity. The style of them, moreover, bespoke the school in which the speaker had received his education, 'the best of all schools'... the school of honest labour. No word-painting in them. No verbiage to becloud and oppress. The thought clear as crystal; and the diction conveying it with a naturalness and a force, which made it at once understood and felt by every hearer" (Marshall, *Historic scenes in Perthshire*, 164).

the village which was once a Royal residence, having been told how Robert III (1340-1406) occupied Logierait as a hunting seat. Further, as the youngest of eight children, and no stranger to sibling conflicts, he would have been reminded time and again by his "arbiter" father how the village was once the seat of the Court of Regality. Here the Lords of Athole administered feudal justice from the twelfth century until the abolition of hereditary jurisdiction in 1748. Hence, the village of his birth was aptly named: "*Logie* meaning a hollow, and *rait* meaning arbitration or settlement of differences — Logierait, thus interpreted, being the hollow in which differences were judicially settled."[5] One wonders whether disputes in the Stewart household were "judicially settled" in the mind of the young Alexander!

As Alexander traced the lines of the village jail, where such justice was often served, he may have imagined himself as the infamous Rob Roy MacGregor (1671-1734), who made good his escape from that prison in 1717, thus adding to his legend. Indeed, there was plenty of folklore in this small village that would capture the fears and dreams and occupy the time of a young lad. However, if asked what village figured prominently in his life's story, I have no doubt that Alexander Stewart would have answered, "Moulin."

The place of his rebirth: Moulin, Perthshire

Only a few miles distant from Alexander Stewart's birthplace, nestled beneath Ben Vrackie mountain was the sister village of Moulin; and like Logierait, it too was not without its claims to Scottish lore. One such historical event that had burned itself into the national consciousness of Scotland was the Battle of Killiecrankie. The peace of this beautiful gorge, just northwest of Moulin, was shattered in 1689 when the first shots of the Jacobite Rebellion were fired — the purpose of the cause was to restore the exiled Stuarts to the throne of Scotland. The Stewart family's parish minister commented thus:

---

5 Marshall, *Historic scenes in Perthshire*, 162.

26 FROM SCOTLAND TO CANADA

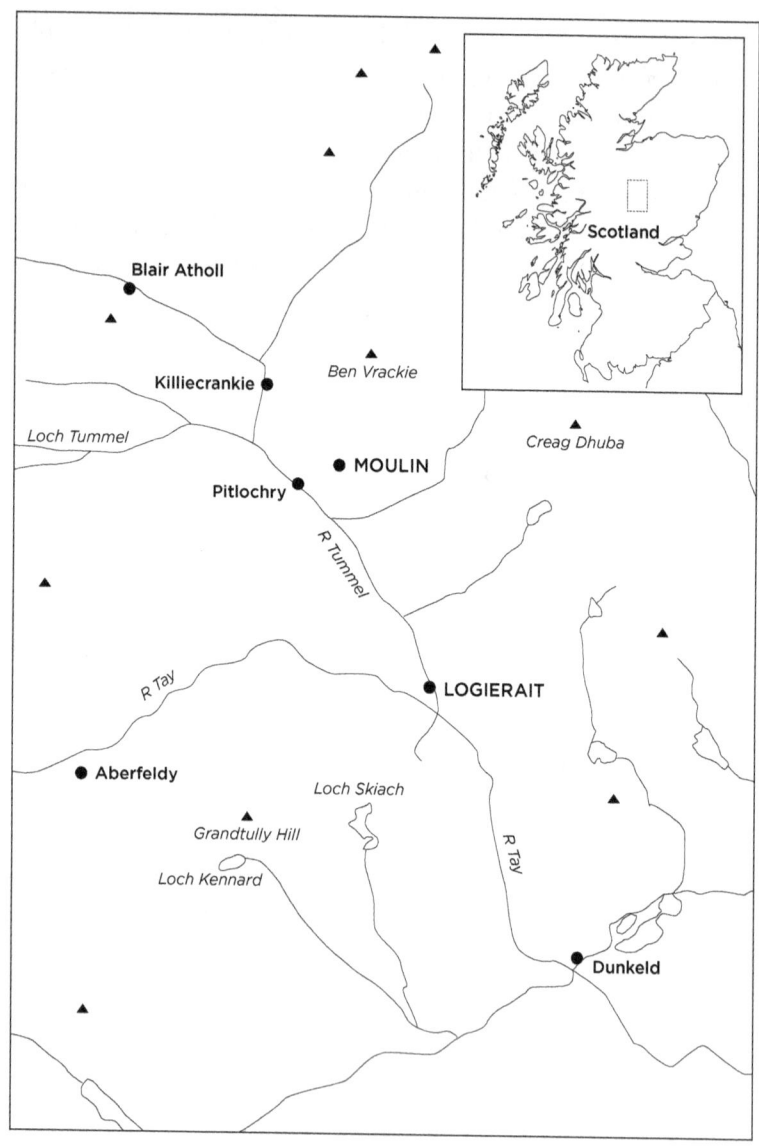

LOGIERAIT, MOULIN AND ENVIRONS

One day I rode out of my way on purpose to see the pass of Killicranky, a deep, narrow gully, of about a mile long… its very silence was grim. I recollected the many tales I had heard of goblins and demons being seen or heard to yell in this den. I began to think the vulgar faith in such apparitions not so unnatural as I used to account it. Such is the influence of local scenery over the imagination, and the power of the imagination over the understanding.[6]

Moulin had a castle as well—actually, the remains of a castle. Young Alexander would likely have been discouraged from taking a closer look at the *Chaisteal Dubh Mhaothlinne* (the Black Castle of Moulin), for the structure itself was unstable, and if this attribute did not inhibit Alexander's curiosity, the old castle's reputation certainly would have. Local tradition spoke of a time when certain doomed and infected citizens were shut up in the castle to prevent one of the many plague infestations from spreading. Thereafter, the castle was always associated with pestilence. Consequently, this engendered a healthy respect, or rather a fear, among the Moulinites. In fact, it deterred them "from meddling with the ruins, and applying the stones to any of the purposes of modern utilitarianism."[7] Indeed, there was much in and around this village that could stir the imagination of a child and even ignite the superstition of an adult! Interestingly, the town's history of warfare and the blackness of its castle's history were merely reflective of the people's state before God: a state of continual rebellion and utter ruin.

Late eighteenth-century Moulin was in spiritual darkness. The Stewart family lived without God, and the parish minister himself did not know Jesus Christ. This is not to say that the Highlanders

---

6 Alexander Stewart, *Memoirs of the late Rev. Alexander Stewart, D.D. One of the ministers of Canongate, Edinburgh; to which are subjoined, a few of his sermons* (Edinburgh: Wm. Oliphant & Co., 1822), 21-22. This book was authored anonymously by James Sievewright.

7 Marshall, *Historic scenes in Perthshire*, 169.

were irreligious. On the contrary, they had the Scriptures in Gaelic, their native tongue. The New Testament, the Book of Psalms, and the *Catechism* of the Scottish Kirk were all read in their schools. The people had some knowledge of the principal stories of Scripture and also had a cursory understanding of some of the great Christian doctrines. However, on the whole, their knowledge was deficient, superficial, often confused, and incorrect. Very few knew the heart of the Christian gospel: that a sinner may be reconciled to God only through faith in the work of his Son, Jesus Christ. Oh, the visible form of religion was there, but as Moulin's rector *later* reflected, the "heart" was absent:

> Our people were alike strangers to the true fear and true love of God. They had evidently little concern about the present, or the future state of their souls. They attended church, and partook of the sacraments, and rested from their work on the Sabbath. But these outward observances were almost the only appearances of religion. There was little reading of the Scriptures at home; little religious instructing of children; hardly any family-worship; no religious conversation; no labouring in any manner for the meat which endureth unto everlasting life. Even on the Lord's day, most of the time was spent in loitering, visiting, and worldly talk; and other days, religion was scarcely thought of.[8]

Such was the lack of true spiritual character in the Stewart family and in the parishioners of Moulin.

Much of what has been described could be attributed to many other towns in Scotland in the late 1700s. However, God had something spectacular in mind for the region surrounding Logierait and Moulin that would set them apart in the annals of church

---

8   Stewart, *Memoirs of the late Rev. Alexander Stewart,* 28-30.

history. It has already been alluded to that Alexander Stewart would be converted in Moulin but it is the instrument and the extent of a *greater* awakening in this town that makes the story worth retelling.

The conversion of the parish minister

The events surrounding the Spirit's reviving work in the heart of Alexander Stewart, and the approximately seventy Moulinites who received Jesus Christ as their personal Saviour, cannot be fully appreciated without recounting the quickening of Moulin's own parish minister. In his latter years he would receive the degree of Doctor of Divinity and serve as one of the pastors of Canongate, in Edinburgh. However, these "honours" were of secondary importance when he considered his life as a servant of God in Moulin:

> The Lord was now preparing to gather to himself a fuller harvest in this place. He might have removed me as an useless incumbrance, or rather an intervening obstacle, out of the way, and subjected me to the doom of the unprofitable servant; but he was graciously pleased to spare me, and visit me in mercy, and even to employ me as one of his instruments in carrying on his own work. Glory to his name, who commanded light to shine out of darkness.[9]

Alexander Stewart (1764-1821), not to be confused with the subject of this biography, was a "professional" minister. He settled in the parish of Moulin in 1786 at the age of twenty-two. For him, the vocation of pastor was nothing more than a career choice — no divine calling or unction from above, simply an avenue through which he could enjoy the pleasures of this life. Hear his own recollections:

> Although I was not a "despiser" of what was sacred, yet I felt nothing of the power of religion on my soul. I had no

---

9   Alexander Stewart, *An account of the late revival of religion in a part of the Highlands of Scotland* (Edinburgh: J. Ritchie, 1800), 11.

> relish for its exercises, nor any enjoyment in the duties of my office, public or private. [It was] a regard to character, and the desire of being acceptable to my people, if not the only motives, that prompted me to any measure of diligence or exertion.[10]

Stewart goes on to state that he was pleased when a "diet of catechizing" was poorly attended, since that meant his work was the sooner over. As a result, he could turn his attention to the fleshly pursuits that captivated him—among them, playing at cards and reading sentimental novels! As far as his effectiveness as a preacher was concerned, his sermons had little impact, as they only addressed man's *external* actions and never proclaimed man's desperate need of a new heart:

> I had no notion of the necessity of a radical change of principle; for I had not learned to know the import of those assertions of scripture, that "the carnal mind is enmity against God"; that "if any man be in Christ he is a new creature"; and, "that except a man be born of water and of the Spirit, he cannot enter into the kingdom of God." I spoke of making the fruit good; but I was not aware that the tree was corrupt, and must first be itself good, before it could bear good fruit.[11]

Stewart would preach vain and empty words to his congregation for ten long years. However, it was not God's will that it would always be so. For, the Lord of this church desired a "radical change of principle"; indeed, he would replace Stewart's "heart of stone" and graciously give him a "heart of flesh."

And so it was that the weekend of June 22-23, 1796, became one of profound significance for Alexander Stewart and his family.

---

10 Stewart, *Revival of religion in a part of the Highlands*, 6-7.
11 Stewart, *Revival of religion in a part of the Highlands*, 8.

During these two days, Stewart's pretext of religion was replaced by *a religion of the heart*. In particular, the Holy Spirit would use two individuals as agents to lift the "scales" from his eyes: Charles Simeon (1759-1836) of Cambridge and James Alexander Haldane (1768-1851) of Edinburgh. Simeon preached twice on the Sabbath, and presided over the Lord's Supper, and both men had occasion to share the good news of the gospel with the Stewart family. Soon after their visit, Stewart was quick to write a heartfelt thank you to David Black (1762-1806), minister of St. Madoes and later of Lady Yester's in Edinburgh. Rev. Black was instrumental in bringing about the meeting of these three men. Here is an excerpt of that letter:

> What thanks do I not owe you for having directed my two late visitors to call at my cottage, as I have thus had the honour and blessing of entertaining angels unexpectedly. Messengers of grace I must reckon them, as their visit has been thus far blessed to me, more than any outward dispensation of Providence that I have met with. They were so kind as to put up with such accommodation as we could afford them, though our house was a good deal out of order on account of Mrs. Stewart's illness, and spent two nights with us... [Simeon's] sermons, and the conversation and prayers, I have no doubt, of *both* gentlemen, have indeed been eminently blessed to me. Since I first entered on my sacred office, I have not felt such a lively season as the last week has been. I had some private conversation, too, with my kind friend, Mr. Haldane, which proved not a little edifying to me. I shall not fail to return his visit when I go next to Edinburgh.[12]

Over the course of the next several months, the reality of his conversion did not wane. In a letter to Charles Simeon, dated

---

12 Alexander Haldane, *The lives of Robert Haldane of Airthrey, and of his brother, James Alexander Haldane* (Edinburgh: The Banner of Truth Trust, 1990), 139-140.

November 25, 1796, Stewart again recounts the visitation with joy: "Ever since the few happy hours in which I was blessed with your company, I have daily thought, with pleasure and gratitude, of the Lord's loving-kindness to me, in sending two of his chosen servants, so unexpectedly and so seasonably, to speak to me the words of life."[13] And so, having wrought a work of grace in the heart of Moulin's minister, the Lord of the church could now begin a saving work in the souls of the parishioners.

The Moulin Revival and the conversion of Alexander Stewart

The salvation of Moulin's minister was only the beginning of the Lord's plan for this village. Following his conversion, an immediate effect was observed in the life of the congregation. Indeed, it could be said that there was no life in the church prior to 1796! Rev. Black echoed this sentiment in a journal entry dated October 9, 1796:

> Greatly comforted of late with accounts from my friend and fellow-labourer Mr. Stewart of Moulin, whose soul has been wonderfully quickened, and much refreshed by a visit from Mr. Simeon of Cambridge, whom I was lead in a very providential manner to introduce to Mr. Stewart's acquaintance. It has proved like the beginning of a new life to him, and I trust the blessed effects of it will be experienced by his people as well as by himself. Indeed, this seems in some measure to be already the case. Blessed be God for this token of his goodness, this fresh evidence of the power of his grace.[14]

Revival winds were beginning to blow! Like the city of Corinth, the Lord had a great many people to call to himself in this place

---

13 Quoted in Haldane, *The lives of Robert Haldane and James Alexander Haldane*, 140.

14 Stewart, *Memoirs of the late Rev. Alexander Stewart*, 108-109.

CHARLES SIMEON
(1759-1836)

DAVID BLACK
(1762-1806)

(Acts 18:10) and among them was a young Alexander Stewart.

The "change in my manner of preaching, excited attention," wrote Rev. Stewart in *An Account of the Late Revival of Religion in a Part of the Highlands of Scotland*. "People began to think more, and sometimes talk together, of religious subjects, and of the sermons they heard."[15] This was the beginning of the awakening in Moulin. It began subtly, and Rev. Stewart himself was not even aware at the time of any deep or lasting impressions having been made. No doubt he viewed the tenets of the Word as new and fresh. Indeed, he noted that he began to preach the fundamentals of Christian doctrine with a new knowledge and confidence. During the next six months, from August 1797 through January 1798, Moulin's minister presented the gospel of Jesus Christ with clarity and conviction. The Spirit who had illumined his mind enabled him to declare with power "that all men are by nature enemies to God, disobedient to his law, and on that account exposed to his just indignation and curse."[16] He no longer addressed his congregation as a group of Christians but rather "as sinners, under sentence of death, and who had not as yet obtained mercy."[17] He focused on Scripture texts such as 1 Timothy 1:15: "This is a faithful saying, and worthy of all acceptance, that Christ Jesus came into the world to save sinners; of whom I am chief" (KJV). Other carefully selected passages included: Matthew 16:26; John 3:4; Romans 3:23; 5:1; 6:23; Galatians 3:10; Acts 16:30; Mark 1:15.[18] However, up to this point, the spiritual seed had only been planted and watered. Another six months would pass before God would produce a spiritual harvest in the town of Moulin.

The Lord's Supper was attended to every summer in Stewart's little parish. Typically, the number of participants numbered between

---

15 Stewart, *Revival of religion in a part of the Highlands*, 20.
16 Stewart, *Revival of religion in a part of the Highlands*, 16.
17 Stewart, *Revival of religion in a part of the Highlands*, 17.
18 John MacInnes, *The evangelical movement in the Highlands of Scotland: 1688 to 1800* (Aberdeen: Aberdeen University Press, 1951), 163.

forty and fifty. Some weeks before the observance of the ordinance, Rev. Stewart instructed his congregation as to the essence of the sacrament and of the necessity of having a "new nature" to participate. The Holy Spirit blessed the pastor's warnings and exhortations in that the number of participants did not surpass a dozen over the course of the summer! How was this a blessing? one might ask. Stewart clearly states that most kept back because they considered themselves in an unconverted state.

> Although the number of communicants was thus, for the time, diminished, yet the number of those who were brought under concern about their eternal interests was increasing. *This concern showed itself chiefly among the younger people under twenty-five or thirty.*[19]

It is interesting to observe that Alexander Stewart had just turned twenty-four years of age.

As the spring of 1799 approached, the revival was at its height. Moulin's minister began a course of sermons on the subject of regeneration that carried on into the month of July. "Seldom a week passed in which we did not see or hear of one, two, or three persons, brought under deep concern about their souls, accompanied with strong convictions of sin, and earnest enquiry after a Saviour," wrote Stewart.[20] It was at this time that the heart of the subject of this biography, Alexander Stewart, was made alive to the truths of the gospel! This was a true revival—one that flowed solely from the Holy Spirit through the exposition of God's Word. In recording the nature of this spiritual renewal, Rev. Stewart noted:

> It is observable that the work of conversion has been begun and carried on among this people, in a quiet manner without any confusion, and without those ungovernable

---

19 Stewart, *Revival of religion in a part of the Highlands,* 21-22. Author's italics.
20 Stewart, *Revival of religion in a part of the Highlands,* 26.

agitations of mind or convulsions of the body, or shrieking or fainting, which have often accompanied a general awakening in other places.[21]

Many years later, Alexander Stewart would echo the words of his spiritual father regarding the true nature of regeneration and revival:

> Some preachers have experienced so and so, and it would be sacrilege, in their view, to apply the blood of Christ in any other way. If one iota of their experience is awanting, though this may have been all the workings of a natural mind, all is wrong—the person is pronounced unfit for the gospel. Others lead their hearers, not to the gospel of Christ, but to religion, as they call it, and exhort their hearers to strive to get *this* pearl of great price. And what is this religion; this pearl of great price? Why it is a violent agitation of the body, something like the ague, the palsy—or some nervous disorder. This is called a work of God: a work of God without regard to the gospel, and in which it has no hand! This is without any knowledge of the Son of God, whom to know is eternal life! Yea, the faith of the gospel, without this conversion, as it is called, is made light of—and such as have not had these agitations are pronounced as destitute of experimental religion. No wonder such teachers deny perseverance, for it is not easy for those who are in health to persevere in fits. A healthy person may be surprised into fits for a time, but when his groundless fears are over he keeps calm. But to

---

21 Stewart, *Revival of religion in a part of the Highlands,* 28. Two generations earlier, Jonathan Edwards (1703-1758) was also careful to distance the true marks of revival from its excesses. In an answer to those who critiqued the Great Awakening in America he wrote *The distinguishing marks of a work of the Spirit of God* (1741) and *Thoughts on the revival in New England* (1742).

be serious upon this subject, those who have had these agitations without the faith of the gospel cannot stand in the faith, for they never had faith. When they fall, they fall not from God, for he never knew them, nor they him.[22]

In all, seventy individuals would come to true faith and repentance in Jesus Christ as their Saviour and Lord.[23] Further, the influence of these converts appears to have extended even to those who did not experience a change of heart. Specifically, Rev. Stewart cited the dissipation of a long cherished ritual in this part of Scotland: the revelry surrounding *late wakes*. During these occasions, those who assembled to watch the body of a deceased neighbour would engage in late-night carousing, noisy sports and excessive drinking. Thankfully, wrote Stewart, "This unnatural custom…is almost wholly discontinued in this part of the country."[24] Thus, common grace was evident in the valleys and straths of Perthshire.

Stewart also wrote of this time: "I have no doubt that the concern about religion, which has been lately awakened in this place, is already the ground of much rejoicing among the angels before the throne."[25] Indeed, Rev. Black echoed Stewart's sentiments, and gave voice to those on earth who added their praises to the angel's chorus. He had opportunity himself to preach at Moulin and verify firsthand the report he had heard. From the outset of his visit, it was plain to him that this was not a revival engineered by man: "Such a revival I never witnessed before—it is truly the doing of the Lord, and marvellous in our eyes."[26] In particular, the Moulinites he interviewed bore testimony to the grace that God had worked in their hearts. Black found that these were a people whose souls

---

[22] Alexander Stewart, *Two essays: the first, on the gospel; the second, on the kingdom of Christ; and a sermon on baptism* (York: Colonial Advocate, Wm. Lyon Mackenzie, Printer, 1827), 36.
[23] Stewart, *Revival of religion in a part of the Highlands*, 30.
[24] Stewart, *Revival of religion in a part of the Highlands*, 35.
[25] Stewart, *Revival of religion in a part of the Highlands*, 4.
[26] Quoted in Stewart, *Memoirs of the late Rev. Alexander Stewart*, 162.

had been made alive to the things of God, having "a keen appetite for the Word of God, and an evident love for the Saviour... A deep sense of unworthiness, and a strong affection for one another."[27] Finally, he remarked that,

> Dear Mr. Stewart himself is mercifully preserved humble amidst all the honour that God is conferring upon him. O may the good Shepherd watch over him, and the dear flock committed to his charge! And may the divine influence be spread abroad throughout all our congregations, that everywhere there may be a shaking among the dry bones, and that a great harvest of souls may be gathered to the Saviour![28]

Amen! Surely, this was no ordinary visitation of the Holy Spirit.

And so, young Alexander Stewart, a Scotsman and son of the Highlands, became a Christian during the revival in Moulin. As time went on, a desire to know his Lord better and to proclaim God's love to his countrymen would begin to consume him. Alexander often shared his experience, in casual conversation, of being one of those converted by the instrumentality of Mr. Stewart, Moulin, Perthshire.[29] The revival of Moulin also kindled in him a much deeper longing—a longing to be employed full time in the building of Christ's church.

---

27 Quoted in Stewart, *Memoirs of the late Rev. Alexander Stewart*, 163.
28 Quoted in Stewart, *Memoirs of the late Rev. Alexander Stewart*, 163.
29 Entry for December 5, 1832, in "Rev. William Proudfoot Diaries." (Lawson Memorial Library, University of Western Ontario, London, Ontario, Canada).

Section 2

The influence of the Haldanes

1800-1808

Chapter 2

Alexander Stewart's call to the ministry

A year and a half passed following Alexander's conversion in the spring of 1799. As he continued to sit under the teaching of Moulin's rector, God was making it clear to him that he would be more than just a flax merchant.[1] He would be a minister of the gospel. A need for intensive theological training was obvious, but where would he go and to whom should he look for guidance? Providentially, he would not have to face these decisions alone, for the Lord gave Alexander a helpmeet.

On November 16, 1800, Alexander Stewart married Janet Douglass (1770-1848) in the parish church of Logierait, Scotland.[2] She was the daughter of James Douglass and likely baptized on June 10, 1770.[3] Though four years his senior, she was definitely a kindred spirit, for she too was converted in the revival of Moulin, as her obituary in July 1848 states:

---

1 *Parochial registers*, County Perth, Parish Perth, Scotland.
2 *Parish registers of Logierait & Moulin*, Perthshire, Scotland.
3 *Parish registers of Logierait & Moulin*, Perthshire, Scotland.

On Lord's Day, the 23rd instant, after a lingering illness which she bore with Christian patience and fortitude, Janet Stewart, age 78, widow of the late Alexander Stewart, formerly Pastor of the Baptist Church in this City — The deceased was a native of the Highlands, Perthshire, Scotland, and in early life was one of the many converts to the faith of the Gospel under the faithful preaching of the celebrated Mr. Stewart, the Parish Minister of Moulin. Through a long, and latterly a weary pilgrimage, she exhibited the strong and living characteristics of the true Christian; and she died as she had lived, with the calm and unruffled hope of a glorious resurrection to eternal life, through Jesus Christ our Lord. The savour of her name will be long cherished in the recollection of her numerous friends.

"The sweet remembrance of the just
Like a green root survives and bears
When dying nature lies in dust."[4]

The two were convinced of the Lord's desire for them to spread the good news of Christ's kingdom. But would it be as a minister in the established church? No, Alexander Stewart's call would follow the example of another. It would be this man's influence and pattern of evangelism that would guide Alexander and Janet over the next eight years, and throughout the course of their lives. So, it is to the story of James Alexander Haldane that we now turn.

The model of gospel ministry: the itinerant preaching of James Haldane

No doubt the Stewarts heard the story of their pastor's visit with James Alexander Haldane and of his choice counsel that fateful weekend a few years before. But it was more than this that persuaded them to follow in his footsteps. Haldane's theology and methods of

---

4 "Death notice of Janet Stewart." *The Examiner* (Toronto: July 26, 1848).

JAMES ALEXANDER HALDANE
(1768-1851)

disseminating the gospel were appropriate—no, needed—for the times Scotland was facing. Indeed, the state of religion in Scotland was bleak at the beginning of the nineteenth century. Alexander Haldane (1800-1882), the son of James Haldane, wrote in *The lives of Robert Haldane of Aithrey and of his brother, James Alexander Haldane* that this was a darkness that "might be felt." As to the cause of the religious gloom that cast its veil over the country, Alexander Haldane left no room for conjecture. The infidelity of Adam Smith (1723-1790), David Hume (1711-1776) and their coadjutors, which had first infected the Universities and seats of learning, "had gradually insinuated its poison into the ministrations of the Church."[5] Hume, for example, was a consistent empiricist, contending that all that we can know in the universe is limited solely to our sense-experience. He rejected any notion of divine revelation. Hence, men of the Word were needed, and the Lord raised up James Haldane as a pattern for others to imitate in the task of evangelizing the lost of Scotland.

Alexander Stewart found in James Haldane a life that he could both relate to and emulate. On the one hand, it bore a likeness to his own, for Haldane was also a layman with no formal theological training, having been brought up for a career on the sea. On the other, Haldane possessed a tremendous zeal for the Lord and a concern for his fellow countrymen. His desire initially manifested itself in the village of Gilmerton, south of Edinburgh, where he preached his first sermon on May 6, 1797.[6] It was, however, an extended missionary venture that attracted the attention of others. His heart's yearning is clearly reflected in this journal entry written just prior to his first tour to northern Scotland and the Orkneys in 1797:

---

5 Alexander Haldane, *The lives of Robert Haldane of Airthrey, and of his brother, James Alexander Haldane* (Edinburgh: The Banner of Truth Trust, 1990), 130-131.

6 George Yuille, ed. *History of the Baptists in Scotland, from pre-Reformation times* (Glasgow: Baptist Union Publications, c.1926), 55.

We would not here be understood to mean that every follower of Jesus should leave the occupation by which he provides for his family to become a *public* preacher. It is an indispensable Christian duty for every man to provide for his family; but we consider every Christian is bound, whether he has opportunity, to warn sinners to flee from the wrath to come, and to point out Jesus as the way, the truth, and the life. Whether a man declare those important truths to two, or two hundred, he is, in our opinion, a preacher of the Gospel, or one who declares the glad tidings of salvation, which is the precise meaning of the word *preach*... Such are some of the arguments which have satisfied our minds that we have a right to preach the Gospel, founded both on reason and on the Word of God. We formerly hinted that our situation in life enabled us to undertake the journey without interfering with necessary avocations, and we deemed the low state of religion a sufficient call for us to go to the highways and hedges, and endeavour to compel our fellow-sinners to lay hold on the hope set before them in the Gospel. The writings of laymen in defence of Christianity have always been considered peculiarly important, as there is less ground to suspect such men of interested motives, and the clergy are naturally led to refer to such writings when the enemies of the Gospel have ascribed their zeal to ambition and priestcraft. Strange, then, if we might not *speak* on subjects on which we might have written.[7]

Haldane's itinerant tour of the north was so blessed of God that many others felt called to evangelize. They would come from all walks of life, recognizing and rejoicing in the fact that "God has chosen the foolish things of the world to put to shame the wise,

---

7 Haldane, *The lives of Robert Haldane and James Alexander Haldane*, 155-156.

and God has chosen the weak things of the world to put to shame the things which are mighty; and the base things of the world and the things which are despised God has chosen, and the things which are not, to bring to nothing the things that are" (1 Corinthians 1:27-28, NKJV). The next course of action was self-evident to the mission-minded Haldane: an organization was needed to facilitate the sending of these additional workers into the field and thus to stem the tide of moderatism.

While it is not known whether Alexander Stewart was ever an agent for "The Society for Propagating the Gospel at Home," it is apparent that he concurred with its purposes and with those the organization employed. James Alexander Haldane, who was instrumental in its founding and setting out its objectives, was one of the voices who declared on January 11, 1798:

> It is not our design to form or extend the influence of any sect. Our sole intention is to make known the Evangelical Gospel of our Lord Jesus Christ. In employing itinerants, schoolmasters, or others, we do not consider ourselves as conferring ordination upon them, or appointing them to the pastoral office. We only propose by sending them out, to supply the means of grace wherever we perceive a deficiency.[8]

Among several men who were commissioned by the Society as itinerants was a former member of the Scotch Secession church, William Ballantine (d. 1836). He was dispatched to the north to labour in places like Thurso and Elgin where a great awakening had followed the preaching of James Haldane.[9] We will see later that Stewart held Ballantine in the highest esteem—advocating Ballantine's ministry, and thus the Society's aims, and maintaining a friendship with him that would eventually span the Atlantic

---

8 Haldane, *The lives of Robert Haldane and James Alexander Haldane*, 193.
9 Haldane, *The lives of Robert Haldane and James Alexander Haldane*, 194-195.

Ocean. However, the Society was not without its enemies and as is often the case when the truth of Jesus Christ is sown, the devil and his legions demonstrate that they are always ready to undermine its planting.

The purpose of the June 2, 1799, edict of the General Assembly of the Church of Scotland was to silence the likes of Haldane and his "vagrant teachers." In particular, the Assembly prohibited all persons, who were not licensed in Scotland, from preaching the gospel in any place under their jurisdiction. In addition, they resolved that a pastoral admonition be addressed by the Assembly to all the people under their charge.[10] This pastoral letter came a day later on June 3. Four thousand copies were ordered printed and circulated, and it was appointed to be read from the pulpit of every parish the first Sunday after it had been received.[11]

> The pastoral admonition attacked by name the "Society for Propagating the Gospel at Home," and charged the *itinerant teachers* with "intruding into parishes without any call," "erecting in several places Sunday-schools," and "connecting these schools with certain secret meetings," "censuring the doctrine of the minister," as "opposed to the Ecclesiastical Establishment of the land" and acting "as if they alone were possessed of some secret and novel method of bringing men to heaven."[12]

Furthermore, the procurator of the church was empowered to proceed legally against these unauthorized teachers of Sunday Schools. This was accomplished on the strength of certain obsolete Acts of the Scottish Parliament directed against "papists" and "malignants."[13] William Ballantine was prosecuted at the Inverness

---

10 Haldane, *The lives of Robert Haldane and James Alexander Haldane*, 256.
11 Haldane, *The lives of Robert Haldane and James Alexander Haldane*, 257.
12 Haldane, *The lives of Robert Haldane and James Alexander Haldane*, 258-259.
13 Haldane, *The lives of Robert Haldane and James Alexander Haldane*, 258.

justiciary court in September 1799 on the grounds of his unauthorized celebration of marriages[14] and Haldane and his followers were to be delivered into the hands of the civil authority. (It should be noted that these declaratory acts were not rescinded until May 1842.) However, it did not matter to James Haldane and his followers for they saw the clear intent of the edict. The Act was passed not to exclude *heresy* from pulpits, but to exclude *truth*. Therefore, they would not be muted!

Haldane and the Society were strengthened in their resolve to spread the Word. Like Israel of old, "the more they were oppressed, the more they multiplied and spread" (Exodus 1:12). The Moderates' oppression of the itinerants only tended to heighten the interests of the Scottish people, in whom God had placed an insatiable hunger for the truth of the gospel. It is this fact that likely galvanized Stewart's decision to cast his lot with the Haldane camp. A quarter of a century later Alexander Stewart would echo the sentiments and the determination of James Alexander Haldane and his followers:

> I consider it my duty to use every means in my power to propagate the gospel of Christ—to point out the nature of his kingdom—and the ordinances he has set on foot in that kingdom… and while my Lord and Master enables me I am ready to defend his kingdom with its doctrine and ordinances:—nor shall I desist from the combat because I have not a silver mounted sword to fight with. I know the sword of the spirit, and I shall not fail to wield it against every enemy, in the calm spirit of the gospel of peace.[15]

---

14 Deryck W. Lovegrove, "Unity and separation: contrasting elements in the thought and practice of Robert and James Alexander Haldane." In Keith Robbins, ed. *Protestant Evangelicalism: Britain, Ireland, Germany and America c.1750-c.1950. Essays in honour of W.R. Ward* (Oxford: Basil Blackwell, 1990), 166.

15 Alexander Stewart, *Two essays: the first, on the gospel; the second, on the kingdom of Christ; and a sermon on baptism* (York: Colonial Advocate, Wm. Lyon Mackenzie, Printer, 1827), preface.

The time to prepare for ministry had come, and Stewart logically turned to one who could facilitate the theological training needed to become a herald of the gospel message: Alexander sought out his mentor's brother, Robert Haldane (1764-1842).

Preparing for gospel ministry: Robert Haldane's Theological Seminary

Robert Haldane, like his younger brother, was a man of the sea. Having finished his service in the Navy, Robert retired to the life of a country gentleman on his estate of Airthrey, near Stirling. However, "his generous mind was captured by the illusive hopes begotten of the French Revolution, and aroused from spiritual torpor."[16] Fuelled by William Carey's (1761-1834) "plunge into the abyss of Indian Heathendom," Robert's chief desire was to plan another Indian mission. However the British East India Company would not sanction the scheme, and in 1796 the plan was abandoned. Happily, Haldane conformed his will to God's, and thus he turned his attention to advancing Christ's kingdom in Scotland.

Robert could preach; his first sermon was given in a barn at Weem, near Aberfeldy, in April 1798.[17] Further, Robert could give; his resources undergirded the erection of many chapels and, for Alexander Stewart and others like him, provided a place to study the Word of God.

The idea for a theological seminary was born in the year 1798:

> [Robert] conceived the idea of educating a number of pious young men for the ministry, who might be selected, as in primitive times, from the various occupations of life, on account of their piety and promising talents, to receive instruction. Natural ability was to be one requisite, but

---

16 Yuille, *History of the Baptists in Scotland*, 55.
17 Yuille, *History of the Baptists in Scotland*, 55.

evidences of a state of grace were to be the first indispensable consideration.[18]

For nine years the able tutors of Robert Haldane's Theological Seminary trained and prepared men to go into the harvest fields of Scotland.[19] It was to this "School of the Prophets'" that God would lead Alexander and Janet Stewart—a chosen path that would further expose them to the Haldane's godly influence.

Along with the other "pious young men," Stewart studied for

---

18 Haldane, *The lives of Robert Haldane and James Alexander Haldane*, 232-233.

19 Alexander Haldane provides us with a brief historical survey of those years:

"I. The *first* class began in January, 1799, under the tuition of Mr. Ewing. In December, 1800, this class completed their term of study, and were sent to different stations as preachers. In it were John Munro, George Robertson, &c.

II. The *second* class commenced in January, 1800, at Dundee, under Mr. Innes. In this class were a few who had been catechists, and who were found to possess talents capable of being trained for the ministry. In the early part of 1801, all of this class were removed to Glasgow, and were under Mr. Ewing for fifteen months. In it were Dr. Paterson, Alexander Thomson, &c.

III. In 1801, the *third* class began in Dundee, under Mr. Innes, but its students met with a very serious interruption, being sent for a time to supply stations with preaching at the end of the first year. They, however, came to Edinburgh in 1804, and finished their term of study. In this class were Francis Dick, Alexander Kerr, &c.

IV. The *fourth* class began in Edinburgh, in 1802, under Messrs. Aikman and Wemyss, with the addition of Mr. Stephens, towards the close of the second year. In it were William Newry, Peter McLaren, &c.

V. In 1803, a *fifth* class was organized under Messrs. Aikman and Wemyss, and Stephens, Mr. Cowie taking Mr. Aikman's place during the second year. In it were Dr. Russell (Dundee), John Watson (Musselburgh), &c.

VI. The *sixth* class began in 1804, under Messrs. Wemyss, Stephens, and Cowie, for the first year, but were under Mr. Cowie alone during the second year. In this class were Alexander Knowles, John Black, &c.

VII. The *seventh* class assembled in 1805. In it were William Orme, John Neave, &c. This and the next class were under Messrs. Cowie and Walker.

VIII. The *eighth* class met in September, 1806. In it were Thomas Smith (Rotherham), Robert Aikenhead, &c. Mr. Cowie resigned the tutorship in the spring of 1808.

IX. A *ninth* class was formed in the end of 1807, and was under the care of Mr. William Walker till December, 1808, when the Seminary was given up, after having sent out nearly 300 preachers" (Haldane, *The lives of Robert Haldane and James Alexander Haldane*, 329-330).

two years with a vacation of six weeks in each year. By his own account he was educated in Edinburgh.[20] Through some ancillary evidences, one can deduce that he was in the *fourth* class, under the tutelage of James Haldane's good friend John Aikman (1770-1834).[21] Stewart's view of education was quite in harmony with the emphasis of the seminary:

> It is too common, in our day, to consider preaching a trade. Hence men send their sons to college to learn them to be ministers, the same as to learn them to be physicians or lawyers. But there is a very great difference between the different callings. Law is learned from the statutes of the land etc. Physic is learned by a minute acquaintance with the human body, and its diseases and a knowledge of medicine—but divinity is only learned by the teaching of the Holy Spirit. We do not despise human learning, but value it as an excellent handmaid to Christianity—but many in this case exalt the handmaid and despise the lawful wife.[22]

The course of study was quite rigorous. Alexander and the rest of the students received lectures in systematic theology, English grammar and rhetoric, and the Greek and Hebrew languages. Once per week, Alexander was required to deliver a sermon before the class, while John Aikman would make some concluding observations. As with all the students, Stewart was financially supported,

---

20 J.G. Hodgins, ed. *Documentary history of education in Upper Canada, 1790-1840*, Vol. 1 (Toronto: Warwick Bros. & Rutter, 1894), 251.

21 The *Parochial registers*, County Perth, Parish Perth, indicate that Alexander and Janet's first child, Catherine Oswald Stewart was baptized on February 6, 1803, by Rev. James Alexander Haldane, Minister of the Dissenting Congregation in Edinburgh. She was named for Robert Haldane's wife, Catharine Oswald. Further, in 1827 Stewart states that he had attended to the ordinance of the Lord's Supper for twenty-four years (Stewart, *Two essays*, 71). Presumably, Stewart commenced administering the Lord's Supper after the completion of his theological studies, sometime in 1803.

22 Stewart, *Two essays*, 42.

had medical attendance when needed, his education and books were given to him, and he had access to a large and well-selected library—all at the expense of Robert Haldane.[23]

Stewart, while certainly appreciating this theological training, always hearkened back to God's call on his life and recognized that this fact was paramount when considering his suitability as a minister of the gospel:

> Human learning however good in its place, and extensive in its acquirements, will never teach one particle of the saving knowledge of the gospel. All the learning absolutely necessary for preaching Christ crucified, is such a knowledge of languages to be able to speak with propriety—otherwise, to be able to convey truth in a plain, simple, intelligible manner; so as to be understood by the weakest capacity. A man who is truly taught by God, with this degree of learning, will both instruct the people of God, and convince gainsayers.—Whatever more knowledge he can acquire, in the original languages etc etc. will be useful to himself and others; but the knowledge of the statutes of Heaven is the chief thing. This is the true ministerial qualification. If a Demosthenes had the degree of Barrister conferred upon him, he could not act without the knowledge of the statutes of the land—nor could he act as a Divine, without the knowledge of the pure gospel though created Dr. of Divinity, Bishop, or Pope. It is in the school of Christ the gospel is learned. All his people, and ministers, are taught of him. He acknowledges no others.[24]

Thus, with his studies finished, a wife and now a newborn daughter, Catherine (1803-1832), to support, Stewart awaited God's guidance for a missionary station in which he could exercise his gifts.

---

23 Stewart, *Two essays*, 330.
24 Stewart, *Two essays*, 42.

The impact of the two years Alexander Stewart spent in direct contact with the Haldanes cannot be understated. Alexander would always carry with him the example of James Alexander Haldane as an itinerant missionary, and of the beneficence of his brother Robert. It was now his turn to be an "angel of mercy" to a perishing world. Stewart was to be among the "choice spirits": those efficient preachers who were sent out from the seminaries, men befitting the times in which they lived, men who were "raised up in mercy."[25]

---

25 Stewart, *Two essays*, 331.

Chapter 3

Missionary to the north of Scotland

Like so many other graduates of Robert Haldane's Theological Seminary, Stewart wasted little time in bringing the light of the gospel to his countrymen. However, it should be observed that the state of religion in Scotland had changed since the revival in Moulin. After James Haldane's last extended missionary tour was completed in 1805, and as a result of the influx of graduates from Robert Haldane's seminary, the number of faithful ministers of the gospel throughout the country was greatly increased. These missionaries, as they were called, could be found "preaching in every village and Highland glen; and in every locality they had their schools and lay agency."[1] These graduates were almost the only promoters of Sabbath schools and the only distributors of religious tracts in the destitute parts of Scotland. Thus, it was imperative to Stewart that he be used in a situation or place that was devoid of any sustained witness. Alexander's burden

---

1 Alexander Haldane, *The lives of Robert Haldane of Airthrey, and of his brother, James Alexander Haldane* (Edinburgh: The Banner of Truth Trust, 1990), 352-353.

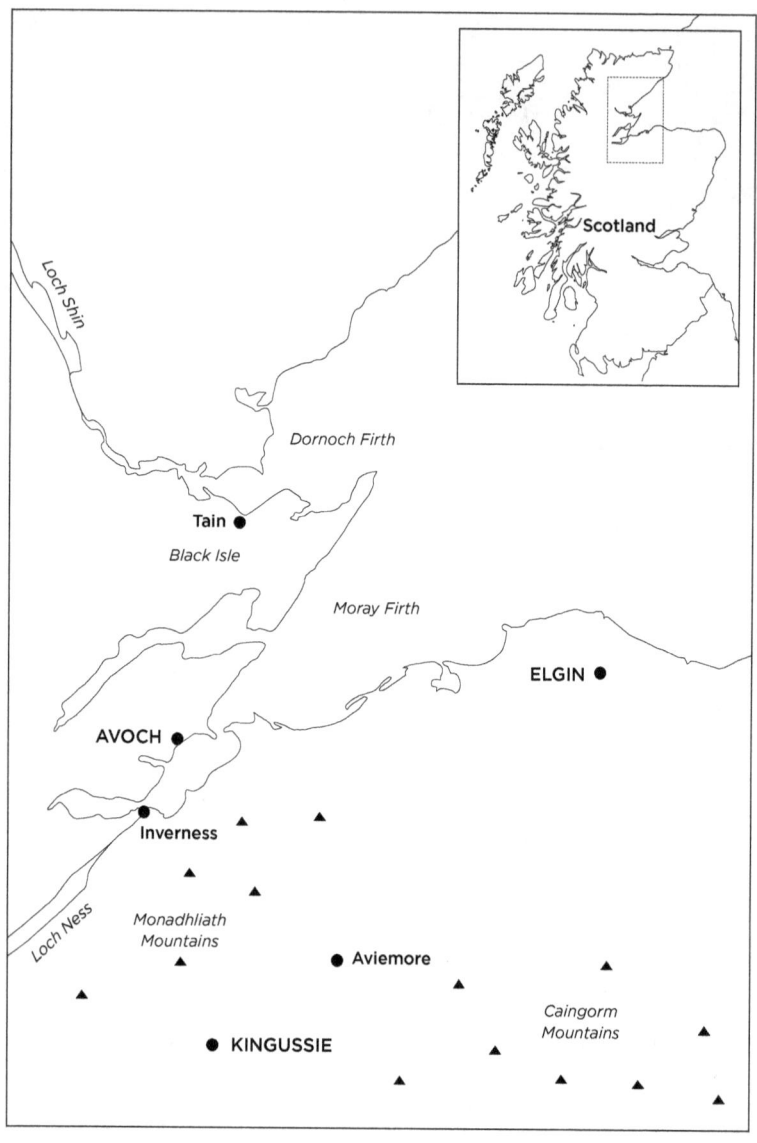

THE EASTERN
SCOTTISH HIGHLANDS

was for the people in the north of Scotland and, while the records for this period of his life are scant, a few missionary stations have yielded up some of their secrets. Doubtless the towns of Kingussie, Avoch and Elgin would ever remain dear to Stewart's heart.

Missionary to Kingussie

Kingussie, a small highland village nestled beside the River Spey in the foothills of the Cairngorm and Monadhliath Mountains, some seventy-five kilometres north of the village of Moulin, was the first scene of Stewart's missionary activities. Alexander and his family likely arrived at this centre of Highland Scotland early in 1806.[2] Here there was a small church formed as a result of the dividing of the Independent church at Rothiemurchus for the geographical convenience of the membership in 1805.[3] The new Kingussie church was led by William Hutchison (1781-1850) who pastored in that place until his death.[4] It is not known in detail nor in what capacity Stewart assisted Hutchison with the work. Nevertheless, it is obvious Alexander Stewart was needed in Kingussie. He preached the Word, assisted in administering the ordinances and fulfilled all the duties of a minister of the gospel. And, true to his itinerant nature, he continued to look for other missionary opportunities.

Missionary to Avoch

Alexander's next ministerial post was likely in Avoch—a hamlet located on the Black Isle overlooking the Moray Firth, not far

---

2 *General account of Congregationalism in Scotland from 1798 to 1848 and particular accounts referring to separate counties.* Typescript, n.d. (*c.*1848), Section 10 (Glasgow: Congregational Union of Scotland Archives), 7.

3 Donald E. Meek, *The Independent and Baptist churches of Highland Perthshire and Strathspey.* (Transactions of the Gaelic Society of Inverness, Vol.LVI, 1991), 282.

4 His gravestone bears the following inscription: "Here lies Wm. Hutchison's remains or dust/His soul in glory now enjoys its rest/By heavenly aid he ran the Christian race/At twenty years he knew the path of peace/For fifty years he served the church below" (Meek, *The Independent and Baptist churches of Highland Perthshire and Strathspey*, 319.)

from the city of Inverness. It is not surprising that he decided to come here with his little family for one of his fellow seminary students preceded him to this tiny community.

Alexander Dewar (1785-1849) attended Robert Haldane's Theological Seminary in either 1803 or 1804 making him, at the very least, an acquaintance of Alexander Stewart.[5] Upon completion of his studies in June 1805, Dewar was sent by the "Society for Propagating the Gospel at Home" to Inverness where he preached from July to October. By the end of October, Dewar was in the village of Avoch where he would serve as minister of its congregational church until his death on August 30, 1849. It would be interesting to speculate on the communication that passed between Dewar and Stewart, which brought about the latter's coming to Avoch. However, the only thing that can be deduced from contemporaneous records is that Stewart was there by the spring of 1807 and was therefore present during the founding days of the church (Dewar baptized Alexander and Janet's second child, James, on May 7, 1807 in Avoch).[6]

The village of Avoch itself had little in its external appearance that would attract anyone to it as a sphere of ministry. There was a smattering of cottages dotting the landscape but "the charms of refined manners and cultivated society were not to be expected in such an obscure spot."[7] Further, there was no chapel or parsonage built at that time. The description of the meeting house reminds one of the scene in Troas (Acts 20:7-12) where Paul delivered a lengthy discourse to his hearers: "The place of meeting was a long narrow house, without any partitions, closely seated with forms,

---

5 William D. McNaughton, ed. *The Scottish Congregational ministry, 1794–1993* (Glasgow: The Congregational Union of Scotland, 1993), 35.

6 The *Parochial registers*, County Perth, Parish Perth, indicate that Alexander and Janet's second child, James Stewart, was baptized 7 May 1807 by Rev. Alexander Dewar, Minister of the Dissenting Congregation in Avoch.

7 Robert Kinniburgh, ed. *Fathers of Independency in Scotland; or, Biographical sketches of early Scottish Congregational ministers. A.D. 1798–1851* (Edinburgh: A Fullarton & Co., 1851), 396.

and often as many were without doors as within—all hanging with profound attention upon the lips of the preacher."[8] Nevertheless, as one nineteenth-century historian of the Congregational Church in Scotland recorded:

> There was...at that period among these humble villagers something that fully compensated for the absence of some of those external appendages. There were a few eminently pious, praying people, there was deep inwrought concern of soul among many that spread like a moral infection; there was a spirit of hearing that diffused itself from the village to the surrounding country, and an inextinguishable thirst for the word, which nothing but the free publication and cordial reception of the unadulterated gospel of the grace of God could allay.[9]

Alexander Stewart, his wife Janet, their four-year-old daughter Catherine and their infant son James, remained in Avoch only for about a year. In all probability they did not leave until the church was rooted to such an extent that Alexander Dewar could continue the pastoral responsibilities alone. God's timing is always perfect, and in his providence another friend was now beckoning Stewart for assistance.

Missionary to Elgin

William Ballantine had been in the town of Elgin since 1801.[10] He ministered to the Free Presbyterian congregation on Moss Street until the end of 1803. From January 4, 1804, Ballantine served the Congregationalists, resigning his charge three years later. The edifice for the Congregational church had been erected at Robert Haldane's

---

8 Kinniburgh, *Fathers of Independency in Scotland*, 396.
9 Kinniburgh, *Fathers of Independency in Scotland*, 397.
10 McNaughton, *The Scottish Congregational ministry*, 10.

own expense.¹¹ Before leaving Elgin, Ballantine was concerned that the flock had a suitable under-shepherd—one whose sentiments and character he was familiar with and approved of. He requested that Alexander Stewart "come and labour among them for a season upon trial; and if the Church deemed him a fit person they might afterwards give him a call to the pastoral office."¹² Alexander responded to Ballantine and accept the church's invitation, likely arriving in November 1807.

However, the eight months that Stewart would spend in Elgin would not be easy, for they would reflect the tumultuous times that the Independents were facing in Scotland at large. Many of the chapels that had sprung from James Haldane's missionary tours were not initially concerned with the *minutia* of operating a church—they were content with worshipping God and receiving instruction from his Word. This also can be said of their ministers:

> At first, they had all the *prestige* which belonged to the Reformers in the Church in which they were educated, but after the institution of Congregationalism they lost this advantage, and became shackled by divisions in their own camp.¹³

So, 1808 would become a watershed for Congregationalists in Scotland, and also a period of spiritual enlightenment—a time when once again Stewart would reflect the influence of the Haldanes.

---

11 George Yuille, ed., *History of the Baptists in Scotland, from pre-Reformation times* (Glasgow: Baptist Union Publications, c.1926), 92.
12 *General account of Congregationalism in Scotland*, Section 10, 8.
13 Haldane, *The lives of Robert Haldane and James Alexander Haldane*, 353.

Chapter 4

Alexander Stewart the Baptist

Alexander Stewart's change of view as to the nature and meaning of the ordinance of baptism can be seen as a natural progression. In fact, he would not be the only Dissenting minister of the gospel to change his sentiments. By 1807, the whole Congregationalist movement would be thrown into turmoil over issues pertaining to church order. Even the Edinburgh Tabernacle, over which James Haldane presided, was not immune to this theological advance. Commenting on the church's beginnings and development, Haldane reflected that the tabernacle was founded as a place where "people of the world" could gather and hear the good news of Jesus Christ. There was little regard given to "forms of external arrangement or Church order." In fact, many of its members still partook of the sacrament in the established church. However, James Haldane recognized that it was normal, in the course of the development of a church, to consider "the apostolic order of primitive churches," and that such a consideration would necessarily produce difference of opinion, accompanied by divisions.[1] Furthermore, of all the treatises given on the nature of church governance, none had more impact on the churches of Scotland than William Ballantine's "withering blast from the north."[2]

Ballantine and the apostolic order of the primitive church

On March 31, 1807, in the town of Elgin, a pamphlet was written that would change the course of history for the Dissenting churches of Scotland. Its title is self explanatory: *Treatise on the elder's office shewing the qualifications of elders, and how the first churches obtained them; also their appointment, duties & maintenance; the necessity of a presbytery in every church; and exhortation, and the observance of every church ordinance on the Lord's Day, in order, amongst other ends, to the obtaining of elders.*[3] Some historical accounts have been emphatic in recording that the church in Elgin — and Scotland as a whole — would have been much better without Ballantine's discourse! For instance, one such record attests that Ballantine's preaching lost the "pointed searching edge" that it had when he first arrived in Elgin. More specifically, he had become preoccupied with the order of the Lord's house, introducing exhortation among the brethren and public discipline on the Lord's Day.[4] In consequence, evangelistic fervour waned and the congregation experienced a reduction in its strength. The account concludes: "Their effect upon the Church,

---

1 Alexander Haldane, *The lives of Robert Haldane of Airthrey, and of his brother, James Alexander Haldane* (Edinburgh: The Banner of Truth Trust, 1990), 354.

2 This phrase has been borrowed from Kinniburgh's *Fathers of Independency in Scotland*.

3 Interestingly, Ballantine's pamphlet was printed by Edward Lesslie (1764-1828) in Dundee. The Lesslie family would later emigrate to Canada and Edward's son, James (1802-1885), would become instrumental in the work which Alexander Stewart would pastor: March Street Baptist Church.

4 The ordinance of mutual exhortation was based on a literal interpretation of 1 Corinthians 14:31. It differed from preaching in that it could be offered by *any* male member "able" to address the congregation. It also allowed the eldership to identify those whom God had called to the eldership.

the congregation and the mind of the public was highly injurious. A spirit of speculation and contention crept in, and the congregation was reduced to a mere shadow."[5] However, this was not Ballantine's express intent nor is this a conclusion that finds agreement among all church historians. Hear Ballantine's thrust, as set out in his preface:

> The end proposed in these pages is the prosperity of the churches of Christ—to lead them to greater exertion for their own edification, that they may obtain from Jesus every blessing to render them perfect and entire, wanting nothing. There is a fullness in him for this end; and he is exalted at God's right hand to bestow it. If his churches are in any way benefited by this attempt in leading them to look up to him for every blessing, and to pay a greater regard to his word in all things, the writer of these pages will rejoice. May Jesus bless this attempt, dispel the darkness and prejudices of our minds, lead us into all truth, and make us shine as lights in the world.[6]

Lest one assumes that Ballantine wavered from his introductory purpose, one only has to read his concluding words and observe the consistency of his heartfelt desire for the church's prosperity:

> It must be confessed, that the subjects handled in the foregoing pages, are of great importance to the prosperity of the churches of Christ. If what is said upon them is deduced

---

5   *General account of Congregationalism in Scotland from 1798 to 1848 and particular accounts referring to separate counties*. Typescript, n.d. (*c*.1848), Section 10 (Glasgow: Congregational Union of Scotland Archives), 8.

6   William Ballantine, *Treatise on the elder's office shewing the qualifications of elders, and how the first churches obtained them; also their appointment, duties & maintenance; the necessity of a presbytery in every church; and exhortation, and the observance of every church ordinance on the Lord's Day, in order, amongst other ends, to the obtaining of elders* (Edinburgh: J. Ritchie, 1807), v-vi.

from the word of God, it becomes us readily to obey. The author is aware, that, in attempting to state what he judges is very clearly taught in the Scriptures concerning the elder's office, he has at every turn met prejudices deeply rooted in the minds of even believers themselves. But, beloved brethren, we ought implicitly to receive the word of God, however contrary it is, as it must be, to all our former notions in religion. We can in no other way be divested of those prejudices that obstruct our growth in the knowledge of God's will, but by receiving with meekness every part of his word.[7]

The repercussions of Ballantine's written exhortations, on the eldership and the structure of the church, were swift. Like the Bereans of old, pastors across Scotland committed themselves to prayer and studying the Scriptures, seeking to discern God's will in these matters. One itinerant minister—Alexander Stewart himself—"had gone into all these peculiarities" and was convinced of the Scriptural truth of Ballantine's arguments.[8]

This examination of the structure of the church and its eldership naturally led to an analysis of church membership. And, a re-evaluation of the ordinance of baptism soon followed.

The baptism of the James Haldane

James Alexander Haldane had often thought about the doctrine of believer's baptism even prior to his considerations on church government. However, he had refrained from pursuing this matter out of a fear of diminishing his usefulness in gospel ministry. Nevertheless, the recurrence of doubts in his mind about infant baptism led him to conclude that he had not fully fathomed the subject. Towards the end of 1804, he determined to search the Scriptures and commit the matter to prayer, asking that the Holy Spirit would lead him to a

---

7 Ballantine, *Treatise on the elder's office*, 135.
8 *General account of Congregationalism in Scotland*, Section 10, 8.

proper understanding of the ordinance. This he did over the next few years, examining the Word and consulting the evangelical divines on the subject. As he progressed in these disciplines, his doubts as to the biblical support for infant baptism steadily increased—so much so, that on one occasion, when asked to administer the ordinance, he refrained. "(He) was obliged to inform the Church, that, although his mind was not made up to become himself a Baptist, yet that, at present, he could not conscientiously baptize children."[9] Finally, he resolved that the more *simply* he followed the Lord, the more *useful* he should in reality be. By March 1808, James Haldane was baptized; his brother Robert followed later that year.[10]

It should be highlighted that James and Robert Haldane always regarded baptism, and thus participation in the Lord's Supper, as a matter of forbearance.[11] They consequently always distanced themselves from those who exhibited a bitter and intolerant spirit in these matters. In fact, on one occasion, while walking by the side of one of his plantations on the undrained moss at Auchingray, James stopped and pointed to the slow and stunted growth of some young trees, as contrasted with the rapid growth of those which had been planted on prepared soil. He said, with a smile, "There is a picture of Sandemanianism. There is life, but its expansive powers are contracted and dwarfed."[12]

The news of James Haldane's baptism spread quickly throughout the Scottish countryside. Not surprisingly, many who had been educated at the Seminary and sent by the Society would likewise

---

9 Haldane, *The lives of Robert Haldane and James Alexander Haldane*, 359.
10 Yuille, *History of the Baptists in Scotland*, 58.
11 Haldane, *The lives of Robert Haldane and James Alexander Haldane*, 359, 380.
12 Haldane, *The lives of Robert Haldane and James Alexander Haldane*, 380. Note: John Glas (1695-1773) was a Congregationalist who, along with his son-in-law Robert Sandeman (1718-1771), sought to restore what they regarded as correct New Testament church administration by a plural rather than a single eldership. Both men, in Haldane's opinion, carried the principle of non-forbearance further than any other. The main tenet of Sandemanianism was the belief that saving faith is "bare belief of the bare truth."

re-address their views on the baptism issue. A certain itinerant preacher in the town of Elgin would also search the Scriptures for an answer.

The baptism of Alexander Stewart

Within three months of James Haldane's baptism, Alexander Stewart would also be immersed in the waters of baptism as a testimony to God's redeeming grace in his life. In fact, it is probable that Stewart went to Edinburgh to have Haldane administer the ordinance.[13] According to a typescript account of the history of the Congregationalist movement in Scotland, this change was definitely not desirable:

> Mr. Stewart, though generally approved of as a preacher, was not invited by the Church to the pastoral office. It was as well he was not. Before he had been twelve months in Elgin he adopted Baptist sentiments. Mr. James Haldane had gone into these views only a few months before Mr. Stewart. He soon followed. This was a new and unexpected stroke to the Church already reduced to a mere skeleton. They had not in the least suspected this change, as he had only a few weeks before expressed himself very fully and strongly in favour of Paedo-baptist principles. It came upon them like a peal of thunder. When he announced himself as having adopted Baptist principles, he wished the Church to say if he was to be continued? Several of the members with seemingly little ceremony, or previous enquiry, adopted the same sentiments. This seemed like the death blow to the little flock. They were poor, few in number, and much dispirited. But there was among them a pious praying remnant, who prayed and mourned and wept over the desolations of Zion.[14]

---

13 Yuille, *History of the Baptists in Scotland*, 92.
14 *General account of Congregationalism in Scotland*, Section 10, 9.

However, there are multiple perspectives of history—especially church history! Hence, from a Baptist point of view, Stewart's enlightenment produced spiritual fruit. For, upon his return from Edinburgh, he instructed many others to search the Scriptures in regard to the nature of baptism. "These formed themselves into a Church of about 30 members in 1808."[15]

Alexander Stewart's adoption of Baptist sentiments was not mindless. That is, it was not solely a reflex response to his mentor's action a few months before. Rather, it came about through a simple, yet thorough, examination of the Scriptures. The end result of his study produced in him a desire to obey and follow the example and express command of his Lord, regardless of the consequences. In particular, the Spirit enabled Alexander to recognize that the tradition of infant baptism was totally unfounded in New Testament church practice. Years later, Stewart would put this challenge to his hearers, as testimony to this fact:

> Let those who contend for infant baptism point out any such passage and we will believe them. Our statutes say that all males above sixteen years of age, shall work on the high-ways—who would infer from this that infants must be militia-men, and work on the roads merely because the statute does not expressly forbid their doing so? Yet such is the absurd reasoning used respecting the subjects of baptism.[16]

Furthermore, he realized that infant baptism was an invention of man—a necessary solution that resulted from the corruption of the gospel of Jesus Christ in the early days of Christendom:

---

15 Yuille, *History of the Baptists in Scotland*, 92.
16 Alexander Stewart, *Two essays: the first, on the gospel; the second, on the kingdom of Christ; and a sermon on baptism* (York: Colonial Advocate, Wm. Lyon Mackenzie, Printer, 1827), 80.

Infant baptism began first about the third century. It arose from a wrong view of baptism itself and of the way of salvation. It was first contended that baptism was necessary to salvation—then that infants had as much need of salvation as others—and that, therefore, infants should be baptized.[17]

Finally, Stewart acknowledged the spiritual dangers inherent in the doctrine of infant baptism citing this example:

> We recollect of a minister of the church of Scotland, upon sprinkling a child of as ungodly a man as himself...coming to the parents and shaking hands with them saying—"I wish you much joy of your new made christian." Might we not ask if the children of the devil could make an infant a christian by sprinkling water upon its face! Are there none in Canada that think children are turned from heathenism to christianity by this charm? Alas! there are not a few—yet these new made christians in a few years turn out to be the children of the devil and do his works. They go astray from God telling lies, swearing etc. Yea some of these parents that vow, and swear to bring them up in the nurture and admonition of the Lord, teach them to lie and cheat their neighbours.[18]

Lest it be thought that after 1808 Alexander Stewart's ministry became unbalanced, let us hear his words on the matter:

> Some will be apt to say that we make everything of baptism: no! we make it what it is: a pointed commandment of Jesus Christ, which must be attended to at the risk of his displeasure; but we place every one of his command-

---

17 Stewart, *Two essays*, 81.
18 Stewart, *Two essays*, 98.

ments on the same level. All must be attended to in their proper places. Those who believe must be baptized—they must join themselves to the people of God—love the brethren—obey all Christ's commandments, and attend to all his ordinances. This is a true manifestation of christianity. It is the character of God's people that they tremble at his word—that they know Christ's voice, and follow him—that they hear and obey the apostles.[19]

The eight years following Alexander Stewart's conversion in Moulin, culminating with his baptism in June 1808, were ones of profound spiritual significance. These were the years of his spiritual infancy, a time when his thoughts and ideas were molded by the Word of God and where his Christian life emulated the practice of his spiritual parents. In the years that would follow in Perthshire, in Upper Canada and throughout his spiritual manhood, the influence of the Haldane brothers would be unmistakable. The Christian graces of truth and charity would appear time and again and the heart of the itinerant evangelist would always shine through:

> Some will think we are keen to *make people baptists*. This we deny... We are not keen to make baptists. We would not, on any consideration, baptize one in whom we had not the fullest confidence as a christian. We are keen to get people converted to God, and then we would urge such to be baptized, and to observe all things that Christ hath commanded. This is our faith in the word of God... We are not among those that court controversy, but we shrink not from the fullest investigation of our faith and practice. We are very confident of having the right side of the question, and we know the more it is examined, controverted, and opposed, it will become the plainer. We wish every

---

19 Stewart, *Two essays*, 87.

man and woman to be fully persuaded in their own minds. Blind obedience is not acceptable to God. It is the duty of every hearer and reader, to "prove all things, and hold fast that which is good" [1 Thessalonians 5:21]. To "try the spirits whether they are of God" [1 John 4:1]. May the Lord open the eyes of sinners to see the gospel—and the eyes of believers to see his whole will as revealed in the scriptures. If the above have either of these effects our labour will not be in vain; and if otherwise we are confident we have done a duty which we owed to God, and to his professed people.[20]

---

20 Stewart, *Two Essays*, 89.

Section 3

Baptist missionary: from the Highlands to Upper Canada

1808-1818

Chapter 5

A church home in Perth

The itinerants of the first decade of nineteenth-century Scotland were kingdom builders in their own right. In fact, they adopted a method of church planting that had been established in New Testament times. "I planted, Apollos watered, but God gave the increase" (1 Corinthians 3:6, NKJV), stated the apostle Paul. Likewise, in the Highlands, the Haldanes sowed the seed and the missionaries watered—and both waited on the Holy Spirit for the fruit.

As a field preacher, Alexander Stewart had assisted at the beginning of at least three fledgling congregational works: Kingussie, Avoch and Elgin. This pattern would continue despite his change in sentiments on the subject of baptism. During his journey to Edinburgh in June 1808, it is probable that he was told of the need for a missionary in Perth. Whether he responded to an exhortation or whether the prospect of being closer to home and family enticed him, Alexander returned to Elgin for his family knowing that Perth would be his next avenue of service for the Lord.[1]

Historical overview of the Baptists of Perth

Some historical records indicate that the Baptists were in Perth as early as 1785.[2] However, like so many other Baptist works in Scotland, the extant church, which exists as a viable congregation today, was born out of a division over the issue of believer's baptism in 1808. The seed of the congregation in Perth was planted when the Independents formed themselves into church fellowship in 1798 under the leadership of James Garie (1762-1801).[3] In 1800, an edifice was erected in South Street through the benevolence of Robert Haldane. From 1801 to 1806, several men gave oversight to the congregation. In 1807, three men began sharing the pastoral responsibilities of the flock: William Orme (1787-1830), John McRobbie (b. 1762?) and John Stalker (b. 1775).[4] It is the story of their disagreement over church order and the ordinance of baptism that would set the stage for Alexander Stewart's entrance in the fall of 1808.

John Stalker and John McRobbie were set apart by the congregation as elders early in 1807. The church devoted the morning of each Lord's Day to exhortation by these brethren, who would give a short discourse in rotation. The afternoon and evening meetings of these Independents were given to pastoral preaching, and cases of discipline were conducted at public meetings.[5] William Orme, who had finished his studies at Robert Haldane's Theological

---

1 George Yuille, ed., *History of the Baptists in Scotland, from pre-Reformation times* (Glasgow: Baptist Union Publications, c.1926), 92.

2 Yuille, *History of the Baptists in Scotland*, 165.

3 William D. McNaughton, ed., *The Scottish Congregational ministry, 1794–1993* (Glasgow: The Congregational Union of Scotland, 1993), 453.

4 Robert Kinniburgh, ed., *Fathers of Independency in Scotland; or, Biographical sketches of early Scottish Congregational ministers. A.D. 1798–1851* (Edinburgh: A Fullarton & Co., 1851), 125.

5 Kinniburgh, *Fathers of Independency in Scotland*, 126.

Seminary in 1807, was ordained by Stalker and McRobbie in February 1808 and was asked to preach regularly at the two latter Sunday sessions.[6] This structure of leadership and Sunday worship was typical of Congregational churches of the day. However, William Orme soon felt that this "normative" order of Christian worship did not tend to edification. Further, he was so thoroughly convinced of its contrariness to the pattern of the early church that he abandoned it *at once*. As a result, pastoral preaching was adopted at all three meetings on the Lord's Day.[7] Hard feelings, no doubt, arose within the eldership of the church.

During the same time, the issue of baptism had come to the forefront. Surprisingly, William Orme did not follow in the footsteps of his benefactors, the Haldanes. John Stalker and John McRobbie did. The church in Perth was emulating the pattern of dissolution and rebirth that had been experienced by countless others throughout the counties of Scotland. "Indeed, it would seem that the Congregational churches in Perthshire were severely weakened by the dispute, and that the Baptists became the more prominent body."[8] Elders McRobbie and Stalker separated from the church with twenty of her members but soon returned to re-occupy the Perth tabernacle[9] after Orme and the Congregationalists were requested to leave by its owner, Robert Haldane.[10] But, owing to their small numbers, the Baptists vacated the tabernacle and collected to meet in Arnot's Schoolroom in Parliament Close — and waited upon God to increase their strength and send them a helper.[11]

---

6 McNaughton, *The Scottish Congregational ministry*, 121.

7 McNaughton, *The Scottish Congregational ministry*, 126.

8 Donald E. Meek, "Evangelicalism and emigration: aspects of the role of dissenting evangelicalism in Highland emigration to Canada." In Gordon MacLennan, ed. *Proceedings of the first North American Congress of Celtic studies* (Ottawa: 1986), 20.

9 "Tabernacle" was the name given to those edifices erected throughout Scotland through the generosity of Robert Haldane.

10 Kinniburgh, *Fathers of Independency in Scotland*, 127.

11 Yuille, *History of the Baptists in Scotland*, 166.

Worshipping with the Baptists of Perth

Alexander Stewart was God's chosen vessel to assist the Baptists of Perth, and his close relationship with this body of believers would span ten years. These Baptists, who now met on Tay Street, were truly his church family.[12] They would witness him mature spiritually as he exercised his talents. They would also rejoice with Alexander and Janet as God blessed them with one final addition to their family: a second son, Alexander (1811-1885).[13] Fortunately, Stewart left a journal covering a portion of these years from 1812 to 1815.[14] A partial roll of members has been extracted from this record and can be found in Appendix A. Further, the entries recount details of some thirty-four Sabbaths and give a good impression of what a typical Lord's Day was like at the Baptist church in Perth.

Stewart's writings indicate that the Congregational pattern of three Sunday worship services was taken up by the Baptists of Perth: one gathering in the morning, one in the afternoon, and one in the evening. Each meeting was opened and closed with prayer and each featured a sermon. The morning session also included an exhortation by at least one of the leading men of the church. In addition, Alexander records that the founders of this congregation, John Stalker and John McRobbie, still participated actively in the worship services. However, it appears that McRobbie's contribution lessened, for the journal shows that he only gave one Sabbath exhortation over a period of four years.[15] Further, if we can deduce

---

12 Yuille, *History of the Baptists in Scotland*, 287.

13 The *Parochial registers,* County Perth, Parish Perth, Scotland, indicate that Alexander Jr. was born on July 30, 1811, in the Middle Church Parish Perth, *but was not baptized.*

14 Alexander Stewart, "Sermon Notes 1810"; "Notes on the Baptist church at Perth, Scotland, 1812-1815"; "Register of sermons preached chiefly at York, Upper Canada, 1827-1833"; "Marriage register, 1830-1840"; "Returns of subscribers for *Essays on the gospel and the kingdom of Christ.*" (Louis Melzack Collection, Thomas Fisher Rare Book Library, University of Toronto, Toronto).

15 Entry for December 6, 1812. "Notes on the Baptist church at Perth, Scotland." (Melzack Collection, Toronto).

anything from the preaching statistics left in the account, it is that at least three men shared in the eldership of the church. The journal shows that Alexander Stewart, John Stalker and John McFarlane shared the responsibilities of preaching equally.[16] Their discourses were not solely for the edification of believers, rather they were also evangelical in nature. In fact, they demonstrated a fervent desire to reconcile men and women to God the Father, through the blood of his Son, Jesus Christ. Alexander's text on April 5, 1812, gives evidence to this fact:

> Listen to Me, you stubborn-hearted,
> Who are far from righteousness:
> I bring My righteousness near,
> It shall not be far off;
> My salvation shall not linger.
> And I will place salvation in Zion,
> For Israel My glory (Isaiah 46:12-13, NKJV).

Matters of Christian fellowship

The Baptists of Perth took the matter of church discipline seriously. They were zealous to maintain a Christ-like, regenerate church membership. Moreover, matters of Christian fellowship were made part and parcel of the worship services of the church. One such case was brought before the church during the afternoon gathering on June 14, 1812. It is of particular interest because it involved the deceit of a servant to her employer, Alexander Stewart. Alexander had engaged Ann Campbell to serve his family for a specified number of months starting in February of that year. While under contract to the Stewart family, Ann found a more desirable position

---

16 Stewart gives details of 100 services from 1812 to 1815. Of these, Stewart preached at 26, Stalker at 23 and McFarlane at 25. Of the remaining 26 services, two individuals stand out: Robert Pullar (b. 1782), who preached at 9 services, and William Candie (b. 1764?), who preached at 8. (Note: McFarlane is mentioned in Yuille, *History of the Baptists in Scotland*, 287.)

with a Mrs. Walker. In order to legitimize the move prior to serving the remainder of her term, she falsely stated to an acquaintance that there were no terms mentioned when she was employed and that she was therefore at liberty to leave. She compounded this falsehood, by confiding to yet another individual that she would sever her relationship with the Stewarts whether the contract existed or not. This she did on May 11 under the pretence of bad health. By May 12 she was under the employment of Mrs. Walker. Owing to the fact that Ann Campbell was a member of the Perth Baptist church, the matter was brought before the other elders of the congregation, John Stalker and John McFarlane. Unfortunately, after a month of investigating the facts of the case, the matter was brought before the church: whereupon "the Church decided that she had sinned and had not repented & she was separated by prayer in her presence."[17]

The fall tour of 1812

While the Baptist church in Tay Street, Perth, was Alexander Stewart's church home, he was by no means limited by his responsibilities to them. Both he and his church were outward looking. That is, they recognized that the message of the gospel must be extended beyond the environs of Perth. As such, the elders and leading men of the congregation were sometimes absent from their fellowship, preaching to other gatherings that had need. This was second nature to Alexander Stewart for he was fashioned in the mold of James Alexander Haldane. Truly, it could be stated that, "The Haldane preachers were trained first and foremost as itinerant evangelists, and their role as pastors of churches was secondary."[18] Being one of God's chosen instruments to bring the message of salvation to the Highlands was a calling Stewart could never deny;

---

17 Entry for June 14, 1812. "Notes on the Baptist church at Perth, Scotland." (Melzack Collection, Toronto).

18 Donald E. Meek, *The Independent and Baptist churches of Highland Perthshire and Strathspey.* (Transactions of the Gaelic Society of Inverness, LVI, 1991), 287.

and it is most certainly what he was remembered for, as evidenced by his obituary: "On Friday last, the Rev. Alex. Stewart… formerly a missionary to the highlands of Scotland, his native country."[19]

While his training had prepared him for the role of the evangelist, other aspects of his person made him especially suited to the task. First, he was an individual who considered no obstacle too large in the spreading of the gospel. Or, to put it another way, no Scottish nook was too insignificant to be overlooked. Second, his zeal for the lost was matched by a concern for the material well-being of his countrymen. Lastly, and unlike the Haldane brothers, he was cut from the same cloth as the ordinary Scots themselves—in that he spoke the same language and lived the same lifestyle.[20] And so, throughout Stewart's tenure with the Baptists in Perth, he continually sought opportunities to travel and preach the good news. In addition, it should be noted that Stewart likely acted as an agent for his home church. This is apparent from the fact that leading men from the Perth congregation often accompanied or met Stewart at different points on his missionary journeys. At the same time, mention should be made of the Baptist Itinerant Society. This organization was formed by Christopher Anderson (1782-1852) and George Barclay (d. 1838) and "…was the pioneer in the Baptist effort to evangelize the Gaelic Highlands."[21] Hence, church and missionary society worked together in chorus to proclaim salvation through Christ alone to the people of Scotland. Fortunately, a glimpse of one such evangelistic effort in 1812 is preserved for us in Stewart's journal.

Starting in mid-October, Alexander embarked on a missionary trip that would take two weeks and cover approximately 300 kilometres. It not only would touch the Highlands of Perthshire but would also take him to North Lanarkshire, midway between

---

19 "Death notice of Rev. Alexander Stewart." *The Examiner* (Toronto: June 24, 1840).
20 Meek, *Independent and Baptist churches of Highland Perthshire and Strathspey*, 276.
21 Yuille, *History of the Baptists in Scotland*, 71.

82   FROM SCOTLAND TO CANADA

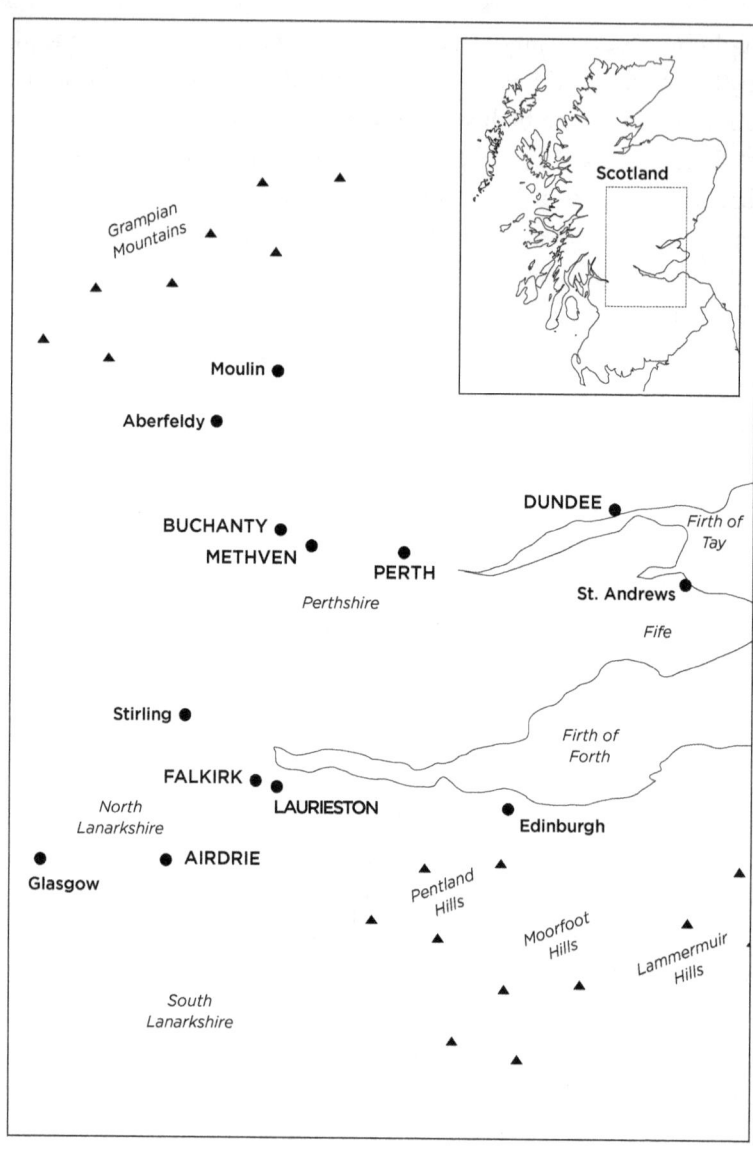

PERTHSHIRE AND LANARKSHIRE

Glasgow and Edinburgh. Further, if one can gather anything from Stewart's Scripture texts on these occasions, his purpose was twofold: to evangelize the lost and to instruct believers in the things of God.

The first week of the tour was spent ministering in the environs of Perth.[22] Stewart travelled twenty kilometres west to the village of Buchanty accompanied by John Lothian, a member of the Baptist church at Perth, and one who often took a turn at giving an exhortation from the Scriptures. Stewart's text for the morning service of October 11 was Colossians 3:12: "Therefore, as the elect of God, holy and beloved, put on tender mercies, kindness, humility, meekness, longsuffering" (NKJV). In the evening, the two headed back towards Perth, and ministered to the believers in Methven. Again, Stewart ministered from Paul's epistle to the Colossians, this time from Colossians 1:28: "Him we preach, warning every man and teaching every man in all wisdom, that we may present every man perfect in Christ Jesus" (NKJV). After the evening service, Stewart and Lothian were met by John McFarlane and returned home to Perth.

The following Sabbath was spent preaching at the Baptist church in Dundee, and again Stewart was attended by a prominent member of his home church, this time Peter McNaughton. At both meetings, Alexander expounded from the book of Psalms. In the morning, from Psalm 127:4: "Like arrows in the hand of the warrior, so are the children of one's youth" (NKJV). And, in the evening, from Psalm 36:7-8: "How precious is Your lovingkindness, O God! Therefore the children of men put their trust under the shadow of Your wings. They are abundantly satisfied with the fullness of Your house, and You give them drink from the river of Your pleasures" (NKJV). The two men returned to Perth by coach, confident that the Lord would use the Word that was preached in Dundee: "So shall My word be that goes forth from

---

22 Entry for October 11, 1812. "Notes on the Baptist church at Perth, Scotland." (Melzack Collection, Toronto).

My mouth; it shall not return to Me void, but it shall accomplish what I please, and it shall prosper in the thing for which I sent it" (Isaiah 55:11, NKJV).

Alexander Stewart next turned his attention to North Lanarkshire. Like the Highland churches, many of the Baptists groups here owed their existence to the work of the Haldanes. Alexander's first stop was Airdrie, on Friday, October 23. In addition to preaching on Psalm 84:11, it is probable that Stewart had an audience with his benefactor and friend, Robert Haldane. In fact, it is likely that Stewart was at the Airdrie church at Haldane's invitation, for Robert Haldane had purchased the estate of Auchingray in 1809 near Airdrie "and may be regarded as the first pastor of the Airdrie Church."[23] Although, Stewart records that there were only a dozen hearers that Friday night and that the village itself was "a dull like place," the reunion with Haldane must have been sweet and far from dull.[24] On Sunday, Stewart gave two discourses to a small audience in Falkirk.[25] In the morning, he exhorted from John 15:2: "Every branch in Me that does not bear fruit He takes away; and every branch that bears fruit He prunes, that it may bear more fruit" (NKJV). In the afternoon, Stewart preached on the same text that he had used in Airdrie. Finally, Stewart concluded what must have been an exhausting tour in nearby Laurieston.[26] Here he preached an evangelistic message to a "full house." It was a call to be reconciled to God: "Then he said to them, 'Thus it is written, and thus it was necessary for the Christ to suffer and to rise from the dead the third day, and that repentance and remission of sins should be preached in His name to all nations, beginning at Jerusalem. And you are witnesses of these things'" (Luke 24:46-48,

---

23 Yuille, *History of the Baptists in Scotland*, 214.

24 Entry for October 23, 1812. "Notes on the Baptist church at Perth, Scotland." (Melzack Collection, Toronto).

25 Entry for October 25, 1812. "Notes on the Baptist church at Perth, Scotland." (Melzack Collection, Toronto).

26 Entry for October 25, 1812. "Notes on the Baptist church at Perth, Scotland." (Melzack Collection, Toronto).

NKJV). The next morning Stewart returned to his home in Perth by coach.

Alexander Stewart: *itinerant*. This was God's vocation for him. Moreover, the Lord of the church was using these experiences in Perth to prepare Alexander for another, perhaps a greater missionary endeavour. Stewart was like many other ministers of the gospel in Scotland: "Surviving journals indicate that they were men of outstanding commitment, who were not deterred by poor roads, (or) rough seas…"[27] In God's providence, it was now time for Stewart to meet with the "rough seas"—it was time for Stewart to journey with his family to Canada and, in that far away place, bear witness to his Lord and Saviour, Jesus Christ.

---

27 Donald E. Meek, "Evangelical missionaries in the early nineteenth-century Highlands." *Scottish Studies*, Vol. 28 (Edinburgh: 1987), 11.

Chapter 6

Baptist missionary to Canada

Monday morning, May 25, 1818: Alexander, along with his wife Janet and their children Catherine, James and Alexander Jr., stood on the pier at Greenock and peered out over the waters of the Firth of Clyde.[1] Scotland behind them, the ship *Camilla* and Canada before them. One wonders what thoughts went through Stewart's mind during these final moments prior to sailing? In all likelihood he conjured up half a lifetime's worth of remembrances: his childhood in Logierait; his conversion in Moulin; his training in Edinburgh; his missionary endeavours in the Highlands; his eldership in Perth. Certainly, he would carry all these experiences to Canada, however, the familiar places of Scotland he would leave behind forever. Truly this was a solemn occasion.[2] Did his extended

---

1 "Letter from Alexander Stewart, Canada." *New Evangelical Magazine and Theological Review*, Vol. V (London: 1819), 76.

2 The thoughts behind this scene have been taken from Donald E. Meek, "Evangelicalism and emigration: aspects of the role of dissenting evangelicalism in

family accompany him? Did the brethren of Perth Baptist church offer him words of encouragement and comfort? This was a picture that would remain in his mind's eye for the duration of his life. Indeed, this was the culmination of months, or perhaps even years, of wrestling with God's leading.

Alexander knew his determination to move to Canada was in the will of God. For most men at the age of forty-four, to even consider uprooting a family and starting over was unimaginable. However, the Lord of Creation had brought to pass several circumstances that made Stewart's choice an obvious one. And yet, the decision must have been heart wrenching. For, he would leave both his station at Perth Baptist church and his beloved Scotland, never to return.

Reasons for emigration

During the second decade of the nineteenth century, Scotland witnessed waves of her sons and daughters leaving her shores for distant lands. That the Stewart family left during this time, points, in part, to their reasons for emigrating. But why did they leave? Many newspapers of this period record for us a general answer to this question. For instance, here are the words of the June 12, 1819, edition of the *Aberdeen Chronicle*:

> EMIGRATION FROM England, Scotland and Ireland to the United States and Canada, goes on to a very great extent; and we cannot help expressing our surprise, that this fatal symptom of decay should be attributed to excess of population. Our cities, the population of which would never be kept up without constant supplies from the country, have no doubt increased in population, as trade and manufacturers have flourished—but the peasantry, and class of small farmers, have rapidly diminished in numbers

---

Highland emigration to Canada." Gordon MacLennan, ed. *Proceedings of the first North American Congress of Celtic studies* (Ottawa: 1986), 16.

during the last thirty years. The increase of luxury, has brought into disuse the plain and fare and homey apparel of former times, and excessive taxation bars the early marriages that formerly took place. In manufacturing towns the youth are corrupted in morals, while their bodies are debilitated, and from these causes, without assigning others equally or nearly equally operative, we may conclude, that no excess of population occasions emigration; but the very natural wish to leave a country, where the lower classes can with great difficulty obtain the prime necessaries of life, for another, where its comforts, and a fair prospect of independence, are the rewards of honest industry.

In short, people left because they wanted a better life for themselves and their children. Further, the Stewarts and the people of Perthshire had experienced poor harvests from the years 1810 and 1815, which fuelled this "natural wish to leave a country."[3] In addition, yeomen farmers who were used to employing run-rigs[4] in their farming operations were displaced as the industry moved towards modernization. Also, the linen industry, which employed many people in Perthshire, collapsed, leaving many without a steady source of income. While a "spirit of independence… was encouraged by the new economic forces, both in landlord and tenant… it also taught the people to take decisions about their own earthly futures, even if these decisions were to lead them to the other side of the Atlantic."[5]

One such Perthshire minister who saw his congregation undermined by the constant outflow of immigrants was William

---

3 Meek, "Evangelicalism and emigration." 20.
4 "Rig" is the Scottish idiom for a strip of land associated with a croft. "Run-rigs" are sequences of those strips of land, many of which are still visible in some areas of Scotland.
5 Donald E. Meek, *The Independent and Baptist churches of Highland Perthshire and Strathspey.* (Transactions of the Gaelic Society of Inverness, Vol.LVI, 1991), 277-278.

McKillican (1776-1849).[6] McKillican resigned his charge at the Acharn Congregational Church in 1813 and cited that the principal cause of his removal was "the extent of emigration from the churches in his part of Perthshire."[7] McKillican himself left for Upper Canada[8] in 1816, and ministered in the township of Glengarry until his death. While, it is not known whether Alexander Stewart experienced the same sort of dilemma in Perth Baptist church, one can be certain that he left the church in capable hands. This was his character. Indeed, Stewart always exhibited a burden for the lost and was ever conscious that the Lord would use him in a station that was devoid of an able witness.

While Alexander Stewart's readiness to emigrate likely reflected something of his social status, it definitely reflected his itinerant missionary calling. Stewart surely knew there was a shortage of ministers in Canada. However, he could only know the *extent* of this need once he was residing in his new country. In a letter to his friend William Ballantine, Stewart shows the fire of his missionary zeal after having had a chance to examine the vast province of Upper Canada:

> This is a land of darkness, and a barren wilderness. It would make one's heart bleed to take a survey of this most extensive country… when he considers the scanty means of religious instruction which the people possess. Eight Church of England clergy, eight Presbyterians, a few Methodist,

---

6 William D. McNaughton, ed. *The Scottish Congregational ministry, 1794–1993* (Glasgow: The Congregational Union of Scotland, 1993), 95.

7 Meek, "Evangelicalism and emigration." 28.

8 The provinces of Upper and Lower Canada existed as British colonies from 1791 to 1841. Upper Canada was generally comprised of present-day Southern Ontario, Canada, and until 1797 it included the Upper Peninsula of the State of Michigan, United States. Its name reflected a position closer to the headwaters of the St. Lawrence River. Lower Canada covered the southern portion of the modern-day Province of Quebec, Canada, and the Labrador region of the present-day Province of Newfoundland and Labrador, Canada.

and a few Baptist preachers, are all the religious instructors they have. Will not the very souls of the people of God with you *ache* at this account? Does it not cry to them, "Come over and help us?" Shall those on whom the Lord has bestowed talents for preaching his gospel shrug up their shoulders and say, "It is far off!" or, "The journey is expensive"? Shall the rich add house to house, and field to field, and content themselves with giving a few pence to the fellowship on the Lord's day, while such a country exists in the creation of God, destitute of the gospel, and they have easy access to send preachers to it? Shall they still use the old argument of covetousness, and say, "We must look to our families" and, "We do not know what we ourselves may yet want"? Is not this at once refusing God that which he has bestowed upon them? Is not this distrusting him for their own support, and that of their families?—"Let the rich be rich in good works" was the language of Paul and what is or can be a better work, than to send the gospel to perishing men? Some will tell us, how zealous we ought to be in keeping the unity of the spirit, &c. and in attending to all the Lord's ordinances in his church, and how we ought to consider the wants of our brethren, while they totally neglect the conversion of the ungodly. Does not the language of Jesus apply to such, "Those things ought ye to have done, and not to leave the other undone"? Let us attend to the ordinances, love and support our brethren; but let us not see our fellow creatures, our *brethren*, according to the flesh, perishing for lack of knowledge, while we have any ability to help them. Shall we continue to pray, "Thy kingdom come," and never attempt to use the means by which it is to come, *viz.* by the preaching of the gospel? Those on whom God has bestowed the gifts of an evangelist, are enjoined upon their peril to use those gifts, or he will require them of them; and those who have the good things of this life are bound to bring them on their way after a godly sort, that they may go forth, taking nothing of the Gentiles. I truly shudder when I think of men who are members of the churches of Christ, and who have thousands of pounds and care nothing about the accounts of the state of the world; and give perhaps a few shillings or pounds for the spread of the gospel.[9]

Thus, like the apostle Paul's vision and subsequent call to Macedonia, Stewart was convinced that God wanted him and his family in Canada.

The transatlantic voyage

The ship *Camilla* would take forty-nine days to cross the Atlantic Ocean, arriving at the Port of Quebec on July 13.[10] As for the voyage itself, Alexander Stewart would later recount that "nothing remarkable happened," although he confessed that he and his family "were a good deal afraid, from the want of knowledge of a seafaring life."[11] And it seems ocean travel did not agree with his constitution, as he experienced bouts of sea sickness for nearly half the trip! Owing to this ailment, Stewart did not preach while on board the ship. Writing to William Ballantine in October 1818, he recalls:

> A Mr. Henderson, a Burgher Minister, from Carlisle, who was a cabin passenger, preached to us twice every Lord's day. As I was some time sick, and particularly as I perceived

---

9 "Letter from Alexander Stewart, Canada." *New Evangelical Magazine and Theological Review*, Vol. VI (London: 1820), 124-125.

10 *The Montreal Gazette*, July 22, 1818. *The Gazette* also records that the ship carried 109 settlers.

11 "Letter from Alexander Stewart, Canada." *New Evangelical Magazine and Theological Review*, Vol. V (London: 1819), 76.

Mr. H. preached the gospel, I did not preach any while in the ship. His doctrine was the purest I ever heard from any of that connexion. I hope the Lord will bless his labours in Canada. I wish there were hundreds like him in this country. He is to settle in St. Andrew's (formerly Cairo), Lower Canada.[12]

The Stewart family did not stay in Quebec but boarded a large steamboat of 600 or 700 tons and landed at Montreal on July 15. Having arrived at British North America's largest city — with no specific view as to where to "fix their tent" — Alexander and his family decided to spend the next two weeks in planning and prayer. As Stewart so succinctly puts it in his letter to Ballantine: "Here we made a pause and began to look about us."

A survey of his new country

In Montreal, Alexander located accommodation for his family with some Baptists from the old country. These folk had left the churches of Glenlyon and Aberfeldy in 1817. Stewart states, "I got my family lodged in a room belonging to some of these brethren. We had three small rooms for three families. It is common for emigrants to take one room for three or four families. The rents are so high, that they cram as many as the floor will contain beds for after heaping their trunks one above another."[13] Stewart consulted with one of these men in particular. His name was John Menzies (1779-1859), and he would become Alexander's constant companion for the next eight years. Joseph Ash (1808-1895), nineteenth-century historian for the Church of Christ Disciples, Canada, gave this description of the character of Alexander's new friend:

---

12 "Letter from Alexander Stewart, Canada." *New Evangelical Magazine and Theological Review*, Vol. V (London: 1819), 76.

13 "Letter from Alexander Stewart, Canada." *New Evangelical Magazine and Theological Review*, Vol. V (London: 1819), 76-77.

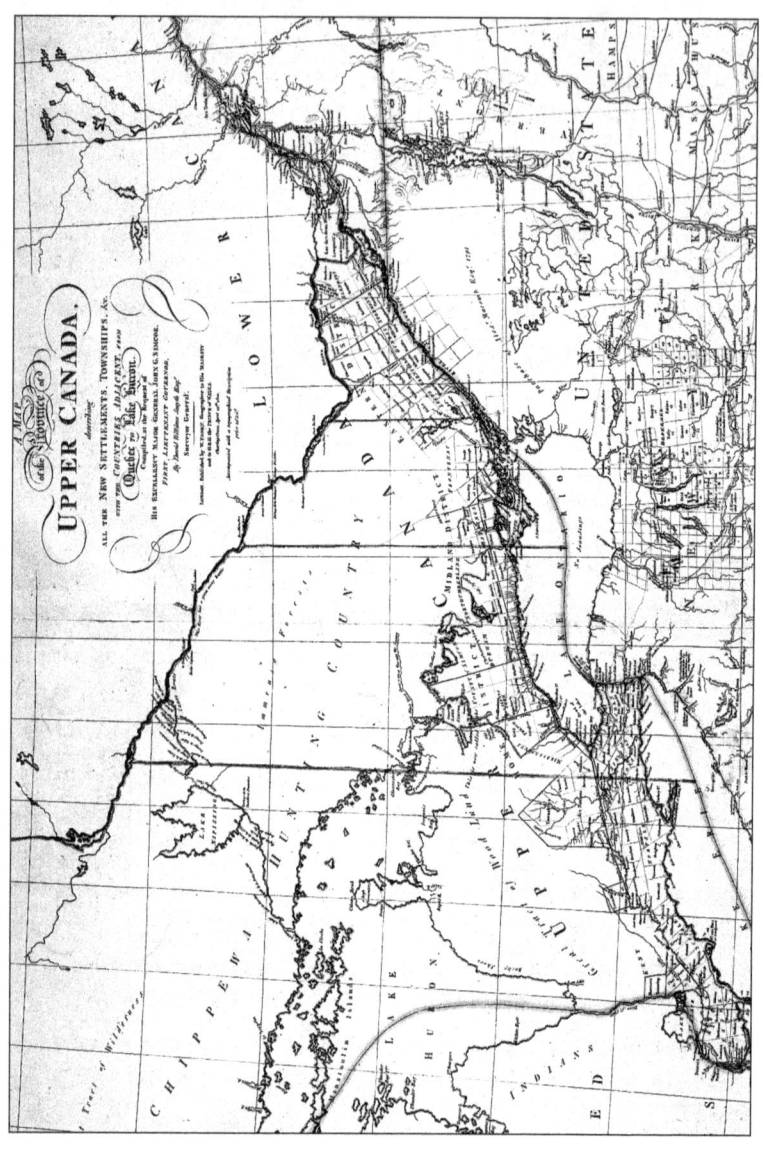

UPPER CANADA
(1800)

Elder (John) Menzies was a remarkable man; a fine speaker, of untarnished morals, a careful student of the Bible, a hard worker at his business (blacksmithing and farming); a man of strong faith, warm zeal, and deep piety. Religion with him was an every day matter; his memory and knowledge of the Scriptures was hard to be equaled and not to be surpassed. So great was his knowledge of the Bible, that, if asked where any passage was, in the whole Bible, he could tell the book, chapter and verse, and even what part of the verse. We used to call him the "living, walking concordance." He was so constant in his Bible studies that he kept his large Bible on his bench, read a few verses, then work, and think of what he had read; and so on, day after day and year after year. He preferred preaching in his native tongue, which was Gaelic.[14]

After having had an agreeable Lord's Day meeting with Menzies and the others, Stewart determined his next course of action and set off on Tuesday, July 28, 1818, to view Upper Canada alone.

Alexander travelled seventy or eighty miles west and arrived at the township of Glengarry, Lancaster County, Upper Canada, on Saturday, August 1. Here he met with some "kindred spirits": Baptists from his home county Perthshire! They had emigrated in 1815 through the assistance of the Colonial Office and were from two of the churches established on Loch Tay through James Haldane's evangelistic campaigns.[15] Some came from the Baptist church in Lawers, and the majority from the church in Killin.[16] Alexander gives this account of the weekend spent with this congregation:

---

14 Joseph Ash, "History of the rise and progress of our cause in Canada." *Christian Worker*, Reminiscences, Nov. 1882 to Feb. 1884.

15 See Marianne McLean, *The people of Glengarry: Highlanders in transition 1745-1820* (Ottawa: McGill/Queen's University Press, 1993), 151ff.

16 Stuart Ivison and Fred Rosser, eds., *The Baptists in Upper and Lower Canada before 1820* (Toronto: University of Toronto Press, 1956), 94-95.

> This church has, I think, seventeen members in it, chiefly males, and Allan McDearmid and Peter McDougal are their Elders. They appeared very happy, and the life of godliness is as much seen among them as I have ever witnessed in any church in Scotland. I preached to them twice on the Lord's day, and once on Monday, and they seemed truly thankful for the opportunity… Close by these brethren Mr. McKillican has taken up his residence; he preaches in three places alternately, taking in one or two more places occasionally. Allan McDearmid preaches one Lord's day out of two at seven miles distance; the people come well out to hear, and good has been done there. That is the only place where Gaelic is particularly necessary, and as four of the church besides Mr. McKillican can preach in that language, I think that part of the country well supplied.[17]

It is crucial to note again Alexander's desire to serve in a place that needed a voice to proclaim the gospel. If there was one thing that surfaced from the weekend spent with the church in Lochiel it was that his gifts could be best used elsewhere.

> The brethren were anxious that I should settle there, but I told them that, however much I valued Christian society, I had one most serious objection to settle with them, *viz.* that there were too many preachers in one place already considering the state of the country at large. Of this objection Mr. McDearmid saw the force; besides I could get no land in that place to support my family, unless I had a large sum of money to purchase a good clear place.[18]

---

17 "Letter from Alexander Stewart, Canada." *New Evangelical Magazine and Theological Review*, Vol. V (London: 1819), 77.

18 "Letter from Alexander Stewart, Canada." *New Evangelical Magazine and Theological Review*, Vol. V (London: 1819), 77.

The question remained: Where *did* God want him to minister?

The decision to settle in York

Alexander would spend the next six weeks traversing the countryside, going as far west as York,[19] the capital of Upper Canada. His express intent from the outset was to survey the province and find a place where he could provide for his family, plant a church and preach the good news. York was to be that place. Perhaps he came to this conclusion because he felt his ministry would have the greatest impact on the province's seat of government? Or, perhaps the prospect of settling at the centre of the colony's commerce and land distribution network attracted him? It was likely a combination of these things. Furthermore, York did not yet have a Baptist testimony. Thus, after much prayer, Alexander stated succinctly, "Having taken a view of York and of the country coming and going, I came to the conclusion, on my arrival at Montreal, to remove to York."[20]

From Perth, Scotland, to York, Upper Canada,—this was God's direction for Alexander Stewart and his family. It is difficult for believers in the twenty-first century to comprehend a missionary call such as this. To be sure, missionaries continue to be raised up today, but global communication "at the touch of a button," and travel at supersonic speeds did not exist for the Stewarts in the first quarter of the nineteenth century. For them, communication often took months, and journeys often took just as long. To leave one's home country for the mission field was often an *irrevocable* decision. With that said, Alexander was content with God's will and immediately set to work on establishing a gospel witness in his new country—a witness that continues to this day.

---

19 The modern-day city of Toronto.
20 "Letter from Alexander Stewart, Canada." *New Evangelical Magazine and Theological Review*, Vol. V (London: 1819), 77.

Section 4

The first Baptist church, York, Upper Canada

1818-1820

Chapter 7

The mission field at York

Alexander and his family left Montreal and arrived at York's harbour in the latter part of September 1818, secure in God's leading. The trip itself was a difficult one. Stewart wrote,

> This was a very tedious journey of 400 miles on fresh water, which took us three weeks. We really thought we should have been buried in Lake Ontario by a storm. We were in a small schooner, as we thought it would convey us sooner than the steam boat; but I think we have learned a lesson of caution. However, our God was still kind, we suffered nothing, only some of our luggage got very wet with the heavy rains.[1]

Having already surveyed the town of 1,000 inhabitants a month

---

1 "Letter from Alexander Stewart, Canada." *New Evangelical Magazine and Theological Review*, Vol. V (London: 1819), 77.

earlier, Alexander was somewhat cognizant of York's advantages and disadvantages. Nonetheless, his observations were cursory and hence, perception did not always coincide with reality. For instance, he hoped that the capital of Upper Canada would be a place of financial opportunity and that its government would unconditionally welcome a preacher of the gospel. The verity of the situation was that York was beginning to feel the effects of an economic recession, the result of a senseless war.[2] Further, Stewart would eventually find out that the secular powers gave preferential treatment to only one kind of clergyman. Indeed, York was a place fraught with its own difficulties and peculiar characteristics. Yet, Alexander Stewart did see clearly in one area: York lacked a Baptist witness. It was therefore a place where God wanted him to spread the unadulterated message of salvation through Jesus Christ. But, what specifically was Stewart's new-found mission field like?

York's physical attributes

York was a quarter-of-a-century new in 1818. The town founded by Sir John Graves Simcoe (1752-1806) in 1793 had already experienced much turmoil in its short history. From the initial construction of its crude infrastructure, through its burning by the Americans in 1813, to its rebirth thereafter, the town grew while always retaining its basic outline. Visitors who sailed the *Crazy Jane* into its harbour were seldom impressed.[3] John Duncan, who

---

2 On April 27, 1813, as part of the War of 1812, the "Battle of York" ended in the town's capture and plunder by American forces. The surrender of the town was negotiated by John Strachan (1778-1867), rector of the Anglican Church. American soldiers destroyed much of Fort York and set fire on the parliament buildings during their five-day occupation. The many acts of arson and looting committed by the American troops at York became (in part) the pretext for the later "Burning of Washington" by British troops. On December 24, 1814, the Treaty of Ghent put an end to hostilities and returned the borders of the United States and British North America to their pre-war state.

3 Between 1816 and 1819, the schooners *Crazy Jane*, *Catherine* and *Asp* transported passengers and freight between Fort George (present-day Niagara-on-the-Lake) and York.

travelled through Canada and the United States from 1818 to 1819, left this description of the Upper Canadian outpost:

> The town consists of one street lying parallel to the lake, and of the beginnings of two or three more at right angles to it. I saw only one church, which had been very much out of repair, but some workmen were employed in putting glass into the windows. The garrison is to the right of the town, and consists of a barrack flanked by a battery and two block houses; they are all of white-washed wood, and have a showy appearance from the water. The harbour of York might be a good one if a well sheltered bay were all that were necessary to form it, but the entrance is narrow and difficult, and in time of war it is completely defenceless.[4]

Not all recorded accounts were as unfavourable as Duncan's. On the contrary, some were astounded at one of the town's most peculiar man-made features. This enduring attribute caught the attention of a former Scottish shepherd named James Laidlaw (b.1763). In a letter to his brother he penned,

> There is a road goes Straight North from york into the Cuntry for fifty mills; and the farm Houses almost all Two Story High; Some of them will have as good as 12 Cows, and four or five Horces; they are Growing very ricth, for they pay no taxes, but Just a perfict trifell, and rids in ther gig, or Chire, Like Lords.[5]

---

4 Edith Firth, ed. *The town of York, 1815-1834* (Toronto: University of Toronto Press/Champlain Society, 1966), 304.
5 Firth, *The town of York*, 307. Note: James Laidlaw, from Ettrick, Selkirk, Scotland, emigrated to Canada in 1818 and had fellowship with the Baptists in York. His story was recorded in York's *Colonial Advocate* on January 18, 1827. Here is an exerpt:

> ...time being bad in Scotland after the War and old Sheperds Like me being not Much thought of when we get old I thought of coming to America and

Of course, the road that Laidlaw was referring to was Yonge Street. Further, his statement of the economy is curious and even misleading. Perhaps it was his first impression. For truthfully, York's citizens had witnessed the full spectrum of the economic cycle.

In an address two decades after the War of 1812 had ended, John Beverley Robinson (1791-1863), Attorney General in 1818 and prominent in York politics, stated that the war benefitted the capital of Upper Canada. He said,

> It must be acknowledged…that the mercy of Heaven has signally accompanied these afflictions. The war to which I allude produced of course many cases of individual suffering and affliction; but in its consequences it was highly favourable to our future prosperity. Its events characterized the people in an eminent degree for a firm adherence

---

there was an Advertisement in one of the Edinburgh News Papers in the year 1816 that any Body that wished to go to Canada Goverment wold take them out free of Expence and they were to Write to a Mr Campble in Edinburgh so I Wrote Mr Campble telling him what famiely I had that I had five sons and told him there age and I wanted to know houw much land each of us ould get, so he wrote me that I was a very fit hand to go to America having so many sons and that I ould get Two hundred acers for myself and Like ways for Every one of my sons that was come of age but I could not get away as stock was so low and it could not be turned into money but times was better in two years so I sold all that I had and came away 1818 and I had to come out on my own Expence for by this time there was no word of Bringing any to Canada So I came to york and went through all there offices acording to acte of parlement I sopose and aye the other Dollar to pay but they ould give us only one Hundred acers Each, and that was to be drawn by Ballat if it was good Land we were the better of if Bad we bid Had with it if there Map and it was capable of cultivation I belive the Cribblers in york ould tak the last Shilling that a poor man has before they ould do anything for him in the way of getting land for in one of their offices they were crying it is five and sixpense five and sixpense and only Marking Two or three words, but I will pas them for they are an avericious Set I am Realy feard that the Devl get the must part of them if they do not bethink themselves in time, I Sopose that they never read the tenth Commandment, or they ould not Covet there Nighbours money…

to the British Crown; and it had the effect of calling into notice the great natural advantages of the country, and making them familiarly known to many persons in Europe of intelligence and influence. It introduced capital, and gave a spur to enterprise, and it prepared the way to that rapid acceleration towards prosperity which we now witness.[6]

Likewise, Alexander Stewart expressed a cautious optimism in regard to York's potential:

> In this place a man could live well if he had a house and a cow of his own. But we pay five dollars per month for a single room… A quart of milk is a York shilling, that is, 12 cents. We have flour however at five dollars per barrel of 196lb.; butcher's meat at from 5d to 6d per lb. British money. If the Lord spare us to get fifteen or twenty acres of land cleared, I think we shall do well, but it is not easy doing this by one hand…this is a poor man's country. A labourer just now gets one dollar per day, and a constant servant from eight to twelve dollars per month, with bed, board, and washing. But the great thing here is the lands, where though one has great trials at first, he comes to ease, and if diligent even to affluence at last. The farmers here are most independent men; they are not like the depraved drunken rabble that are in Lower Canada, but are almost to a man respectable.[7]

However, in the months immediately after Stewart's arrival a period of economic depression was coming to fruition. Peace did not immediately bring prosperity. In fact, it brought about a provincial government who no longer demanded either produce or

---

6 Firth, *The town of York*, 349-350.
7 "Letter from Alexander Stewart, Canada." *New Evangelical Magazine and Theological Review*, Vol. V (London: 1819), 78.

labour. Further, its inauguration kick-started a resumption of the import trade, ending the scarcity of manufactured goods, causing prices to drop drastically, and forcing some smaller merchants into bankruptcy. Finally, it opened the doors to immigration, flooding the market with surplus workmen. By 1819 a depression had developed which lasted until about the year 1822.[8] Notwithstanding these changing perceptions of the town's physical and economic characteristics, each inhabitant's recorded observations had the most basic thing in common: the mission field at York was new, with little of the present day's comforts and conveniences. Hence, those who were to plant churches here were certainly pioneers. They were hard-working, and courageous. In addition to these attributes, the Stewart family would have to cultivate and exercise perseverance as they faced yet another one of York's obstacles: its administration.

York's political attributes

In general, the government of York was not inclined to show impartiality to the portion of its citizenry who were ministers—specifically Baptist ministers. Initially, Stewart expressed a hopefulness that this would not be the case; that it would be different than it was in Scotland. One can sense his gladness and excitement as he wrote of his prospects:

> There is a house belonging to Government which I think I shall get to preach in, as the Governor is a friend to the preaching of the gospel; so much so that I have got a grant of 200 acres of land because I am a preacher, while others get only 100 acres. These lands I got the grant of last week, but I have not yet located. I wait for a township to be surveyed very soon within 15 miles of this town.[9]

---

8 Firth, *The town of York*, xxiii.
9 "Letter from Alexander Stewart, Canada." *New Evangelical Magazine and Theological Review*, Vol. V (London: 1819), 78.

We shall address the location of Stewart's land grant in chapter 9. For now, it is sufficient to state that prejudice and favouritism were alive and well in York. Yes, the new lieutenant governor, Sir Peregrine Maitland (1777-1854), was sympathetic to the gospel. But it was not he, nor the elected members of the Legislature, that governed Upper Canada. The governor would soon discover that he was impotent to affect change. The principal of oligarchic rule dominated Upper Canadian politics. Of course, this was detrimental to the views of many Nonconformist churches. Conversely, it furthered the aspirations of one church: the Church of England.

John George Lambton, better known as Lord Durham (1792-1840), summarized the impact of oligarchic rule on the electorate. In his famous report of 1840, which was the catalyst in bringing about "responsible government" to the British North American provinces, he recorded that Upper Canada had long been entirely governed by a party commonly known as the "Family Compact": "...a name not much more appropriate than party designations usually are, inasmuch as there is, in truth, very little of family connection among persons thus united."[10] This body of men possessed almost all the highest public offices, thereby wielding their influence in the Executive Council and maintaining their grip in the legislature by means of their dominance in the Legislative Council. Thus, Durham stated, "Successive Governors, as they came in their turn, are said to have either submitted quietly to its influence, or after a short and unavailing struggle to have yielded to this well-organized party the real conduct of affairs."[11] Of course, this statement would also apply to the likes of Lieutenant Governor Maitland. In addition, Durham observed that the adherents of the Family Compact were almost exclusively members of the Anglican Church, and concluded that "the maintenance of the

---

10 R. Coupland, ed. *The Durham Report* (Oxford: Oxford University Press, 1946), 81.

11 Coupland, *The Durham Report*, 81.

claims of that church has always been one of its distinguishing characteristics."[12]

Alexander Stewart, on the other hand, was a Baptist and firmly believed in the separation of church and state, having "the conviction that any formal link between Church and State was indefensible, being intrinsically harmful to true religion."[13] Given York's political climate, however, it was not always in his best interest to associate with a dissenting congregation, let alone to lead one. Nevertheless, Stewart would remain true to his convictions and his calling, while the Anglican Church enjoyed its preferred status.

York's religious attributes

York's religious climate can be described as encompassing two extremes: order and experience. "(T)hese two cultures battled each other in the pulpit, the press, the legislature, and the fields, villages, and towns of the colony as they fought for the allegiance of people who had yet to form completely their ways of understanding and shaping the new world to which they had come."[14]

The Anglican Church, pre-eminent in politics, was the "orderly" religious presence of York in 1818, a position it had maintained since the town's founding. Proponents of the established church maintained that since salvation was a "slow and gradual process" the populace needed continual instruction on how to live a life of moderation and order. Consequently, they required "a well-educated and resident clergyman…churches to house the faithful, and schools and teachers to educate the youth of the province."[15] These objectives were only to be sustained by a state-supported church,

---

12 Coupland, *The Durham Report*, 82.

13 Deryck W. Lovegrove, "Unity and separation: contrasting elements in the thought and practice of Robert and James Alexander Haldane." In Keith Robbins, ed. *Protestant Evangelicalism: Britain, Ireland, Germany and America c.1750-c.1950. Essays in honour of W.R. Ward* (Oxford: Basil Blackwell, 1990), 167.

14 William Westfall, *Two worlds: the Protestant culture of nineteenth century Ontario* (Montreal: McGill University Press, 1989), 45.

15 Westfall, *Two worlds*, 23.

"…without which society could not be saved."[16]

Thus, the Anglican Church in Upper Canada enjoyed several advantages over other religious bodies. First, it received direct financial assistance from the government. This financial "upper hand" was further augmented by its original land endowments, which were becoming increasingly more valuable. Second, elementary, secondary and college education were closely linked to the Church of England. This provided the Church with a pool of ordained ministers who were utilized both in the town and in the country. Third, the Anglicans were united in their belief in the union of church and state and in their unique position within the Province of Upper Canada. Lastly, and perhaps most importantly, was the outstanding ability of the Anglican Church's rector, John Strachan (1778-1867).[17] "Thus the history of St. James' Church, with its strong leader, privileged position, financial solvency, and congregational unity, differs from that of every other church in York."[18]

At the other extreme were the "experiential" Methodists and their radical evangelicalism. Rooted in the itinerant ministries of Hezekiah Calvin Wooster (1771-1798) and Nathan Bangs (1778-1862), Methodism espoused a salvation that was "sudden and immediate, the dramatic experience of being overwhelmed by the redeeming spirit of God."[19] The people of Upper Canada seemed to be especially suited to the evangelistic "tent meeting" methodology of the Methodists. Indeed, this denomination enjoyed enormous numerical success in Upper Canada.[20] During Nathan Bang's

---

16 Westfall, *Two worlds*, 23.

17 St. James was established in 1797 and is the oldest congregation in the city of Toronto. John Strachan took up his post as rector of St. James in York just prior to the War of 1812. During the Battle of York, it was Strachan who negotiated the surrender of the city with American general Henry Dearborn (1751-1829).

18 Firth, *The town of York*, liv.

19 Westfall, *Two worlds*, 26.

20 William Westfall estimates that, assuming a one-to-fifteen ratio is used, there would be an estimated 26,000 Methodist adherents out of an Upper Canadian population of 70,000 in 1810, or 37 percent (Westfall, *Two worlds*, 122).

itinerancy from 1804 to 1808, he succeeded in persuading many of the unchurched to become Methodists and was also successful at drawing new-world Baptists into his Wesleyan fellowship. However, the War of 1812 and its resultant anti-Americanism would disrupt Methodism's hegemony over Protestant life in the colony, as republicanism became equated with religious enthusiasm.

As these two cultures clashed, Baptists sought to find their place in the Upper Canadian religious landscape. In 1818, the Baptists were a nonentity in the capital and had made little impact in the rest of the province. Still, it is strange that the most prominent settlement in Upper Canada did not have a Baptist work, whereas Baptist clergymen served many of the colony's towns and villages. Alexander was aware of this fact for he received this survey of the Baptist cause by George Barclay (1780-1857), minister at Cramahe:

> I have this evening had a visit from Mr. Barclay, the person whom Mr. Buchanan sent here two years ago from Fife. He teaches a school and preaches 90 miles down the lake, and he gave me an account of a number of Baptist Churches in this country. I shall give you the account as I took it down from his lips about two hours ago. In Augusta and Elizabeth townships there is one church, Mr. William Carson (nephew of Mr. A. Carson, Tubermore, Ireland), pastor; he has baptized, since July 1817, 126 persons. —Gananaqua, a church, number unknown, Mr. Abington elder. —Bastard, from 50 to 60 members, a Mr. Stephens elder. —Thurlow, 40, preachers James Hulse and Joseph Win. —Bodden, 30, no preacher. —Crammy, 36, George Barclay elder. —Carrying Place, 15, no preacher. —West Lake, number unknown. —Haldimon, 60, no regular preacher. —Whitby and Darlington, 25, John Joy and David Buck preachers. —Markham, 20, Joshua Wilkinson preacher. —At Forty Mile Creek, a church, number unknown, but must be numerous, as they support Mr. Upford wholly in

preaching; he is their elder.—At Long Point, on Lake Erie, there are three churches, and one at Malden, but the numbers are not known at either place. There is a Mr. Crawdle and a Mr. French elders in that quarter. There was a Missionary Society formed at Haldimon, county of Newcastle, Nov. 10, 1817. They have sent out some preachers, though but a few as yet.[21]

Perhaps the lack of a Baptist church in York was due in part to the strength of the Anglicans or to the transitory nature of the town's population. This is not to say that there was never a prior Baptist witness in York. Certainly, much of the capital's populace remembered fondly the works of itinerant missionaries such as Rev. Caleb Blood (1754-1814), Rev. Peter P. Roots (b.1765) and Rev. Nathaniel Kendrick (1777-1848).[22] Unfortunately the years of war, from 1812 to 1815, negated the possibility of further Nonconformist missionary activity. Needless to say, when the Stewarts arrived they were needed as the "fields were white for harvest" (John 4:35).

Practical hands-on experience is the missionary's best educator.

---

21 "Letter from Alexander Stewart, Canada." *New Evangelical Magazine and Theological Review*, Vol. V (London: 1819), 78.

22 Rev. Caleb Blood was sponsored by the Shaftsbury Association of Vermont who sent him to minister in York in 1802. He "created such a favourable impression among the people that Nathaniel Kendrick, who followed him six years later over the same route, could report that everywhere Mr. Blood had visited he was held in grateful remembrance." [See Stuart Ivison & Fred Rosser, eds., *The Baptists in Upper and Lower Canada before 1820* (Toronto: University of Toronto Press, 1956), 65.]

Rev. Peter P. Roots came to York in 1805. "He rode, on the average three thousand miles each year, and preached three hundred sermons." (See Ivison & Rosser, *The Baptists in Upper and Lower Canada*, 79.)

Rev. Nathaniel Kendrick, also sponsored by the Shaftsbury Association, came to York in 1808. "Of his tour as a whole, which included a large area of New York State, as well as Upper Canada, Kendrick reported, 'I was absent from home eighty-five days, and rode 1280 miles, preached 62 sermons, attended and heard 11 sermons preached by other ministers, attended two church meetings, twice administered the Lord's Supper, baptized two persons, attended several conferences and met with two Associations.'" (See Ivison & Rosser, *The Baptists in Upper and Lower Canada*, 54.)

Truly, one can be apprised of a mission field's particular advantages and disadvantages before embarking and still be unprepared for what awaits. Two centuries ago, settlers and missionaries alike had little foreknowledge of what physical, economic, political and religious conditions existed in the New World. And yet, despite this lack of information, Alexander Stewart knew the Lord wanted him in York. It is the story of his church-planting work there that truly begins the history of all who call themselves Baptists in the city of Toronto today.

Chapter 8

York's first Baptist church

It should be understood that the Stewart's desire to build a Baptist work in York was a conviction that was held by others as well. John Menzies likely became convinced of York's need after Stewart's summer excursion to the town and the subsequent report of its prospects to him and the brethren in Montreal. In a letter written to a friend from the "old country," Menzies recounts the events that led to his decision to join Stewart in York:

> Before I left my native country some of my friends were telling me that my lot probably might be cast where I would not have a chance of a godly society. I told them that, I was determined in the strength of the Lord not to be without a meeting as long as the Lord would enable me, but after we landed at Montreal my property was so much reduced… For the want of means I had to stop at Laprairie for a year, where after some time we had some prospects

in the things of the world, but alas my mind had some wounded feelings, such as, where is now your resolutions, that you would not be without a meeting? You have put yourself from the people of God; and there is nothing around you but rank idolatry and an unknown tongue and the few that can speak English you cannot speak to them with freedom. I continued in that place for a year, and a long year it was to me and my wife, where we could not see one living soul, except some few days we could go to Montreal and we hade to cross nine miles of river, there was a few friends from Glenlyon there at that time, and we kept always a meeting when we could go over the river… O, I could wish that my voice could reach to the deciples of Christ and warn them against putting themselves from the means of grace. Brother Stewart from Perth and family came out then and we came up with them to York (now Toronto)…[1]

Thus, the Menzies and the Stewarts were to be God's chosen vessels in planting York's first Baptist church.

The church's founding

Alexander and John wasted little time in canvassing the town for the purpose of assembling a Baptist meeting. As Menzies succinctly put it: "…when we spent a few days there we found out a few desciples that were like sheep that had no 'shepard.'"[2] Likewise, in his account to William Ballantine, Stewart also provided some details of their "gathering the sheep" of York, in the early days of October. He first sought out Thomas Carfrae (1766-1834) with whom he had long been acquainted as the leader of the praises of James Haldane's Tabernacle Church in Edinburgh. The Carfrae family

---

1 John Menzies, "Letter to Elder Archibald Cameron, January 12, 1841." (Canadian Baptist Archives, McMaster University), 2.
2 Menzies, "Letter to Elder Archibald Cameron, January 12, 1841." 2.

was within five miles of York. Here, Stewart preached in a schoolhouse to a "pretty good congregation" on two successive Lord's Days, October 4 and 11. On the following Sunday, Stewart preached in the Methodist meeting house in York to about 150 hearers. Satisfied that his canvassing activity was sufficiently complete, Alexander resolved on gathering a Baptist meeting together "to attend to the ordinances of Christ and hold forth the word of life in that populous district."[3] "Holding forth the word of life" in York — this was Alexander's chief aim. It was a desire that would find its fulfillment in the founding of a Baptist church.

Lord's Day, October 25, 1818. "We formed the first Baptist Church that ever was in that place," penned John Menzies.[4] In fact, nine charter members congregated for the church's inaugural services (see Appendix B). It is obvious that Alexander Stewart was the preacher and pastor of this little flock and it is probable that John Menzies was its first deacon. On that first Sunday, Stewart preached in the morning from Acts 2:24: "…whom God raised up, having loosed the pains of death, because it was not possible that He should be held by it." In the afternoon, the church attended to the ordinances. How happy they must have been on that special day! Stewart exclaimed to Ballantine,

> We had much comfort. Brother Stephens gave a very excellent exhortation. I hope we shall have many of the saved added to our number. Pray for us, that the word of the Lord may have free course and be glorified. We have doubtless a great field here for doing good, but without the outpowering of the Holy Spirit our labour will be in vain, and this perhaps may be given through your prayers.[5]

---

3 "Letter from Alexander Stewart, Canada." *New Evangelical Magazine and Theological Review*, Vol. V (London: 1819), 77-78.
4 Menzies, "Letter to Elder Archibald Cameron, January 12, 1841." 2.
5 "Letter from Alexander Stewart, Canada." *New Evangelical Magazine and Theological Review*, Vol. V (London: 1819), 78.

Truly, the mission field was great and surely the Stewarts and the Menzies looked forward to nurturing the saved and evangelizing the lost in the ensuing months.

The church's life

It is not known whether Lieutenant Governor Maitland made good on his promise to secure a hall for Stewart to hold a Baptist meeting. In any case, it wouldn't have mattered to Alexander. For, his missionary experience had taught him to be content with the Lord's provision. The important thing was that the gospel was being preached—period. James Laidlaw, who was likely added to the church's number in 1819, commented simply on the blessings received during this time: "We like this place far better than the States; we have got Sermon three times Every Saboth; they are the Baptists that we hear."[6] It seems that the Scottish pattern of an exhortation and three sermons each Lord's Day was adopted in this Upper Canadian context. Furthermore, Laidlaw's letter pointed to the need for a Baptist presence by contrasting its teaching with the other denominations now present in York:

> ...there is no Presbetaren minister in this Town as yet, but there is a Large English Chapel, and a Methidest Chapel; but I do not think that the Methidests is very Sound in their Doctrine; they Save all infants, and Saposes a man may be Justified to day, and fall from it to-morrow; and the English Minister reads all that he Says, unless it be his Clark Craying always at the End of Every peorid, good Lord Dliver us. If Tom Hogg ould Come Over and hear the Methidests one day, it oul Serve him Craking about it for one Year; for the minister prays as Loud as Ever he Can, and the people is all doun on there knees, all Craying, Amen; So that you Can Scarce hear what the prest is Saying; and

---

6 Edith Firth, ed. *The town of York, 1815-1834* (Toronto: University of Toronto Press/Champlain Society, 1966), 307.

> I have Seen Some of them Jumping up as if they ould have gone to Heaven, Soul and Body—but there Body was a filthy Clog to them, for they always fell down again, altho crying, O Jesus, O Jesus, Just as he had been to pull them up through the Loft. They have there field meetings, where they preach night and day for a week, where Some thousands atends; Some will be asleep, and Some faling down under Convictions, and others Eating and Drinking![7]

Yes, the Lord was using the Baptists in York and was blessing their efforts. In fact, by the time Stewart wrote his second epistle to Ballantine on August 30, 1819, the number of members had increased:

> I believe I told you when I wrote last, that we had formed a church, and were only nine in number: I have now the satisfaction to state, that our number is increased to twenty; this, however, is chiefly by emigrants from the Old Country, the name here given to Britain and Ireland. We have not yet heard of any instances of conversion, but we have heard of several who profess to have been better instructed in spiritual things.—We feel indeed confident, that the Word of the Lord shall not return unto Him without accomplishing the end for which he sent it, and that we shall yet see its abundant fruits. At all events, I consider it my duty to labour to the utmost of my power in the gospel of Christ; and I know that my "labour shall not be in vain in the Lord."[8]

---

7 Firth, *The town of York*, 307. [Note: Laidlaw's letter was sent to *Blackwood's Magazine*, Edinburgh, by the Ettrick shepherd James Hogg (1770-1835), who was a noted Scottish poet and likely a cousin. Hogg explained that Laidlaw became obsessed with North America and emigrated when almost fifty years old, although some of his sons refused to accompany him. The Thomas Hogg mentioned in the letter was an Ettrick tailor.]

8 "Letter from Alexander Stewart, Canada." *New Evangelical Magazine and Theological Review*, Vol. VI (London: 1820), 124.

Unfortunately, their service to the community of York would be short-lived. John Menzies wrote, "…we continued about a year and a half, during which time several came to the place and joined the church."[9]

The church's dissolution

Several factors contributed to the church's disintegration in the early months of 1820. For the Stewart family, the first reason was financial. While Alexander had served as the Common School's first teacher, the remuneration was not sufficient to support his family.[10] In addition, given the economic downturn in York, he began to contemplate other opportunities. Stewart stated,

> I still lament with you that the concerns of this life stand as a bar in my way. I have a family to support,—that is a first duty, and I cannot at present devote more of my time than I now do, to preach the gospel: but I look forward to a period when I shall, if the Lord will, be more engaged in his immediate service. Without support from a foreign quarter, which is a thing I see not the least prospect of, it is impossible for me to preach much through the week.[11]

This burden was obviously a constant distraction to Stewart and, along with the responsibility of preaching three times every Sunday, it must have taken quite a toll on him, his family and his church. And yet, Alexander always exhibited a desire to do more.

> I employ myself on the Lord's day as much as I can. I preach forenoon [morning], afternoon, and evening. *Important as my station is here as a preacher of the gospel, I do lament the want*

---

9 Menzies, "Letter to Elder Archibald Cameron, January 12, 1841," 2.
10 Firth, *The town of York*, 98.
11 "Letter from Alexander Stewart, Canada." *New Evangelical Magazine and Theological Review*, Vol. VI (London: 1820), 124.

of opportunity to go about a little through the country to preach. I comfort myself with Paul's example at Ephesus. Perhaps the Lord may yet open here a great and effectual door. He may save many people at this place, and why should I murmur or repine at his will?[12]

Certainly, the itinerant's heart was still beating in Alexander's breast!

A final factor that must be considered was the existence of internal dissension within the church. John Menzies gave evidence of this cause when he wrote,

> Shortly before we left Toronto a few members embraced new sentiments, and altho, they were baptized and were several years with the churches in the Old Country, they withdrew from the church and maintained that they did not believe the Gospel till then and were not baptized.[13]

To paraphrase, it appears that a portion of the membership disputed the validity of the baptism they received in Scotland, as it occurred when they were unregenerate. Having been converted in Canada, they probably requested baptism a second time as profession of their new-found faith, citing the example of the New Testament church. It is not known whether or not there was an attempt at a resolution. Regardless, the parties involved eventually left the church. Thus, with the membership depleted, and with limited economic prospects, Stewart resigned his charge at the Common School and the church and prepared to move away from York.

Did the Baptists of York disband altogether? This question is difficult to answer. For, between the spring of 1820 and the fall of 1826, no records have been found that would indicate the Baptists ever maintained a formal meeting. However, one thing is certain:

---

12 "Letter from Alexander Stewart, Canada." *New Evangelical Magazine and Theological Review*, Vol. VI (London: 1820), 124. Author's italics.

13 Menzies, "Letter to Elder Archibald Cameron, January 12, 1841," 2-3.

York and its people would always be a cross that Alexander Stewart wanted to bear. So much so, that he would eventually return and rally the Baptists and finally call York his home.

Section 5

Itinerant preacher in Esquesing and environs

1820-1826

Chapter 9

Norval: the church in the woods

"We came to the woods on the 13th of March, 1820," stated John Menzies.[1] Carved out of that wild territory was the new village of Norval in the township of Esquesing, some eighty kilometres northwest of York. The township itself was given its name by Lieutenant Governor Maitland, deriving its origin "from the magnificent pine timber with which it was formerly covered, the word signifying in the Indian tongue, 'The Land of the Tall Pines'."[2] In fact, its creation took place in the neighbouring township of Toronto on October 28, 1818. On that date, the chiefs of the Otter and Eagle tribes of the Mississauga Nation put their totems on "Treaty 19"—an agreement to buy a large

---

1 John Menzies, "Letter to Elder Archibald Cameron, January 12, 1841." (Canadian Baptist Archives, McMaster University), 3.

2 J.H. Pope, *Illustrated historical atlas of the County of Halton Ontario* (Toronto: Walker & Miles, 1877), 55.

tract of land in the Home District.³ But why did Menzies and Alexander Stewart, along with many of York's Baptists, choose to settle in this wilderness?

Opportunities in "the Woods"

Alexander always maintained that his "first duty" was to provide for the needs of his family. Obviously, the land grant that Lieutenant Governor Maitland had given was of paramount importance in satisfying Stewart's domestic obligations. In addition, the concept of *spiritual kinship* should not be overlooked in the relocation decision. For, Stewart and the Baptists of York, like many Highland churches, "perceived themselves as a small 'clan'—in the world, but not of the world—making its way through many trials and tribulations to its real destination in Heaven."⁴ Thus, in April 1819, it is not surprising that Alexander banded together with six of York's Baptists and presented a joint application to the Lieutenant Governor requesting a location in Toronto Township (see Appendix C). The petition is unique in that these men asked that the usual method of drawing by lot be set aside so that they might all be located in one place for the purposes of attending to the ordinances of the Lord Jesus Christ. Eventually, these Baptists were located in Esquesing rather than Toronto Township. The Stewart land grant of 200 acres was located in Lot 7, Concession 11, just south of Norval.⁵ The Menzies family settled the east half of Lot 8,

---

3 Richard Ruggle, *Norval on the Credit River* (Erin: Press Porcepic, 1973), 10.

4 Donald E. Meek, "'The fellowship of kindred minds': some religious aspects of kinship and emigration from the Scottish Highlands in the nineteenth century." In *Hands across the water: emigration from Northern Scotland to North America* (Aberdeen: Aberdeen and North East Scotland Family Historical Society, 1995), 22.

5 *Abstracts of Deeds Esquesing Township, Halton County*, Public Archives of Ontario. Alexander finished his settlement duties and paid his administrative fees likely by 1826. He was finally awarded the patent (private ownership of a crown land parcel) to Lot 7, Concession 11 on November 23, 1827. He also purchased Lot 5 Concession 11, another 200 acres, from Richard Bristol in 1820. This was subsequently sold on November 15, 1821.

Concession 10, next to the Stewarts.[6] Also, Thomas Stephens (1771-1833), who gave the exhortation at the first service of the Baptist church at York, moved from Markham township and settled the east half of Lot 8 and 9, Concession 11.[7] Further, former York Baptist church members such as James Laidlaw and Thomas Fyfe (b.1774?) also cast their lot close by the others, though they did not add their names to the joint petition.[8] Stewart's intent was to work the land to support his family, and he was not alone in this purpose. Certainly, all of these families were confident that the land would yield enough produce to ensure their material well-being. In addition, the new locale presented Alexander with another opportunity.

The people of Esquesing, and of the other townships in the vicinity of Norval, sorely lacked spiritual instruction. They were also, few in strength, numbering just 424 souls in the year 1821.[9] Alexander Stewart longed to preach to them. Hence, given his experience, Alexander contended that he possessed all the instruments necessary to engage in an Upper Canadian itinerant ministry. Citing the pillars of the early church as an example, he exclaimed:

> The apostles used no craft...sent forth no spies, threatened no worldly punishment. They used no sword but the word of God. They went forth declaring the character of their king, and the love he manifested in redeeming his subjects by laying down his life for them, the glorious privileges and blessings he would bestow on all who would submit to his authority, and the certain destruction that awaited those who would not hear him. They preached, they

---

6 *Abstracts of Deeds Esquesing Township, Halton County*, Public Archives of Ontario. (See also Pope, *Illustrated historical atlas of the County of Halton Ontario*, 55.)

7 *Crown lands and resources records*, Public Archives of Ontario.

8 James Laidlaw settled Lot 5, Concession 3, and is mentioned as one of the earliest settlers in Halton. (See Pope, *Illustrated historical atlas of the County of Halton Ontario*, 55.) Thomas Fyfe settled the west half of Lot 7, Concession 9.

9 *Minute book Township of Esquesing 1821-1891*, Public Archives of Ontario.

prayed, they persuaded men to embrace the truth; and they manifested their own faith in that truth by patience and fortitude, under all their trials and persecutions, and by a life of obedience to the gospel they proclaimed. All the compulsion they used was persuasion, and even in this they did not use the enticing, or ensnaring words of man's wisdom, but by manifestation of the truth in its simplest form, they commended themselves to every man's conscience in the sight of God. "The weapons of their warfare were not carnal, *but mighty through God, to the pulling down of strongholds.*"[10]

Furthermore, Alexander was confident that, in this new environment, he could balance his desire of disseminating the gospel with the necessity of providing for his family.

A proposal made by Stewart to William Ballantine, captures the essence of this certainty, and displays his zeal for the lost. In it, Alexander recommended to Ballantine that the churches in Britain should consult who among them were gifted to preach the gospel and who among them were willing to live by cultivating lands. While the latter trait was of secondary importance, it was nevertheless crucial to the success of Stewart's program. For, "a man who could cultivate lands could soon get into such circumstances as would enable him to preach the gospel without charges."[11] Alexander also emphasized that these individuals "must be men of experience and of tried principles." Simply put, his plan advocated the placing of a Baptist pastor in every township of the province. Each minister could either get 100 acres of land from the government or get a lease of a 200 acre reserve lot for twenty-one years

---

10 Alexander Stewart, *Two essays: the first, on the gospel; the second, on the kingdom of Christ; and a sermon on baptism* (York: Colonial Advocate, Wm. Lyon Mackenzie, Printer, 1827), 54.

11 "Letter from Alexander Stewart, Canada." *New Evangelical Magazine and Theological Review*, Vol. VI (London: 1820), 125.

at $14 per year. "Thus the townships might all hear the gospel; and churches being formed in them pretty near to each other, its influence might be widely diffused in all the fruits of righteousness," wrote Stewart.[12]

Coupled with Alexander's desire to spread the truth was his desire to eradicate error. Stewart impressed upon Ballantine the urgency of bringing his plan to fruition, recognizing that if the Baptists did not seize the moment others would. "And shall we allow those who know not the gospel to exceed us in zeal? Shall zeal for a party overcome zeal for the *truth?*" Stewart asked.[13] While it appears that Alexander's plan was never implemented on a large scale it nonetheless illustrates something of his character. His concluding words to Ballantine, attest to the same: "I hope…that the churches will come forward like a burning and shining light, and cause darkness and ignorance to fly away from the best of countries."[14] Thus, regardless of whether or not there existed support from a foreign quarter, Alexander Stewart decided that he would do his part. But first, he would need to establish a base of operations.

The church in "the Woods"

The Baptist church at Norval, Esquesing Township, was probably formed on Sunday, March 19, 1820, with the meetings held in the home of John Menzies.[15] One can understandably wonder at the ease of Baptist church formation. It should be remembered that gifted preachers were in short supply in the New World, and thus there existed a strong dependence on lay leadership. Further, Baptists were "Independents" in the purest sense of the word: not dependent on a central organizing body. Hence, the Norval assembly was typical

---

12 "Letter from Alexander Stewart, Canada." *New Evangelical Magazine and Theological Review*, Vol. VI (London: 1820), 125.

13 "Letter from Alexander Stewart, Canada." *New Evangelical Magazine and Theological Review*, Vol. VI (London: 1820), 125.

14 "Letter from Alexander Stewart, Canada." *New Evangelical Magazine and Theological Review*, Vol. VI (London: 1820), 125.

15 Menzies, "Letter to Elder Archibald Cameron, January 12, 1841," 3.

of a "Highland" church, identical to the York church in its polity and particularly well suited to the emigrant experience.[16]

The duties of preaching in the Norval church were shared by Alexander Stewart and—"a man of fine education and culture"[17]—Thomas Stephens. However, because of the church's stress on lay leadership, there existed the risk that it "could readily proceed to new or 'enlightened' interpretations of the Scriptures under persuasive leaders."[18] This is, in part, what happened to the Baptists of Norval in the early months of 1821. John Menzies penned,

> …the church…continued about a year, in peace and love, till some differences took place between our two preachers in some worldly matters, which ended in a separation of the church and the most part of them went and joined those very men, that they parted with in Toronto for, what they called, Barean Sentiments.[19]

Thus, the causes of the schism were actually twofold. Further, the order in which Menzies places them is relevant. First, a rift occurred between Stewart and Stephens, the substance of which is not known. Certainly, Alexander possessed strong and, at times, inflexible opinions, and there is little doubt that this must have made attempts at reconciliation very problematic. In consequence, the congregation's loyalties became divided, and the greater number of them followed Stephens. After, and only after their departure, does Menzies mention the second reason for the split. Bereanism or Hyper-Calvinism may indeed have been a legitimate factor.

---

16 Donald E. Meek, "Evangelicalism and emigration: aspects of the role of dissenting evangelicalism in Highland emigration to Canada." In Gordon MacLennan, ed. *Proceedings of the first North American Congress of Celtic studies* (Ottawa: 1986), 22-23.

17 W.H. Trout, *Trout family history* (Milwaukee: Meyer-Rotier Printing Co., 1916), 51.

18 Meek, "Evangelicalism and emigration," 23.

19 Menzies, "Letter to Elder Archibald Cameron, January 12, 1841," 3.

However, more often than not, discord in the church is less a result of doctrinal differences than it is of conflicting personalities. In any event, the church at Norval survived the ordeal and formed itself anew with seven members in March 1821.[20]

Alexander Stewart continued to expound the word and nurture this little band in the woods despite their early trials. Although small in number, the church he built at Norval was now stable. He could, therefore, turn his attention to the communities close by and set a portion of his energy to the ministry of preaching and church planting. For truly, Stewart wanted to fulfill, in some measure, the plan he had communicated to his good friend William Ballantine.

---

20 Menzies, "Letter to Elder Archibald Cameron, January 12, 1841," 3.

Chapter 10

Missionary in "the land of the tall pines"

The five years that followed the schism of 1821 witnessed Alexander Stewart extending his missionary zeal beyond his responsibilities at Norval. In fact, John Menzies commented that "Brother Stewart was very frequent going out to preach, and the Church appointed me to keep up the meeting and administer the ordinance."[1] While these new opportunities gave reason for Alexander to rejoice, this was also a period where he and his family would suffer great loss. However, throughout this time, Alexander continuously sought to please and follow Jesus Christ. Little did he know that his sovereign Lord was leading him towards a field that had previously benefitted from his ministry.

---

1 John Menzies, "Letter to Elder Archibald Cameron, January 12, 1841." (Canadian Baptist Archives, McMaster University), 3.

Joy in Chinguacousy and Eramosa

Alexander Stewart was in his element when he was travelling from village to village, heralding the gospel message. Doubtless he preached in many communities, but only two instances of his evangelizing efforts have surfaced on the pages of recorded history. First, on a Sunday in 1825, when Alexander had occasion to preach in the Township of Chinguacousy. Imagine, for a moment, his discourse, as it is given to an audience on the banks of the Credit River in the open-air. Stewart presents the example of Scripture as several candidates gather in obedience to their Lord's command. Listen, as he passionately expounds on the doctrine of believer's baptism:

> Whatever God commands, his people are bound to obey; if he has placed them in circumstances in which they can obey. There may be circumstances in which it is impossible to obey, such as deep distress. In such cases God will have mercy and not sacrifice. This is quite a different thing from abstaining from baptism for fear of persecution, want of convenience, &c. It has been asked how men can be immersed where there is no water, and that there are some places where water cannot be found. This is trifling with the will of God. Can it be seriously thought that any person would live in a place where there could not be so much water found as would cover his body? Would a man not travel one or two hundred miles for gain or at the command of his sovereign — and is it too hard if it be absolutely necessary, to travel that distance to obey Christ? Where is the man in Canada that could not reach a lake or river?[2]

---

2 Alexander Stewart, *Two essays: the first, on the gospel; the second, on the kingdom of Christ; and a sermon on Baptism* (York: Colonial Advocate, Wm. Lyon Mackenzie, Printer, 1827), 86.

Missionary in "the land of the tall pines" 133

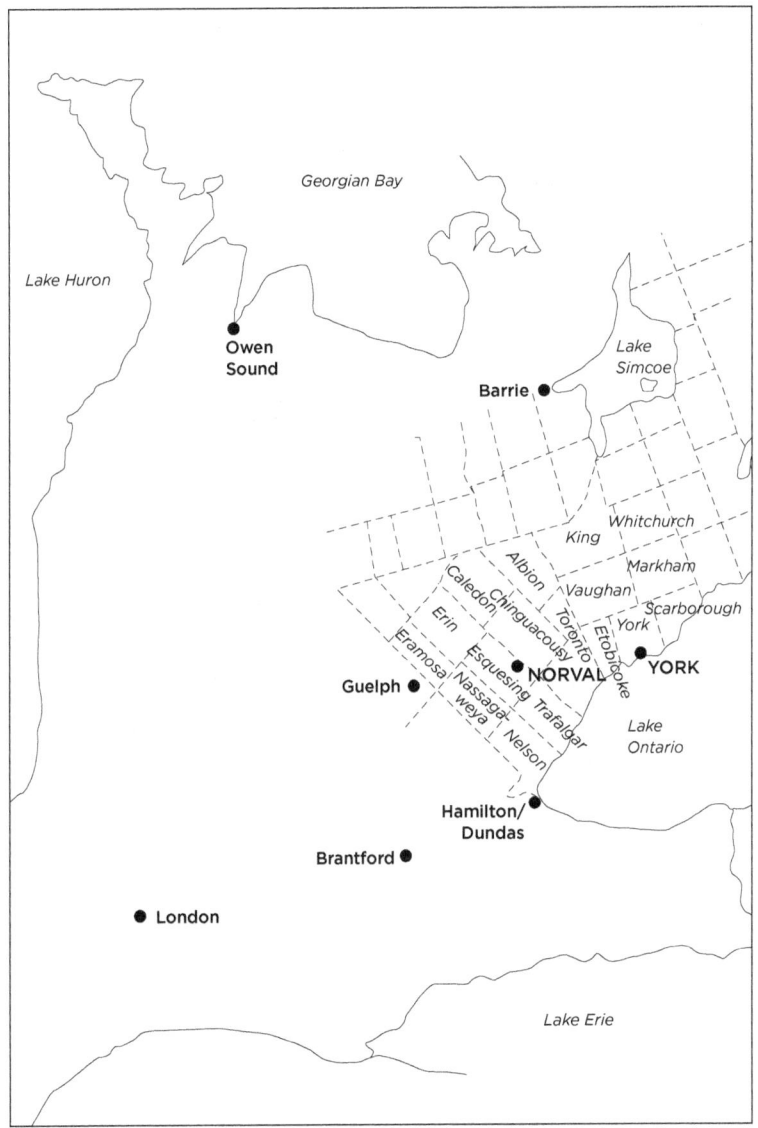

THE TOWN OF YORK
AND SURROUNDING TOWNSHIPS

A second record indicates that Stewart was also engaged in church-planting work. Sometime prior to 1825, Alexander is listed as one of the founding fathers of the church in East Eramosa, thirty kilometres west of Norval. Specifically, the account indicates that "in the beginning" the church was shepherded by the following leading men: David Oliphant Sr., Thomas Stephens, Donald McLean and Alexander Stewart.[3] These preachers of the gospel were further assisted by the arrival of James Black (1797–1886), who had for some time ministered in Aldborough Township in Elgin County.[4] Doubtless, Alexander Stewart cherished these fruits of an itinerant ministry. However, while these were times of joy for Stewart, they were tempered by the many trials and pains experienced at home in Norval.

Pain in Esquesing

From the spring of 1820 to the spring of 1826, the Baptist church at Norval never exceeded ten members.[5] This must have been a source of profound discouragement for both Alexander Stewart and John Menzies. Perhaps too, it says something of the "difficult ground" they were attempting to cultivate for the cause of Christ's kingdom. James Laidlaw, the old shepherd, in a letter to William Lyon Mackenzie (1795–1861), newspaper man and future mayor of Toronto, wrote of the poor character of Esquesing's citizens. The following is an extract of this letter, printed *without* Laidlaw's permission in Mackenzie's *Colonial Advocate*:

> I have taken upon me to write a few Lines to le you kno that the Scotts Bodys that Lives heare is all doing Tolarably well for the things of this world but I am afraid that few of them thinks about what will Come of their Soul when

---

3 Reuben Butchart, *The disciples of Christ in Canada since 1830* (Toronto: Churches of Christ Disciples, 1949), 4.

4 Elder James Black was an itinerant preacher who emigrated to Canada in 1820.

5 Menzies, "Letter to Elder Archibald Cameron, January 12, 1841," 3.

Death there days doth End for they have found a thing they Call Whiskey and a great many of them dabbales and drinks at it till they make themselves worce than an ox or an ass for they Differ among themSelves and men that meets good friends before they pairt is Like to cut one anothers throts Burns Speaks of the Barley Bree Sementing the qurall but the ray Bree hear is almost sure to make Qurall for since the Bodys turnd Lairds Every one if for bring Master and they never consider that there Neighbour is as far up in the world as themselves, but America is a good Contry for a poor man if he is able to work but is a Contry that is full of Rougs that is what I like it worst for for there is very few but will Cheat you if they can if I had known it to be what it is it Should never have seen me…[6]

Like Laidlaw, Alexander Stewart was well aware of the depraved nature of this mission field. In fact, that is precisely why he wanted

---

6 "Letter from James Laidlaw [January 8, 1827]." *Colonial Advocate*, York, January 18, 1827. The fact that Mackenzie printed Laidlaw's letter speaks of his character. When Laidlaw found out that his letter was in the *Advocate*, he became so incensed that he wrote another missive to Mackenzie and added some sage advice:

Esquising March 17th 1827. Very Dear Sir
  This will Let you know that you have done me a very Bad trick in printing my bit simpel Letter that I sent you ye are shurly very scarce of News. I thought that you had more honour in you than Expose an old Body Like me when I told you not to put me in your paper but I will trust no more to you, for the folk hear is so ill pleased out there bits of falts beng told that they Look to me Like stink and when they pass by will scarce say good day. I Like to Live in peace with all my Neighbours but you have put an end to it now. but it was my foley in writing to such a (?) Stump that puts all in your bit ill printed paper that you can get by hook or Crook I Shall say Littel more but if ever I come to you I shall give you your xxxx. I ould give you my advice to read your Bible and it will tell you to do Justice and ove Mercy and walk Humbly with thy God. I remain your Humble Servt. James Laidlaw

("Letters from James Laidlaw, January 8 & March 17 1827." *William Lyon Mackenzie Correspondence*, Public Archives of Ontario, 508.)

to preach the gospel. He shared his Saviour's mindset, "I did not come to call the righteous, but sinners, to repentance" (Matthew 9:13). Hence, Stewart understood that his sole duty was to be the vessel and deliver God's message. And while the results were often disheartening, he left the work of regeneration to the electing grace of God. However, there was a terrible happening that Alexander could have never prepared himself for. Furthermore, it took place in the midst of his own family.

James Stewart, Alexander and Janet's oldest son, died in 1822 at the age of fifteen.[7] The past is silent in regards to the circumstances surrounding his death. Nevertheless, the harshness of life in the wilderness often took its toll on pioneer families. This observation does not make their son's death any less tragic. Mother and father surely suffered through a long period of intense grief. In addition, the Stewart's experienced a loss of another kind. On January 27, 1824, Rev. John Strachan presided over the marriage of John McIntosh (1796-1853) and Catherine Oswald Stewart, in York's St. James Anglican Church.[8] To be sure, Alexander and Janet did gain a son! However, their daughter's removal to York coupled with the recent blow of James' untimely death may have fuelled a latent desire to return to the larger community of York.

Alexander Stewart was certain that God had ordered every aspect of his life. He always recognized that it was his responsibility to discern his Sovereign's will and obediently follow his leading. This he did, in the Highlands of Scotland, in Upper Canada's capital and in "the land of the tall pines." By 1826, he knew God was directing him towards another sphere of service. The Baptists of Norval had a capable and faithful man in Elder Menzies, the "walking concordance." Conversely, the Baptists of York were leaderless. Alexander Stewart's choice was crystal clear: God was calling him back to the town of York.

---

7 Entry for February 24, 1832. "James Lesslie Diaries." (Dundas Historical Society Museum, Dundas, Ontario).

8 Marriage registers of St. James Anglican Church, Toronto.

Section 6

York: the return of a Baptist presence 1826-1829

Chapter 11

Participating in the voice of reform

The town of York saw little demographic change in the six years of Alexander Stewart's absence. Its population growth had been steady, but modest, reaching the 1,700 mark by 1826.[1] There was, however, a political "tempest in a teapot" brewing in the capital between Reformers and Tories. In particular, it centred on a fiery Scotsman from Dundee and his newspaper. While Stewart's relocation to York was prompted by family concerns and a desire to consolidate the Baptists of that town, it also gave him a chance to add a distinctive Baptist voice to the chorus of reform.

Alexander was quite familiar with the inequities parcelled out by a religious group whose status was entrenched in the law of the land. He had witnessed, firsthand, what the General Assembly of the Scottish Kirk was capable of. He was seeing it's like in the Anglican Church in Upper Canada, and given his itinerant, non-

---

1 Edith Firth, ed. *The town of York, 1815-1834* (Toronto: University of Toronto Press/Champlain Society, 1966), lxxxii.

conformist nature, he would not—no, he could not—keep silent. Furthermore, Stewart would not necessarily fight for political equality in the chambers and halls of government. On the contrary, he consistently waged this battle at a *spiritual* level. His vehicle was his pulpit, and his sword, a pen. Oftentimes, as Alexander sought to dispel the prejudices levied against the despised Baptists, his attack was veiled. Hear his words:

> It is generally held out by these hirelings, that dissenters, that go about preaching for nothing, or without hire, are the false prophets. Christ says, "By their fruits ye shall know them." We can find great abundance of the fruits of unrighteousness with those who wear the gowns and bands, and whose religious systems are supported by the law. We ought "to try the spirits, whether they are of God." Let the false prophets, or false teachers, be judged of by their fruits, whether among establishments, or among dissenters. It is not of churches we are now speaking, but of false doctrine, held forth by false teachers. Let us, "prove all things, and hold fast that which is good."[2]

In addition, Stewart also demonstrated the ability to launch a direct assault:

> If we are against the state (a very common charge against the people of God), let them apply the wholesome laws of our country to us. We shrink not from the fullest investigation. We have always denied fellowship to those who have, in any manner, acted contrary to the laws, or against our Sovereign King George. Our conduct, in this respect, has uniformly proved the sincerity of our profession. We *may*

---

2 Alexander Stewart, *Two essays: the first, on the gospel; the second, on the kingdom of Christ; and a sermon on baptism* (York: Colonial Advocate, Wm. Lyon Mackenzie, Printer, 1827), 37.

be charged with being opposed to *their* church, for we boldly affirm that it has not the marks of the church of Christ. Its members and ordinances are quite different from the N.T. churches. Christ's kingdom is not of this world. The introduction of infant baptism was a first corruption—a second was its being made subject to bishops and pontiffs—and lastly its being united to the state. We are sure these are corruptions, yet we wish no downfall of any church, not even the church of Rome, but by the word of God. For this we earnestly pray.[3]

Notwithstanding his methods, Stewart always defended and remained true to his independent, Baptist way of thinking:

Some may think that I speak with prejudice and irritation against other teachers, and that I also would accept of ecclesiastical preferment if I could obtain it. I can assure such they are mistaken. That I abhor the doctrine is true, but I wish their salvation. As to preferment I would not accept of any. I trust I have higher motives.[4]

Those "higher motives" were quickly put to the test, upon his return to York in the spring of 1826.

The Types Riot

William Lyon Mackenzie's choice instrument of striking at Upper Canada's ruling class was in financial trouble by the time Stewart came back to York. In fact, Mackenzie closed the doors of his newspaper, the *Colonial Advocate*, in early June 1826, after publishing what he thought was his last diatribe against the Family Compact. Instead, it was this last Reform "straw" that broke the Tory "camel's" back. On the evening of Thursday, June 8, 1826, a group of young

---

3 Stewart, *Two essays*, 94-95.
4 Stewart, *Two essays*, 44.

Tories broke into the offices of the *Advocate*, smashed some of the equipment and threw the types into Toronto Bay.⁵ As a result, Mackenzie was rewarded £625 damages in a civil suit and the famous War of 1812 veteran, Colonel James FitzGibbon (1780-1863), was entrusted with the task of publicly collecting the money from the leading families of York! Thus, Mackenzie's *Advocate* was back in business, and he would use the printed page to constantly remind his Tory enemies of the incident.⁶

Alexander Stewart watched this whole event unfold. He did not have to get involved. But he did. Quietly and cautiously, he cast his lot into the leading reformer's camp. A letter by a fellow reformer named Jesse Ketchum (1782-1867), sent to Mackenzie a few days after the revolt, illustrates Stewart's concern for the editor of the *Advocate*, and carries with it two concealed suggestions:

> ...I Wrote You Little because I supposed you would have a full account from your own folks respecting the destruction of your property & I had not at time an oppertunety of hearing the Publick expression which I find to be very Strong in your favour. But Mr. Stuart [Stewart] thinks you will not be Safe in York from personal violance but that I think is a wrong conclusion. He also thinks that thear is Leagal proceeding entered against you for Libell. How that may be I do not know But on the whole I think with good management you might git all your things settled...⁷

---

5 "Types" referred to the lead letters that were used to typeset the newspaper.

6 Chris Raible's book, *Muddy York mud: scandal & scurrility in Upper Canada* (Creemore: Curiosity House, 1992), deals with the "Types Riot" and subsequent trial in detail. [Note: Colonel James FitzGibbon was born in Ireland and entered the British Army during the Napoleonic Wars, coming to Canada in 1802. He served in the War of 1812 and was appointed Assistant Adjutant General in 1822. He returned to England in 1846 and later became a military knight at Windsor. (See Firth, *The town of York*, 232.)]

7 Firth, *The town of York*, 98.

First, Stewart wanted Mackenzie to continue the cause of reform, but away from the heat of York. Second, Alexander subtly encouraged Mackenzie to take a respectful and truthful approach when drafting his editorials. Alas, William Lyon Mackenzie did neither of these things. His future assaults exhibited a single-mindedness: win the day at any cost, using any means necessary. While it is true that Stewart was unable to influence Mackenzie's course of action, he would be able to demonstrate his own suggested methods, as his status as an observer would change. Indeed, an opportunity would present itself that would enable Alexander Stewart to address the Establishment directly.

The Common School question

On February 28, 1828, Alexander Stewart petitioned government representatives on an issue that was close to his heart: education. Specifically, Stewart's audience was assigned to examine and report on any executive abuses relating to the keeping of Common Schools in the province. The Upper Canadian legislature had passed the Common Schools Act in 1816. Through its enactment, a group of citizens could receive a grant of up to £25 towards a free school, provided they had twenty pupils and were prepared to subscribe whatever additional funds were needed. Of course, Alexander was well acquainted with York's Common School for he was its first teacher in 1818, resigning that post in 1820. He was succeeded by Thomas Appleton.[8] However, Appleton's tenure was short-lived. Rev. John Strachan and certain members of the Executive Council espoused control of education by the Established Church. Further, they desired to use a portion of the government funds to support a school in which Church of England principles would be taught.

---

8 Thomas Appleton arrived from Yorkshire in 1819. He taught at schools in Scarborough and King Townships, and in 1820 he was appointed schoolmaster of the York Common School. When Maitland established the Central School in York, Appleton moved to a schoolhouse on Colborne Street and continued to teach for some years. (See Firth, *The town of York*, 143.)

Consequently, the government seized the school and Appleton was denied the official grant.⁹ Not surprisingly, these high-handed tactics were never forgotten by the reformers. Appleton protested this action for seven years and finally succeeded in having his case brought before the legislature. Many witnesses were called, including Stewart, for he had unique insight into Appleton's experience. The minutes of Alexander's testimony are as follows:

> The Reverend Alexander Stewart, being examined, stated that he is a Baptist Minister, educated in Edinburgh. A native of Scotland he left it in 1818 for this province, via Quebec. Upon coming to York, he kept a Common School, (the same as that afterwards kept by Mr. Appleton) for about a year and a half, for which he received the Legislative bounty.
>
> He next kept a school in Toronto Township for a year, ending in June 1826. Upon applying for the Legislative bounty, was refused on the ground (as stated by the Reverend Dr. Strachan) that the District Board of Education limited the number of schools to three in that township.
>
> He presented to the District Board a Petition, but received no answer.
>
> He has known other teachers who have been refused the Legislative bounty, and he knows no other reason than the one assigned to himself.
>
> In the other Districts, the numbers have not been so limited. In the Niagara District there were two townships, where six Common Schools were allowed. He does not know of any such limitation in any other District than this.¹⁰

---

9 Firth, *The town of York*, xlvii.
10 J.G. Hodgins, *Documentary history of education in Upper Canada, 1790-1840*, Vol. 1 (Toronto: Warwick Bros. & Rutter, 1894), 251.

It should be noted that the reformers, which included many nonconformist clergymen, always contended for equality of educational opportunity. On this day the reformers were victorious! The legislature condemned the action of the Executive, and there began the long struggle between the two branches of government which continued over many years.[11]

The King's College question

Stewart did not limit his reforming interests to the Common School question alone. He was also interested in the developments that were taking place in higher education. While the full desectarianization of King's College (later the University of Toronto) from the control of the Anglican Church did not take place until the mid 1840s, Alexander's preliminary work on the Central Committee set the framework for a later Baptist's liberating efforts.[12] The first report of the Central Committee was a petition dated June 28, 1828. Stewart and the other signatories advocated that all Christian denominations be recognized in the constitution of the new university.[13]

---

11 Stuart Ivison & Fred Rosser, eds. *The Baptists in Upper and Lower Canada before 1820* (Toronto: University of Toronto Press, 1956), 149.

12 Refer to letter from Wm. L. Mackenzie "To the Members of the Methodist Conference, assembled at Hamilton." *Correspondent & Advocate* (Toronto, June 11, 1835).

That *other* Baptist I refer to was Robert Alexander Fyfe (1816-1878). Fyfe was pastor of March Street Baptist Church from 1844 to 1848 and later Bond Street Baptist Church from 1855 to 1860. He would later become Principal of the Canadian Literary Institute, a position he held until his death. It should be noted that Fyfe was "in the very forefront of the warriors for the equality of all citizens in the ownership, control and use of the national university. Indeed, it may well be affirmed that Fyfe was the most consistent and most persistent of all the protagonists of complete religious equality in secular educational institutions in this long struggle." [Theo T. Gibson, *Robert Alexander Fyfe: His contemporaries and his influence* (Burlington: Welch Publishing Co., 1988), 329.]

13 *First report of the Central Committee on the petition to the imperial Parliament, from Christians of all denominations in Upper Canada* (York: Colonial Advocate, Wm. Lyon Mackenzie, Printer, 1828).

When Alexander Stewart returned to York in 1826, he could have chosen to remain silent regarding the structures of society. As a minister of the gospel he certainly espoused the separation of church and state. But as a private citizen he did not shy away from speaking against unrighteousness, particularly unfairness in education. Thus his presence and point of view were helpful in laying the groundwork for future public reform. However, of prime concern to Stewart was *private* reform and the need to share the good news of Christ's gospel to York's citizenry. As Jesus said, "Make a tree good and its fruit will be good" (Matthew 12:33, NIV).

Chapter 12

Alexander Stewart's theology

It is imperative at this juncture to consider something of Alexander Stewart's theological perspective. For, to understand a man's view of the God of the Scriptures is to understand something of the man himself and of his vision for gospel ministry. Providentially, we are not left to our own musings to wonder at where he stood. During the winter months of 1827, Stewart completed a treatise that he hoped would effectively communicate the Baptist message and eliminate the theological errors he detected around him.¹ It was entitled *Two essays: the first, on the gospel; the second, on the kingdom of Christ; and a sermon on baptism*, and is the only printed record known to exist, that conveys in

---

1 Deryck W. Lovegrove indicates that the Haldane brothers attempted to eradicate error through their theological writings as well. [See Deryck W. Lovegrove, "Unity and separation: contrasting elements in the thought and practice of Robert and James Alexander Haldane." In Keith Robbins, ed. *Protestant Evangelicalism: Britain, Ireland, Germany and America c.1750-c.1950. Essays in honour of W.R. Ward* (Oxford: Basil Blackwell, 1990), 160.]

detail, his theological thought. Alexander's good friend, William Lyon Mackenzie, agreed to run the *Essays* as a serial in the *Advocate* and, in July, printed the work in book form. Fortunately, Stewart's subscription list to his *Essays* has also been preserved. For, inasmuch as the list shows his commitment to reach the lost of his community, it also illustrates his concern to touch the entire province of Upper Canada: from Malahide Township in the west to Glengarry Township in the east.[2] Thus, when Stewart returned to York in the spring of 1826, he came as a man with a completely crystallized theology. This is not to say that his views had changed radically since his adoption of Baptist principles in 1808. In short, Stewart was decidedly a Calvinist; and, it is this fact alone that speaks volumes as to his character and as to the focus of the organizations he founded, nurtured, and left as a legacy.

God's missive and Stewart's bibliology

Foundational to all that Alexander Stewart believed was the regard he had for God's revelation to mankind. Stewart reasoned that because the Bible is God's inerrant Word it must follow that it contains everything that is needful for salvation and for matters of faith and practice. Alexander espoused the principle of *Sola Scriptura*; in his own words he declared, "The bible is enough."[3] Speaking on Christ's kingdom as not being governed by worldly laws, Stewart testified to the primacy of the Scriptures:

> The bible is the christian's book of statutes: to it he pays respect and walks in its light; it is the light to his feet, and the lamp to his path; he hides it in his heart that he might

---

2 Alexander Stewart, "Returns of subscribers for *Essays on the gospel and the kingdom of Christ*." (Louis Melzack Collection, Thomas Fisher Rare Book Library, University of Toronto, Toronto).

3 Alexander Stewart, *Two essays: the first, on the gospel; the second, on the kingdom of Christ; and a sermon on baptism* (York: Colonial Advocate, Wm. Lyon Mackenzie, Printer, 1827), 58.

not sin against God; it is the man of his counsel all the day long. There he sees the will of God written as with a sun beam. Others may heed to their articles, creeds and constitutions, but the new testament is his only guide—there he finds the true faith, the true practice, and the true constitution of the churches of Christ. All the vain attempts of men to improve upon the apostles, is darkening council by words without knowledge. The Westminster divines and others may have been good and wise men, but we affirm that the Apostles were better and wiser, and therefore ought to be heard in preference. Shall we have the old cant brought forward, that these confessions make things plainer? We answer: the holy ghost could speak plainer than any common man. To say that any book is plainer than the new testament, is directly to impeach the wisdom and power of God.[4]

Thus, Stewart considered, "It would be direct rebellion against the Lord, for Christians to admit of any law as their guide not sanctioned by the Apostles."[5]

God's message and Stewart's soteriology

Simply put, Stewart believed that the redemption of men and women is *solely* accomplished through the sovereign grace of the triune God—thereby giving all the glory to God. Because man is *totally depraved*, every fibre of man's being is tainted with sin [ie. "There is none who does good, no, not one" (Romans 3:12, NKJV)]. It is absolutely essential, then, that he has an advocate to act on his behalf to save him. In his *Essay on the gospel of Christ*, Stewart elaborated on this point and spoke of those to whom the gospel is addressed:

---

4 Stewart, *Two essays*, 59.
5 Stewart, *Two essays*, 59.

> The human race are not only sinners in *practice*, but the inherent principle of sin is interwoven in their very *nature*... As such they are under the condemning sentence of the law of God... Not only in this case, but they are utterly helpless; utterly unable to do any thing to save themselves... All that a natural man performs, even his religious services, springs from wrong motives—self love is the spring of all, and destroys all its productions... Present duties, and these duties springing from sinful motives too, cannot atone for past transgressions.[6]

In consequence of this condition, the only thing that sinful man has that would recommend him to God is his "utter pollution and helplessness," stated Stewart. "The righteousness of a just person must be imputed to them or they must perish."[7]

Alexander taught that since there is nothing in a man's personal character that would recommend him to God as a candidate for salvation it follows that God's sovereign choosing of the *elect* before the foundation of the world is *unconditional*. In fact, he wholeheartedly concurred with the apostle Paul:

> But God has chosen the foolish things of the world to put to shame the wise, and God has chosen the weak things of the world to put to shame the things which are mighty; and the base things of the world and the things which are despised God has chosen, and the things which are not, to bring to nothing the things that are, that no flesh should glory in His presence (1 Corinthians 1:27-29, NKJV).

Stewart does not touch on this doctrine in his *Essays*, however, we do find a clear picture of his position in his "Notes on the Baptist church at Perth, Scotland, 1810-1815." Specifically, Stewart wrote

---

6 Stewart, *Two essays*, 20.
7 Stewart, *Two essays*, 21.

of a two-hour discussion that he and Peter McNaughton had with a man surnamed McKinchie on Monday, January 9, 1815. Basically, McKinchie's view was twofold. First, regarding the Holy Spirit's application of salvation, he stated that a sinner first believes the gospel and then is made partaker of the Spirit and at that point the Spirit by the Word converts him. Second, regarding the Father's plan of election in salvation, McKinchie said that God elects all who would believe and foreknew all who should believe. Alexander's response is telling: "With him I differ on both & told him I considered his views detracting from the grace of God and giving the glory at least of the application of salvation to the sinner."[8] It is hardly surprising that on the ensuing Sunday, Elder Stalker preached on the subject "Election—Objections Answered"! Three objections were brought forward for the church's consideration, namely, (1) of partiality in God; (2) of its not being consistent with it being said that God hath no pleasure in the death of the wicked or that he will have all men to be saved; (3) that it is not consistent with the extent of the call of the gospel. Alexander recorded in his journal that John Stalker "ably answered" all three objections.

Stewart also affirmed that God the Son succeeded in atoning for the elect, as the writer of the Epistle to the Hebrews declares, "so Christ was offered once to bear the sins of many" (Hebrews 9:28). To be sure, one drop of Jesus' blood would have been sufficient to redeem a billion worlds. However, his intent was to save *his people* from their sins. Therefore Jesus' sacrifice was efficient to redeem his chosen people alone. Not one drop of his precious blood was wasted! This is the principle of *limited atonement* or *particular redemption* to which Alexander testified:

---

8 Alexander Stewart, "Notes on the Baptist church at Perth, Scotland, 1812-1815." (Melzak Collection, Toronto). Also in the same vein, on January 29, 1815, the membership application of Jess Easson came before the church at Perth. She testified before the congregation that "man believed the gospel of himself then recd the spirit & was converted." Stewart recorded: "On this the church was called & she was refused fellowship."

> He died for sinners, and every sinner that believes in his atonement for sin as the ground of his acceptance before God, is justified. The atonement for Christ is the propitiation for sin, and to the sinner who believes in his character and work, is his righteousness imputed; that is, the work of Christ, or object of the sinner's faith, is imputed to the sinner, and he is thereby justified. His sins are pardoned, and he is made an heir of eternal life.[9]

It is interesting to note how Stewart connects Christ's perfectly completed work of redemption to the *certainty* of a sinner's justification and glorification. For, Alexander believed that the work of Jesus Christ actually *achieves* a sinner's reconciliation and does not merely put him into a position of reconcilability.

Stewart also taught the sureness of the Holy Spirit's application of salvation to the elect. To put it another way, the *grace* of God is *irresistibly* applied to those who God has chosen. Reflecting on the sweetness of the gospel message and the fact that man cannot respond to it, Stewart wrote of the only possible solution for those who are absolutely "dead in trespasses and sins" (Ephesians 2:1):

> ...the sinner can find no fault with the gospel of Christ, yet the perpetual language of his heart is, away with it. He hates—he abhors it. Truth as it is (and his conscience bears witness to its truth), he will not receive it. He hates both the gospel and its author—he has seen and hated, both Christ and his Father. Such is his rooted hatred to the gospel that nothing but Divine power can remove it.[10]

So, will those who are made alive by the quickening power of the Spirit, *reject* the call of God? To even suggest this is to posit a God who is impotent or powerless to save. No, Stewart trusted the

---

9 Stewart, *Two essays*, 22.
10 Stewart, *Two essays*, 38.

words of Scripture, as Jesus stated: "All that the Father gives Me *will come to Me*" (John 6:37, NKJV). God, through the irresistible power of his Holy Spirit, is able to move men's hearts.

Finally, Alexander Stewart believed in the *perseverance of the saints* because he believed in a God who preserves his people and finishes the work he began in them. Stewart proclaimed, "Who can break the seal which Jehovah has fixed on his blood-bought property?"[11] Indeed, Alexander knew well Christ's words when he declared, "And I give them eternal life, and they shall never perish; neither shall anyone snatch them out of My hand" (John 10:28, NKJV). This was a doctrine that was precious to Stewart, and hence he did not mince words with those who thought otherwise:

> Some may reprobate the perseverance of the saints, but such "know not the scriptures, nor the power of God." They say salvation is connected with continuing in faith; this is true; but it is also true that the power of God is engaged in keeping them in the faith, and that the Holy Spirit has sealed them as Jehovah's eternal property… The certain consequence of believing the gospel is everlasting life.[12]

Praise God for his grace!

God's messenger and Stewart's ecclesiology

When Alexander Stewart came back to York his express intent was to replant the Baptist church along "Scottish" Baptist lines. This fact must be distinctly understood, because it represents a change in his views on church order. For, his church in Perth, Scotland, his first church in York and his church in Norval were all "Scotch" Baptist in their polity. Although Scotch and Scottish Baptists were alike in their Calvinism and evangelical doctrine, Scotch Baptist espoused a plurality of elders whereas Scottish Baptists maintained

---

11 Stewart, *Two essays*, 24.
12 Stewart, *Two essays*, 24.

a single-man eldership. "The difference is not trifling when the force of the two separate mind-sets and respective group energies are considered."[13] The question remains why did Stewart discard the notion of a plurality of elders? Although the Scottish Baptists aligned themselves with a growing denomination in England, this does not account for Alexander's new-found allegiance. Perhaps the change was a by-product of his experience. Did he surmise that a one-man pastor-led congregation would be less susceptible to the schisms he had already experienced in Upper Canada? Given the inherent divergent opinions of York's immigrant population, he may have been right in his approach. In any case, he was still a Baptist; and he clearly appreciated the challenges that came with his branch of Protestantism's witness:

> Were Paul to apply now to some existing churches I fear they would refuse him upon very different grounds from those of the church at Jerusalem—some would exclaim, begone Paul, you are not of our tenets—you say our earnest endeavours to keep the law will not save us—you preach salvation by grace only—your faith is too simple for us—you preach individual election to eternal life—you preach the necessity of conversion and being a new creature—you preach perseverance—you put all the clergy on a level, and set a bad example for ministers to work—you are too strict about holy conduct—you are an independent, and have the impudence to order particular churches to settle their own affairs: thus despising bishops, presbyteries, sessions, conferences, &c—you are a baptist—you oppose oratory—you are an enthusiast, a hypocrite, a sectarian—you separated the disciples from the synagogue, though we know the Jewish and the christian churches are one—Be gone! you can have no fellow-

---

13 Claude E. Cox, ed. *The Campbell-Stone Movement in Ontario* (Queenston: Edwin Mellen Press, 1995), 415.

ship with us—it is not fit such a fellow should live. This is no vain picture —it is what Paul's followers meet with daily, and have met with for 1,800 years.[14]

With these preliminary considerations at the forefront, what did the local manifestation of Christ's messenger at York look like and what was it like to attend a Lord's Day gathering of the "despised" Baptists?

Stewart's adoption of the Scottish form of church government did not negate his belief in the two offices of the New Testament church: "The apostolic churches...when in full order, had office bearers, these were bishops and deacons."[15] Speaking on the qualifications for elders, Stewart, not surprisingly, appealed to the practice of the primitive church:

> It is evident the apostles did not look to universities, or colleges, for bishops, though thousands might have become college learned during the period between Christ's resurrection and Paul's writing to Timothy and Titus. They looked from among themselves for persons qualified by the holy Ghost.[16]

In addition, he also sought to put right the responsibilities of the deaconate:

> The deacons were the temporal servants of the church. We have often wondered how the clergy in general, have managed so well to keep the deacons in their own place, while they have usurped so much unlawful authority for themselves—authority never given them by Jesus Christ.[17]

---

14 Stewart, *Two essays*, 67.
15 Stewart, *Two essays*, 68.
16 Stewart, *Two essays*, 68.
17 Stewart, *Two essays*, 69.

Thus, the church at York was given spiritual oversight by one elder, called the "president," while the deacons were given the responsibility of "serving tables" (Acts 6:2). But who did these office bearers serve?

Central to Alexander Stewart's baptistic ecclesiology was the requirement that all members gave testimony of their faith, publicly declaring their union with Christ through believer's baptism.[18] Baptism by immersion was considered a prerequisite to fellowship at the Lord's Table, making Stewart's view of fellowship in the church one of "close communion."[19] Doubtless he reasoned that to partake in a familial meal one must first testify that one *belongs* to the family. Furthermore, it is critical to note that Alexander did not advocate baptismal regeneration. Prominent at this time, were the teachings of two Baptists, Thomas Campbell (1763-1854) and his son Alexander Campbell (1788-1866). Initially, Stewart had admired the Campbells.[20] However, as will be seen in Chapter 15, he would later depart from them over their adherence to the doctrine that baptism by immersion is the *indispensable* testimony to saving faith. Thus, in the 1830s, when many Baptist churches began flocking to the Campbellites or the denomination known as the Disciples of Christ, Stewart held firm. In short, Alexander Stewart never became a proponent of the "Restoration Movement"[21] or a spokesman for Campbellism. He lived the life of a Baptist and believed simply that the ordinance represented and displayed publicly a believer's union with Christ.

---

18 For a fuller picture of Alexander Stewart's views on the subject of baptism, the reader is directed to Appendix D for his only printed sermon.

19 In general, "close communion" is the practice of restricting participation in the Lord's Supper to those who are members of a particular church, whereas "open communion" is the practice of allowing participation in the Lord's Supper to those who are not members of a particular church but profess faith in Christ.

20 Stewart, *Two essays*, 12. Stewart uses Campbell's translation of the Scriptures.

21 The Restoration Movement sought to "reform" the whole church based solely on the pattern of the New Testament without any reference to the creeds developed by the church, orthodox or otherwise.

In accordance with the example and practice of the early church, Stewart contended for the observation of seven acts of worship each Lord's day: public prayers, praise, public reading of the Scriptures, preaching and expounding of the Word of God, the exhortation of the brethren, the fellowship and the Lord's Supper. Of course, the pinnacle of the order of baptistic worship was preaching, which Stewart exclaimed was "the proper work of elders".[22]

Of the remaining ordinances, only three require further explanation. First, the praise offered to God was to be unadorned. Stewart explained, "The first churches sang psalms, hymns, and spiritual songs...but they had neither organs, viols, nor flutes—neither had they singing bands of ungodly people set by themselves—it was the church which sang the praises of God as such."[23] Second, exhortation by the brethren, though uncommon even in Stewart's day, was nonetheless considered important. For, it "provided a natural means for the divine choice of pastoral leadership to become apparent."[24] Alexander believed that this duty was an express command of Scripture and that Christians should attend to it when they gathered together for worship. However, he lamented that it was now "generally thrown out at the doors of meeting houses, to make way for the splendid talents of the preachers."[25] Third, the fellowship, was understood to mean the weekly "collection for the poor and other necessary uses."[26] Hence, Stewart was convinced that each Sunday was the Lord's and as such all these matters of worship were beneficial and should be attended to:

---

[22] Stewart, *Two essays*, 70.
[23] Stewart, *Two essays*, 69.
[24] Lovegrove, "Unity and separation," 171, citing J.A. Haldane, *Observations on... mutual exhortation.*
[25] Stewart, *Two essays*, 70.
[26] Stewart, *Two essays*, 70.

The Lord's day is a memorial of Christ's resurrection, and the Lord's supper is a memorial of his death, and the other ordinances are his commandments, and intended for the growth of the church. Prayer and praise are acts of worship; reading, exhortation, and preaching are the appointed means of edification, or growth in knowledge; and the fellowship is a manifestation of Christian love. How suitable that all these should be attended to at once![27]

God's mission and Stewart's eschatology

Like the Puritans, Alexander Stewart held a very hopeful view of the future of the church in this world.[28] That is to say, he believed that the millennium, or the period prior to Christ's second coming, would gradually and progressively become a "golden age"—one in which the church would go from "strength to strength" and society would become increasingly righteous. Thus, Stewart was optimistic about the increase of Christ's kingdom. Certainly, this aspect of his theology is evident in the emphasis he placed on missions and the many manifestations of his own itinerant heart. One can also deduce this eschatological mind-set simply by noting the hopeful expectation that is conveyed in his hymnology. Indeed, all of Stewart's recorded hymns are optimistic in nature (see Appendix E). Further, the phraseology of his hymn "Dawning of the church's glory" is especially worthy of note:

> My soul, with sacred joy survey,
>   The glories of the latter day;
> Its dawn already seems begun,
>   Sure earnest of the rising sun.

---

27 Stewart, *Two essays*, 71.

28 For an exhaustive study of the Puritan view of eschatology, see Iain H. Murray, *The Puritan hope: a study in the revival and the interpretation of prophecy* (Edinburgh: The Banner of Truth Trust, 1971).

> The friends of truth assembled stand,
>   (A chosen, consecrated band).
> The standard of the cross display,
>   And cry aloud, *"Behold the way."*
>
> The north "gives up," the south no more
>   "Keeps back" her consecrated store;
> From east to west the message runs,
>   All lands, and islands, yield their sons.
>
> Auspicious dawn, thy rising ray
>   With joy I view, and hail the day;
> Thou sun arise, supremely bright,
>   And fill the world with purest light.[29]

The word "dawning" was part of the common language of the Puritans and their spiritual progeny. For instance, Jonathan Edwards, the pre-eminent theologian of the eighteenth century, employed the term in his *Thoughts on revival*. Reflecting on the Great Awakening and the future state of the Christian religion in New England he wrote:

> It is not unlikely that this work of God's Spirit so extraordinary and wonderful, is the *dawning*, or at least, a prelude of that glorious work of God so often foretold in scripture, which, in the progress and issue of it, shall renew the world and mankind. If we consider…what the state of things now is and has for a considerable time been, in the church of God, and the world of mankind; we cannot reasonably think otherwise, than that the beginning of this great work of God must be near…God presently goes about doing some great thing in order to make way for the introduction

---

29 Stewart, *Two essays*, 76. (Suggested tune: Duke Street L.M.)

of the church's latter-day glory...what is now seen in America and especially in New England, may prove the dawn of that glorious day; and the very uncommon and wonderful circumstances and events of this work, seem to me strongly to argue that God intends it as the beginning or forerunner of something vastly great.[30]

Thus, as Alexander Stewart began his reformation efforts in York and considered how he might fulfill the great mission of the church, he did so with passion, zeal and an unbridled optimism:

We pray the Lord may open the eyes of every Pope, Bishop and churchman to see the simple truth as revealed in scripture, and lead them to give simple, but unfeigned obedience, to all the will of God as laid down in the New Testament. *We know our prayers will be heard, though we know not the time.*[31]

---

[30] Jonathan Edwards, "Thoughts on the revival." In *The works of President Edwards*, Vol. 6 (London: Hughes & Baynes, 1817), 54-59.

[31] Stewart, *Two essays*, 96. Author's italics.

Chapter 13

Rallying the Baptists of York

Alexander Stewart commenced Baptist services shortly after securing work and a residence in the spring or early summer of 1826.¹ Accommodation was found on Yonge Street and the first meetings of the Baptists were held in his home.² His reformation efforts were also enhanced by the placement of several notices in the *Advocate*, beginning late in 1826. These advertisements indicate that Stewart's mobilizing efforts met with some success. Each one stated: "A. Stewart… preaches every Lord's day (and will continue to do so regularly) at 11 o'clock forenoon, and at 6 o'clock P.M. in Mr. Patfield's School House."³ The fact that the Baptists were requested to congregate in

---

1 Stewart was a land agent, engaged in effecting the transfer of title to property. His residence was at 76 Yonge Street. Papers relating to his secular employment are held in the Baldwin Room of the Toronto Reference Library.

2 John Carter, "Reminiscences of the Baptists of Toronto." *The Canadian Baptist,* April 22, 1885.

3 Advertisement in the *Colonial Advocate*, December 18, 1826.

JOHN MCINTOSH HOUSE
(76 YONGE STREET, CIRCA 1820S)
ALEXANDER AND JANET STEWART'S
RESIDENCE IN YORK, 1826

a school house shows that the Stewart home did not afford sufficient room for the numbers who attended. In addition, his statement in parenthesis, "and will continue to do so regularly," is worthy of note. For, it was his desire to *never again* leave the Baptists without a meeting in York. Little did Alexander realize that this unassuming rallying cry would start a legacy of almost two centuries of a continuous Baptist presence in York. However, it seems that Stewart's arrangement with Mr. Patfield was only temporary. So, with his proclamation efforts completed, Stewart turned his full attention to locating a long-term church home.

Ministering in Market Lane

Alexander's informal Sunday meetings continued for about a year and led to the formation of a new Baptist church, likely in May 1827.[4] There were two officers in the church: Stewart was the elder or pastor, and Peter Paterson (1780-1844) served as the church's only deacon. The latter came to York from Blantyre, Scotland, in 1819 and may have been part of Stewart's first church planting attempt. The Paterson family have long been associated with the early Baptists of Toronto. In fact, it was through their instrumentality that the Baptists secured a convenient home in Market Lane.

Peter Paterson began a hardware store in York's Market Square in 1821 and brought his sons, David (d.1856), John and Peter (1808-1883), into partnership. Nearby their premises was a suitable meeting hall, owned by the Freemasons. The Patersons approached this society in May 1827, and the minutes of St. George's Masonic Lodge No. 9 record the result of their inquiry: "Bros. Rose and Watson are authorized to rent lodge room to the Baptist congregation at seven shillings and sixpence currency, per month, if they choose to accept the terms."[5] The terms were accepted and the

---

[4] The Baptists were recognized as an organized body by the Masons, when they approached that group in May for the purpose of renting their lodge.

[5] E.O. White, "The first Baptist church in Toronto." *The Canadian Baptist*, August 16, 1906. (Note: The minute was recorded on June 6, 1827.)

Baptists began their Sunday services in October 1827 according to the following stipulations:

> We, Walter Rose and Richard Watson, being fully empowered by St. George's Lodge No. 9 to rent lodge room for the sole use and benefit of a Sunday meeting and none other, and that the said David Paterson, have the free use of the said room on the Sabbath days for a period of six months, and the same be delivered to him in a clean state at seven shillings and sixpence provincial currency, monthly. He shall keep the house in careful and clean state, and deliver it in such state when the congregation leaves off the use of it.[6]

The church rejoiced at the Lord's provision of a new church home. However, for a young Sunday school scholar named John Carter, the new location was not a welcome change: "The Baptist church continued its meetings in the Masonic Hall, but the hall had no attraction for me, for I had been told that Freemasons always kept a skeleton locked up in the cupboard, and I was terrified at the sight of the awful G in the midst of the square and compass."[7] Nevertheless, the church would continue in that place for five years and would experience many instances of God's goodness and grace.

On Sunday, May 18, 1828, a momentous occasion took place in both the life of the church and the life of Alexander Stewart. On that Lord's Day, Stewart was ordained pastor of the Baptist church of York, according to the principles of the Regular Baptists in Britain and America.[8] George Barclay, the preacher from Cramahe who had given Alexander a detailed report of the Baptist witness

---

6 Quoted in White, "The first Baptist church in Toronto."
7 Carter, "Reminiscences of the Baptists of Toronto."
8 "Certificate of Ordination." "Alexander Stewart Papers, York Auxiliary Bible Society Papers." (Baldwin Room, Toronto Reference Library).

MARKET LANE HALL
YORK, 1827

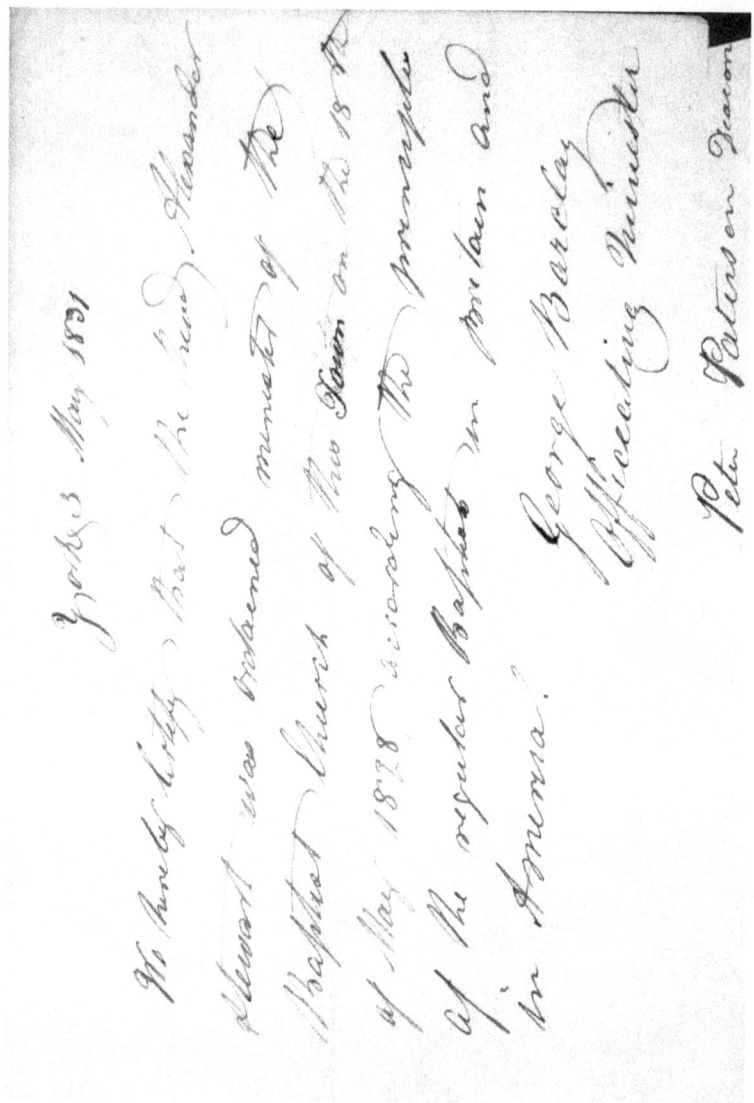

ALEXANDER STEWART'S
"CERTIFICATE OF ORDINATION"
(MAY 3, 1831)[8]

in Upper Canada almost a decade before, was the officiating minister. Even the *Colonial Advocate* joined the congregation in celebration, by reporting the details of the event: "York Baptist Church[9] —This religious society has been formed for some time, but has not, until now, obtained a settled pastor. Elder Alexander Stewart, was, we understand, ordained to the pastoral charge on the Sabbath before last."[10] It goes without saying that Stewart fulfilled all the duties of a pastor previous to this recognition. However, the event demonstrated to the greater community that the Baptists were in York to stay. Furthermore, it signified Alexander's first step on the path to enjoying a privilege often taken for granted by other clergyman—namely, the right to perform *marriages* (refer to chapter 14).

Notwithstanding titles, Rev. Alexander Stewart was always driven to *nurture* the people under his care. One such example of his pastoral concern, has been preserved in the form of a handwritten register. "Sermons preached chiefly in York, Upper Canada," commences Stewart's record in 1827. The account, which primarily lists dates, places and the text of each discourse, provides us with a window into his homiletic methodology. In particular, Stewart used the morning service to preach through various books of the Bible, chapter-by-chapter and verse-by-verse. For instance, from May to November 1827, he preached through Ephesians; from December 1827 to July 1829, Hebrews; and from July 1829 to November 1830, Paul's letter to the Romans. (One would refer to this as *expository* preaching.) The afternoon and evening services were reserved for *topical* dissertations. For example, in the spring of 1827, Alexander spent several weeks on the doctrine of the trinity. Furthermore, his register also illustrates the priority he gave to ensuring the *stability* of the congregation; for, although he still

---

9 The *Advocate*'s reference to "York Baptist Church" shouldn't be taken as the church's given name but simply as a succinct way of distinguishing this religious body from other Protestants in York. The title of the first minute book simply reads: "Minutes of the Baptist church at York."

10 "Ordination of Baptist minister." *Colonial Advocate*, May 29, 1828.

> Thursday Oct. 16. 1829.
>
> Present
> The Revd Alexander Stewart Pres^t
> Messrs Peter Paterson, William Mitchell, Robert
> Yorston and Joseph Wenham.
>
> It was Unanimously Resolved.
>
> First. That a regular account be kept of the transactions of the Church and that Brother Wenham be appointed for that purpose.
>
> Second. That the first Thursday in every Month be a regular Church Meeting to be held as 6 O'clock.
>
> Third. That the following method shall be in future adopted for the admission of Members. viz. Upon the proposal of a Candidate at a Meeting of the Church two of the Members shall be appointed to visit, for the purpose of ascertaining their true Character &: who shall report the same, which report being satisfactory the Individual shall then be requested to state his experience before the Church.
>
> The Candidate being accepted shall be then considered as a Member of the Church, a suitable and convenient time fixed for Baptism, and received into full Communion on the following Sabbath.
>
> All Matters brought before the Church for their consideration shall be decided by a Majority of the Members present—

THE FIRST PAGE OF MINUTES OF
THE BAPTIST CHURCH AT YORK, UPPER CANADA
(OCTOBER 16, 1829)[12]

wanted to preach in various places, the first instance of his being away from York does not occur until September 1828, when he was engaged at Niagara. As soon as Stewart ascertained that the church was "on its feet" he increased the frequency of his other engagements, confident in the membership's abilities to supply able men for the pulpit.[11] But, who were these men, and who were the members of the Baptist church in York?

Unfortunately, no roll of constituent members has survived that lists the membership in its entirety. However, the leading men of the congregation can be extrapolated from the church's minute book, which began recording the affairs of the church on October 16, 1829. On that Thursday night,

> It was Unanimously Resolved.
>
> First. That a regular account be kept of the transactions of the Church and that Brother Wenham be appointed for that purpose.
>
> Second. That the first Thursday in every Month be a regular Church Meeting to be held at 6 O'Clock.
>
> Third. That the following motion shall be in future adopted for the admission of Members—*vis* Upon the proposal of a candidate at a Meeting of the Church two of the Members shall be appointed to visit, for the purpose of ascertaining their views character & who shall report the same... which report being satisfactory the Individual shall then be requested to state his experience before the Church.
>
> The Candidate being accepted shall be then considered as a Member of the Church, a suitable and convenient time fixed for Baptism, and received into full communion

---

11 Stewart enjoyed returning to the townships of Esquesing and Chinguacousy. In 1829, he preached in those places at least 3 times. (See Alexander Stewart, "Register of sermons preached chiefly at York, Upper Canada, 1827-1833." (Louis Melzack Collection, Thomas Fisher Rare Book Library, University of Toronto, Toronto).

on the following Sabbath.

All Matters brought before the Church for their consideration shall be decided by a Majority of the Members present.[12]

The "Brother Wenham" mentioned in this account was Joseph Wenham (b.1795?), an Englishman, who was the bookkeeper of the Bank of Upper Canada from 1822. In addition to Wenham and Stewart, who is recorded as "President" of the society, three other men were present at that first documented meeting—and they came from all walks of life. Peter Paterson was the deacon of the church; James "William" Mitchell (1783-1849) was a tailor by trade and sometimes assisted Stewart with the preaching duties; and Robert Yorston (1802-1892), who was a labourer in York.[13] William Hewitt (1794-1883), who had located on King Street in 1824, began attending the monthly "board" meetings on November 12, 1829, at which time two additional men were set apart for ministry:

> It was recommended by the President that the Church should take into their consideration the propriety of choosing one or more additional Deacons to assist Brother Paterson in the discharge of that duty more especially under the circumstance of his being unavoidably absent at certain times.
>
> Thereupon the Brethren Mitchell & Wenham were unanimously chosen to that office, who having accepted…
>
> It was resolved that they should be set apart by Prayer etc…on the following Thursday Evening.[14]

---

12 "Minutes of the Baptist church at York, Upper Canada, 1829-1833." (Jarvis Street Baptist Church Archives, Toronto).

13 James "William" Mitchell left the Baptists in York in the fall of 1830 and assumed the pastorate of the Baptist church at York Mills.

14 "Minutes of the Baptist church at York, Upper Canada, 1829-1833."

Thus, one can account for six families solely from the first two minutes of the church's books: the Stewarts, Patersons, Wenhams, Mitchells, Yorstons and Hewitts.

Certainly there were others who called the Baptist church at York their home in those early days, and it behooves us to recognize their contribution to this pioneer Baptist effort. (Appendix F lists the known founding families of the reorganized church, along with the approximate dates of their admission into membership and dismissal, where applicable.) Each member shared the responsibility of bearing one another's *physical* burdens, assisting where possible; and *spiritual* burdens, laying them before the mercy seat of God. All in all, the church in Market Lane was growing and probably numbered in excess of forty souls when they realized the Masonic Hall was no longer suitable for their needs.

A plan to build

Of all the evidences that illustrate Stewart's zeal to solidify the Baptist presence in York, none is more poignant than his plan to build a church home. Through an act of Christian charity on the part of one of their brethren, the first stage in reaching this goal was recorded on November 12, 1829, in the church's Minute Book:

> It was mentioned that a Lot of Land had been purchased by Henry Mosley for the purpose of erecting a suitable and convenient place of worship subject to the approbation of the Church offering at the same time to pay the first instalment on the Purchase and to present the amount (£12) as his donation towards the object.
>
> When it was Resolved That the said purchase be confirmed and the Deed of it be made out in the name of Brother Paterson to be held by him on behalf of the Church and We take this opportunity to express our sense of the generous and Christian feeling which produced

such an act of liberality on the part of Mr Mosley.[15]

While it would be a year and a half before an edifice was erected, Stewart and the Baptists of York had cause to rejoice. For, in this blessing, they saw the hand of God and were confident that he would bring their plans to fruition.

The York Auxiliary Bible Society

Alexander Stewart's desire to fulfill Christ's commission did not rest entirely with his pulpit ministry among the Baptists. He always recognized the power of the Scriptures and the importance of every individual having access to the Word of God. In Perth, Scotland, he had participated in the Auxiliary Bible Society as one of its office bearers.[16] The fruitfulness of his experience with that organization left a lasting impression on him. For, upon his return to York, he was driven to found another society, one that would also foster the goal of circulating the Bible.[17] Truly, when it came to the matter of winning the lost, Alexander heartily agreed with the following words: "The experience of ages has shewn, that, as yet no plan has been discovered by which that sacred privilege can be so usefully exercised — that pious duty so advantageously performed, as by promoting institutions for the distribution of the sacred scriptures."[18] On September 19, 1828, the York Auxiliary Bible Society was conceived as a result of Stewart's vision and foresight.[19]

While the chief aim of any Bible Society is readily apparent, the

---

15 "Minutes of the Baptist church at York, Upper Canada, 1829-1833."

16 Alexander Stewart, entry for December 27, 1814. "Notes on the Baptist church at Perth, Scotland, 1812-1815." (Louis Melzack Collection, Thomas Fisher Rare Book Library, University of Toronto, Toronto).

17 Stewart's obituary in the *Christian Guardian* (June 24, 1840) lists him as the "founder of the Bible Society in Upper Canada."

18 *Report of The York Auxiliary Bible Society* (York: Christian Guardian, 1830), 7.

19 Edith Firth, ed. *The town of York, 1815-1834* (Toronto: University of Toronto Press/Champlain Society, 1966), 190. The York Auxiliary Bible Society actually held its first formal meeting in February 1829. It was a branch of the British and Foreign Bible Society. In 1841, it became known as the Upper Canada Bible Society.

specific objectives may be less so. Not only did the York Auxiliary Bible Society aim to distribute the "Sacred Book" among Upper Canada's citizens, but it was also determined to *translate* the Scriptures and bring the Word of God to the First Nation peoples of Upper Canada. The Society's first letter of appeal was drafted in part by Alexander Stewart. It beautifully illustrates these lofty purposes. (The letter is reproduced in its entirety in Appendix G, and speaks for itself.) All in all, the Society was enabled to make 542 individuals "acquainted with the Word" in its first year, as 152 Bibles and 390 New Testaments were distributed throughout York and its environs.[20] Certainly Stewart could echo the words of the apostle John: "These are written that you may believe that Jesus is the Christ, the Son of God, and that believing you may have life in his name" (John 20:31, NKJV).

Alexander Stewart was the first secretary of the Bible Society at York. Initially, he shared these responsibilities with Rev. James Harris (1793-1873), the town's first Presbyterian minister. It was their duty to draft and respond to any correspondence relating to Bible Society matters. Stewart was eager to engage other Christians in this vital work, and it obviously did not bother him to transcend denominational boundaries in achieving this objective. Indeed, this trait of "undenominationalism" and a willingness to make common cause in evangelical ventures was rooted in his experience with the Haldanes.[21] Also, Stewart was probably influential in recruiting the likes of his good friends Thomas Fyfe and John Menzies. This pair served as the president and treasurer, respectively, of the Esquesing branch of the society.[22] Alexander would serve a total of six years in the capacity of secretary and

---

20 *Report of The York Auxiliary Bible Society* (York: Christian Guardian, 1830), 8.

21 Deryck W. Lovegrove, "Unity and separation: contrasting elements in the thought and practice of Robert and James Alexander Haldane." In Keith Robbins, ed. *Protestant Evangelicalism: Britain, Ireland, Germany and America c.1750-c.1950. Essays in honour of W.R. Ward* (Oxford: Basil Blackwell, 1990), 154.

22 *Report of The York Auxiliary Bible Society* (York: Christian Guardian, 1830), 21.

three years as one of its vice-presidents. Given the time he invested in this ministry, one is not surprised to find this epitaph ascribed to him: "He was one of the earliest, most laborious and most persevering officers of the Bible Society in this city…"[23] It is impossible to know how many souls were reconciled to God through the missionary endeavours of the York Auxiliary Bible Society and, hence, through Alexander Stewart's efforts. Certainly, Stewart's secretarial duties put him in contact with many people throughout the province. These were individuals who could never have been reached through his pulpit ministry.

Alexander Stewart could never be accused of being an idle man. Truly, he was an individual who "put his hand to the plow" and did not look back. Upon his return to York in 1826, he not only provided for the needs of Janet, his wife, and his son Alexander Jr., but he sought to elevate the status of the despised Baptists. This he accomplished, by giving the Baptists a voice in politics, by providing leadership in the work of the Bible Society, and most importantly by reforming the Baptist church. Over the ensuing years, Alexander would continue to water the seeds he had planted and wait on God to bring the harvest.

---

23 "Death notice of Rev. Alexander Stewart." *The Examiner* (Toronto: June 24, 1840).

Section 7

Growth in the midst of sadness

1830-1833

Chapter 14

Building March Street Baptist Church

In many church settings, the decision to construct an edifice often leads to a time of discord within the congregation. This was not the case with the Baptists of York. For, following the church's acknowledgement of Henry Mosley's generous gift, the Baptists experienced a period of harmony and growth. Indeed, Alexander Stewart and his congregation could echo the sentiments of King David who wrote: "Behold, how good and how pleasant it is for brethren to dwell together in unity!" (Psalm 133:1, NKJV). In 1827, the church had made the choice to band together. By the end of 1833, the church had bonded together. Arguably, the simple passage of time could have accomplished this change. However, the Lord of the universe brought to pass opportunities and trials through which the membership could express its love for their pastor and each other, and Alexander could recognize and nurture the talents of those in the congregation.

Upholding the "president"

The Baptist church of York supported Alexander with their prayers and through their deeds. This is clearly demonstrated in the instance of Alexander's successful struggle to obtain a license to marry. Stewart was ultimately given this privilege on January 13, 1830. The court accepted the church's argument that they were Calvinistic in doctrine, regardless of the fact that their denominational name was Baptist. Thus, the church and her pastor fell under the terms of the Act.[1] The certificate itself shows how the leading men of the church supported Alexander:

> Be it remembered that as the General Quarter Sessions of the peace holden at the Town of York in the County of York in and for the Home District on the Thirteenth day of January in the year of our Lord one thousand eight hundred and thirty before Alexander Wood Esquire chairman, Robert Stanton and finally William Proudfoot, Christopher Widmer, Charles Small and James Black Esquire, and others Justices of our Sovereign Lord the King assigned to keep the peace in the said District, came Alexander Stewart of York aforesaid, minister of a religious congregation in the said Town of York professing to be Calvinists together with Peter Paterson of the said Town of York Merchant, James Mitchell of the same place Tailor, Joseph Wenham of the same place Gentleman, William Hewitt of the same

---

1 The Marriage Act of 1798 allowed marriages to be legally performed by the Anglican Church, Catholic Church, Church of Scotland, Presbyterian Church, Calvinist Church and Lutheran Church.

Alexander Stewart and the Baptist church at York, Upper Canada, were not the first to try this approach. In 1806, Elijah Bentley, a Baptist minister in Markham, was unsuccessful in his application to the General Quarter Sessions of the Peace. "In some places the argument worked, but evidently not in the Home District." [Stuart Ivison and Fred Rosser, eds. *The Baptists in Upper and Lower Canada before 1820* (Toronto: University of Toronto Press, 1956), 124-125.]

place Shopkeeper, James Ore of the same place Gardener, Henry Mosley of the same place Auctioneer, Robert Yorston of the same place Labourer, and Alexander Thomson of the same place Mason, members of a congregation of Calvinists at York in the County of York in the said District and the said Peter Paterson, James Mitchell, Joseph Wenham, William Hewitt, James Ore, Henry Mosley, Robert Yorston and Alexander Thomson duly examined satisfied the Court that the said Alexander Stewart is the settled minister of the said congregation and was regularly ordained constituted and appointed thereto.[2]

As a result of the backing of his people, Stewart would have occasion to perform precisely 100 marriages between 1830 and 1840 (see Appendix H). In addition, the congregation on Market Lane would be presented with another opportunity to support their undershepherd and his family.

At the end of January 1832, Catherine Oswald McIntosh, the only daughter of Alexander and Janet, a faithful wife and mother of three,[3] was seriously ill. Her illness had a profound impact on the men and women of Alexander's congregation. There seemed to be a oneness of heart and soul as they lifted up Catherine's situation in prayer. James Lesslie, a trustee of the church property, testified to this fact in his diary: "Mr. Stewart — Mr. Scott & Mr. Caldicott preach — subjects solemn and important — the illness of Mrs. McIntosh, Mr. Stewart's daughter, seems to impress the minds of the speakers."[4] In the end, it was the Lord's will to call Catherine home on February 10, 1832. But, the Stewart family, and the church, could take

---

2 "Certificate of Quarter Sessions or License to Marry." January 13, 1830 in the "Alexander Stewart Papers." York Auxiliary Bible Society Papers. (Baldwin Room, Toronto Reference Library).

3 Catherine bore five children, two of whom died in infancy. Her surviving children were Catherine (1824-1899), John (1826-1892) and Ann Jane (1828-1890).

4 Entry for January 22, 1832. "James Lesslie Diaries." (Dundas Historical Society Museum, Dundas, Ontario).

comfort in the knowledge that: "On her death bed was attested the power of faith to support, to comfort, to fill with joy unspeakable and full of glory."⁵ Thomas Ford Caldicott (1803-1869), an eloquent speaker and member of the church, gave a most suitable and impressive sermon at the graveside.⁶ Her obituary appeared in the *Advocate*, and in addition to eulogizing her character, it illustrates, in some measure, the depth of love that the congregation showered upon Elder Stewart and his family:

> Died — On Friday last, at half past one in the morning in the twenty-ninth year of her age, CATHARINE [*sic*], wife of Mr. JOHN McINTOSH, of this Town, shipowner, and daughter of the Rev. Alexander Stewart of the Baptist Church here. This pious and amiable woman was a native of Perthshire, Scotland, whence she emigrated with her parents into Canada in early life; she was greatly esteemed and beloved, and her loss is deeply regretted by a numerous circle of relatives and acquaintances; her manners were mild, gentle and unassuming; she was an affectionate wife; a kind and constant friend; and the tender and watchful mother of three infant children who with her husband survive to lament their early bereavement. The funeral took place on Sabbath last, at half past one in the afternoon; and her mortal remains were interred in the family burial ground in the Potter's Field… A large concourse of the respectable inhabitants of the town and county accompanied the mourners to the place of burial.⁷

---

5 "Death notice of Catherine McIntosh." *Christian Guardian* (Toronto: February 22, 1832), 59.

6 "Death notice for Catherine McIntosh." *Colonial Advocate* (Toronto: February 16, 1832).

7 "Death notice for Catherine McIntosh." *Colonial Advocate* (Toronto: February 16, 1832). Two weeks after her funeral, Alexander returned from Esquesing with the remains of his son, James and re-interred them beside Catherine. The Potter's Field was eventually closed and the family plot was moved to the Necropolis Cemetary

Undoubtedly, the Stewarts deeply appreciated and expected the church's warmth—for the unity of the body was not just a doctrine espoused by their church but, rather, something Alexander had fostered, taught and led by example.

Recognizing the gifts of others

Alexander Stewart was always conscious of the propriety of recognizing gifts in his congregation—even if those talents were similar to his own. Although Stewart had adopted the *Scottish* model of church order, there was still quite a bit of *Scotch* Baptist left in him! In particular, the characteristic of allowing others to exercise their gift of preaching was developed during his time with William Ballantine, in the town of Elgin. As a pastor of a Baptist church, Alexander took to heart this advice from Ballantine:

> It becomes the elders of the churches not to stand in the way of the exercise of the gifts of their brethren. One important part of the elder's duty, is to study and call forth these gifts to action. Much depends on elders in this respect. They are the presidents in the churches. It is their duty to stir up the brethren to the exercise of their gifts, and to afford opportunities for this end. If in almost all the meetings of a church and especially on the Lord's day, there is no gift exercised but that of the elders, this opportunity is not given. If the gifts of the church are not used, it is not possible to know who in them are fit for the elder's office. Let the elders see to it, that this is not their fault. It ought to rejoice your souls, brethren, if there are in the churches gifts for prayer, exhortation and preaching, even superior to your own, if called forth to action. Let them not be dormant through your neglect, or by so conducting yourselves in the house of God, as to remain ignorant

---

in 1856. (See entry for February 24, 1832. "James Lesslie Diaries.")

of their existence. This will neither tend to your own profit, nor to the advantage of your churches. The place you hold is important in this view, that it gives you an opportunity of exciting to action the blessings Christ confers on his churches for edifying themselves in love.[8]

At a meeting of the church, held after the morning service on September 11, 1831, the president recommended that the congregation call Thomas Caldicott to "preach the Gospel among them as occasion might require."[9] In addition, the minutes of the church note that four other men were set apart for gospel ministry:

> The Church met for the purpose of taking into their consideration the propriety of requesting Brother Parson to exercise his Gift as a Public Preacher. When it was Resolved unanimously That he be invited to the discharge of this duty & the Church at the same time follow him in his labours, with their fervent prayer that the Lord may be pleased to own & bless his exertions.
>
> It was also Resolved That the Brethren Paterson, Wenham, Caldicott & Parson having each received the Call of the Church to preach the Gospel they are also requested either of them to so minister the Lord's Supper, in case the Elder should be absent or otherwise prevented.[10]

---

8 William Ballantine, *Treatise on the elder's office shewing the qualifications of elders, and how the first churches obtained them; also their appointment, duties & maintenance; the necessity of a presbytery in every church; and exhortation, and the observance of every church ordinance on the Lord's Day, in order, amongst other ends, to the obtaining of elders* (Edinburgh: J. Ritchie, 1807), 138-139.

9 Entry for September 11, 1831. "Minutes of the Baptist church at York, Upper Canada, 1829-1833." (Jarvis Street Baptist Church Archives, Toronto).

10 Entry for October 2, 1831. "Minutes of the Baptist church at York, Upper Canada, 1829-1833." The 1833 Directory for York lists Timothy Parson (b.1808?) and Caldicott as "preachers." [See *York commercial directory, street guide and register 1833-4, with almanack and calendar for 1834* (York UC: Thomas Dalton, Printer), 96, 123.]

Building March Street Baptist Church 183

THOMAS FORD CALDICOTT
(1803-1869)

Stewart and the church understood the character of these men and so harmony was enhanced. However, it should be noted at this point, that Alexander assumed that this unity would not be disturbed, and did not fully take into consideration the possibility that a "gifted" outsider might upset the balance. But, what of the other members of the congregation? Did Elder Stewart promote an atmosphere of acceptance and love with them?

A notable event

There were several additions to the church's number between January 1830 and July 1832. In fact, the minutes indicate that there was a net gain of eleven members during this period. However, none was more notable than the admission of Henry Tost (or Toast) and his wife into the membership. The examination of the candidates, in and of itself, was uneventful. The minute of November 26, 1831 simply states: "Mr. Henry Tost & Mrs. Tost came before the Church as candidates for admission into the communion of the Church and having made a profession of their faith to the satisfaction of the Church were unanimously accepted."[11] But subsequent to this interview, two weeks of bad weather followed, which prohibited the couple from being baptized. Thus, their full admittance into the body was delayed and consequently they refrained from taking part in the Lord's Supper. Providentially, a suggestion was brought forward that likely averted a time of disunity. Brother Caldicott, acting *pro tempore* for the church's clerk, Joseph Wenham, recorded Alexander's and the congregation's solution:

> Resolved that as a Church formed upon the principle of admitting no one to the fellowship of the Church except such has have been baptized by imersion—that we strictly adhere to this Rule but in consequence of the following

---

11 Entry for November 26, 1831. "Minutes of the Baptist church at York, Upper Canada, 1829-1833."

circumstances (Henry Tost and his wife having applied to the Church to be admitted to its fellowship having professed their faith before the Church to the fullest satisfaction of its members on the 26th of Novr having stated their views of the Ordinance of Believers Baptism and their conviction of its importance and readiness to attend to it The Church then determined to attend to the ordinance on the next morning if the weather permitted—but the weather has been so inclement since that time that it has been quite impracticle to attend to it—the Church sympathizing with Brother Toast and his wife under these circumstances and seeing no probability of the ordinance being administered for some time have met to consult upon the case) and have unanimously determined to receive Brother Toast and his wife to the full fellowship of the Church considering that (from their views of the ordinance and their wish to attend to it and that no moral cause but a natural one has prevented it) they are virtually Baptized—and shall be actually so as soon as circumstances permit—But the Church wish it to be distinctly understood that this act is to form no precedent for admitting any one to the fellowship of the Church who does not view the ordinance in the same light as it does—and moreover even one who does where natural causes do not absolutely prevent attending to the ordinance.[12]

Indeed, this was a unique and unifying occurrence in the life of the church for it shows the people's fervent desire to strive together, without forsaking their stand. Surely, the Baptists of Market Lane were spiritually ready to embark on their first building project.

---

12 Entry for December 10, 1831. "Minutes of the Baptist church at York, Upper Canada, 1829-1833."

Building a church home

The Baptists of York joyfully gave funds towards the erection of their new home beginning in 1830. Among the over 130 individuals who subscribed, special mention was given in the church's books to the gifts of Peter Paterson, Joseph Wenham and the Honourable John Strachan.[13] The construction began at the northeast corner of March (now Lombard) and Church Streets, sometime in 1831. The church contracted the services of James Turner, mason, and Caleb Humphrey, carpenter, to undertake the work.[14] The edifice was in mid-construction when the congregation decided to add a significant detail as a result of the Tost situation:

> Resolved that though the Church approve of Public Baptism administered in the most public water yet to provide for peculiar cases that a Baptistry be dug in the Meeting House and that Brother Patterson see this done as soon as possible.[15]

The Baptist chapel on March Street was almost complete when the congregation commenced holding their services there in the spring of 1832. John Carter recounted the attributes of the building and the demeanour of the people in this way:

---

13 Entry for January 1, 1835. "John Eglinton Maxwell Diary." (Baldwin Room, Toronto Reference Library, Toronto). The original church book was lost but the records were copied. They show that the 130 subscribers gave a total of £260; Paterson, £25; Wenham, £12; and Strachan £2. In regards to the latter's contribution, William Westfall reasons that as Strachan was constantly pleading for government money in an effort to put his church at the centre, he needed to demonstrate that other religious groups, perhaps ones that sustained sedition and rebellion, were making advances in the capital. Thus, "Strachan needed enemies in order to promote his own goals." [William Westfall, *Two worlds: the Protestant culture of nineteenth century Ontario* (Montreal: McGill University Press, 1989), 21.]

14 Entry for January 1, 1835. "John Eglinton Maxwell Diary."

15 Entry for December 10, 1831. "Minutes of the Baptist church at York, Upper Canada, 1829-1833."

Building March Street Baptist Church 187

THE BAPTIST CHURCH
ON MARCH STREET
(1832)

> [The church was] capable of holding 200 when crowded. It had four immense Gothic windows to afford it light—two in front and two in rear, the lot was too narrow to permit of windows in the sides of the building. The pulpit was imposing and massive, and high up above the heads of the congregation. The minister when seated in it could not be seen by the congregation. The church held regular Sunday services in the meeting house before it was finished, notwithstanding the presence of carpenter's benches, lumber, etc, and were thankful to have a church home, and were willing to endure a few inconveniences for a short time.[16]

In addition to Carter's description, the building consisted of two aisles, three sections of seating, and a communion pew, front and centre.[17] Pew rents were collected during this time and thus the more financially prominent members sat near the front of the church. Of course, this did not exclude anyone from attending their three Sunday services. On the contrary, the Baptists were careful to note in the *York Directory* of 1833 that "all hearers are welcomed to a seat."[18] Moreover, the statement that the pulpit was "imposing and massive" is worthy of comment. For, its sheer size illustrates that Stewart and his people gave scriptural teaching and preaching the place of primacy in the church's ministry. Soon after the society's relocation, however, the Baptists would be challenged with another urgent ministry need.

The church's first trial

The cholera epidemic of the summer of 1832 was the type of trial that caused the members of March Street to further unite under

---

16 John Carter, "Reminiscences of the Baptists of Toronto." *The Canadian Baptist*, April 22, 1885.

17 *Jarvis Street Baptist Church; directory and historical sketch* (Toronto: Dudley & Burns, 1897), 51.

18 *York commercial directory...for 1834*, 123.

Stewart's leadership, and to bear each other's physical and emotional burdens. The disease itself is characterized by violent diarrhea, vomiting and cramps, followed by a comatose stage, and often death within twenty-four hours. The epidemic began in India and reached the shores of Great Britain in 1831. It was brought to the British North American colonies when shipping commenced early the following year. "The residents of York watched in fascinated helplessness as it spread inexorably up the St. Lawrence with the immigrants, reaching the town on June 18, 1832."[19] Among the "helpless" who recorded the impact of cholera on the town of York was James Lesslie. His diary provides us with a sad yet gripping account of the cholera's devastating effects:

> *Jul. 8, 1832*
> This day several cases of Cholera—one young woman dies in half an hour!
> *Jul. 22, 1832 (Sabbath)*
> This morning the Cholera car passed our door in the morning to convey some person to their long home—and again as we came out of meeting at noon was it receiving the body of a man who had died in the house opposite—how many cases may have been today I know not.[20]

At the same time, God used this ongoing drama to cause individuals to take stalk of their eternal welfare. Lesslie records:

> *Jul. 7, 1832*
> The cholera still rages around us and many are called to their Eternal state after a few hours struggle with this terrible disease. Oh may these solemn proofs of our frailty—sinfulness & mortality lead us to *Him* "who is as a refuge from the

---

19 Edith Firth, ed. *The town of York, 1815-1834* (Toronto: University of Toronto Press/Champlain Society, 1966), lxiii.
20 Entries for July 8 and 22, 1832. "James Lesslie Diaries."

storm & as the shadow of a great Rock on a weary Soul"
—Then will such a terrific messenger of death be disarmed
of his terrors.[21]

The epidemic affected Alexander's preaching as well. While the biblical texts of his sermons during the summer of 1832 are not known, Lesslie wrote that "the solemnity of the present period forms a subject of almost every public discourse."[22] By the end of the season, the trial was over, and the membership paused and reflected on the town's losses: 555 cases and 217 deaths in York. Historians have noted that these figures are probably low for "at the time the fear and bewilderment of the citizens were increased by the universal belief that all fatalities were not reported and that through incompetence or design the full horror of the situation was being kept from them."[23] Despite the gravity of these statistics, March Street Baptist Church survived this ordeal, and their solidarity was the stronger for it.

Alexander Stewart had drawn closer to his people and his God through his experiences of the early 1830s. From the joy of securing a license to marry and breaking ground for a new church home, to the sorrow of losing his only daughter and enduring the horrors of York's cholera outbreak, Stewart saw that God's timing was perfect. Certainly he could proclaim that "all things work together for good to those who love God, to those who are the called according to His purpose" (Romans 8:28, NKJV). The oneness that these events engendered should not have lost its intensity for some time. But, the town was changing by the mid-1830s, and hundreds of new immigrants were pouring into York, bringing with them their own ideas and ways of doing things. More than ever, March Street Baptist Church needed a multi-gifted and discerning pastor to integrate these new-world Christians into their society.

---

21 Entry for July 7, 1832. "James Lesslie Diaries."
22 Entry for August 5, 1832. "James Lesslie Diaries."
23 Firth, *The town of York*, lxiii-lxiv.

Section 8

Years of decline
1834-1836

Chapter 15

Reasons for dissension

Though the church had the means of efficiently doing the Lord's work, strife and unpleasantness prevailed, which at length culminated in disaster to the church."[1] Unfortunately, Alexander Stewart was unable to keep the Baptists of March Street united in love and purpose. However, to keep their plight in perspective, it should be stated that their downward slide towards disunity and ultimately schism was a trend that was suffered by the majority of York's churches. The Baptists were just the last to fall.[2] But what were the circumstances that

---

1 John Carter, "Reminiscences of the Baptists of Toronto." *The Canadian Baptist*, April 22, 1885.
2 Edith Firth, ed. *The town of York, 1815-1834* (Toronto: University of Toronto Press/Champlain Society, 1966), lii. Firth records that "With the exception of the Church of England, each of the congregations in the period had an oddly parallel history. Each was founded by a small group of dedicated laymen living in York, and each faced two major problems—the finding of a minister and the erection of a building... The most striking similarity among them, however, was that each had a major internal upheaval in the early 1830s."

contributed to the disintegration of March Street Baptist Church?

Alexander Stewart's character

Alexander Stewart was a man of deep convictions and firmly rooted principles. He was not unlike many Scottish Protestants who were fiercely independent and unashamedly Calvinistic in their thinking. Although these are qualities that are needed—indeed, sought after by many a church of Christ—nevertheless, such a mindset often produced a character who was irascible, argumentative and very sure of his own correctness of vision and action.[3] John Carter noted this side of Stewart's character—a side that manifested itself in his later years: "Elder Stewart possessed a disposition which others would not submit to…"[4] At this point, it is sufficient to examine two instances in Stewart's life that shed some light on this aspect of his nature. First, a letter to his old friend, Thomas Fyfe of Esquesing, on December 12, 1833, displays Alexander's unyielding zeal to defend his good name. The letter itself concerns the possible prosecution of a certain John Dewar for perjury. Stewart exclaimed,

> I hate the idea of prosecuting J Dewar for perjury though I can easily prove it, but I also hate the idea of being defamed particularly on oath… I request you will give me a certified copy by the first part of the said affidavit, for which I shall pay you what is just and lawful. I mean to shew that even the despised Baptists can shelter their innocent character under the just laws of the land. I ask no favours. I am willing to publish all my dealings with that man to the world—but private slander I cannot bear.[5]

---

3 W. Stanford Reid, ed. *The Scottish tradition in Canada* (Toronto: McClelland and Stewart, 1988), 120.

4 Carter, "Reminiscences of the Baptists of Toronto," April 22, 1885.

5 Letter to Thomas Fyfe, Esquesing, December 12, 1833. "Alexander Stewart Papers." (Baldwin Room, Toronto Reference Library, Toronto).

Certainly, Stewart had just cause in pursuing vindication in the courts. However, the tone of the epistle is such that one might wonder how he dealt with sensitive issues within his church.

Second, a first impression left on a recently arrived clergyman, also helps in illuminating the "other side" of Stewart's disposition. William Proudfoot (1788-1851) was born in Scotland and landed in York in 1832 as a minister of the United Presbyterian Church, and even had occasion to preach in the Baptist meeting house.[6] Nevertheless, several of Proudfoot's diary entries indicate that he had no wish to foster an ongoing relationship with the Baptist pastor. The insertions speak for themselves:

> Sep. 14, 1832
> Called this morning for Mr. Harris, Mr. Rintoul and Mr. Stewart. I took up residence with Mr. Harris, the Presbyterian minister. Mr. Rintoul, of the Kirk of Scotland received me coolly, as was expected. Mr. Stewart, the Baptist Minister received me very cordially.
> Oct. 8, 1832
> Spent part of the evening with Mr. Stuart... Mr. Stuart is one of the fruits of the revivals in Moulin and Perthshire, and so is his wife. Both assured me that it was there they were first brought to the knowledge of the truth.
> Dec. 5, 1832
> Went into York and called for some acquaintances with whom I had some chat and from whom I heard some scandal. The chief of which was that there is considerable dissension in the Scotch kirk, regarding their minister Mr.

---

6 The United Presbyterian Church was formed in 1820 by the union of the Burgher and Anti-Burgher synods of the Scottish Secessionist Church. Proudfoot actually preached at March Street Baptist Church on two successive Sabbaths: April 7 and April 14, 1833. ["Register of sermons preached chiefly at York, Upper Canada, 1827-1833." (Louis Melzack Collection, Thomas Fisher Rare Book Library, University of Toronto, Toronto).]

Rintoul—The only fault which is stated against him, is, that he *reads* his Sermons... Mr Stewart the Baptist delights in telling of it, though it can affect him I suppose in no way—But he is a man who having a vulgar low mind is gratified by the disturbance, as scandal of any kind gratifies the mob who delight in the mischief which lowers their neighbours... Was considerably disappointed to day in Mr Stewart—I have been now several times in his house, but never heard any thing that could indicate his possessing a literary turn. He is always working as a labourer, covered with mud or lime. His manners the manners of a man of *work*, and forwardness and conceit supply him in the place of ease. He piques himself upon being one of those converted by the instrumentality of Mr Stewart, Moulin, Perthshire, and taking his stand upon that vantage ground he looks down upon almost all others, not of his own denomination, as hardly Xtians, if they be Christians at all. Were I to be much about York I should choose not to cultivate his acquaintanceship. I write not this because of any slight on his part for he has behaved to me as well as he could and certainly acted kindly but I have so often met men of his character and seen so many unhappinesses arising from intimacy with them that I could not willingly come into intimacy with him.[7]

Rev. Proudfoot would eventually settle in London (Upper Canada) but would visit the community again in 1835 and make this telling statement: "Called for Mr. Stewart and Mr. Harris, ministers.

---

7 "Rev. William Proudfoot Diaries." (Lawson Memorial Library, University of Western Ontario, London, Ontario). The Rev. William Rintoul (1797-1851) accepted a call to St. Andrew's Church, York, arriving in June, 1831. In 1834 there were some difficulties with his congregation and Rintoul left St. Andrew's.

The reader should remember that Stewart was also a land agent, and it was not uncommon for him to be covered in "mud or lime."

The former has begun to experience the infirmities of old age."[8] The fact that Alexander was in the twilight of his earthly sojourn should be born in mind in any discussion of his inner character. For, the frailties that coincide with old age often extend to the spiritual as well as the physical being. Indeed, at the age of sixty, Stewart reflected on his walk with the Lord, as Christians are wont to do, and undoubtedly recognized that the "old man" within was still very active, and that sins still beset him. But, praise God, "There is therefore now no condemnation to those who are in Christ Jesus..." (Romans 8:1, NKJV). In conclusion, an examination of Stewart's character cannot alone explain the decline experienced by his church. The composition of the congregation must be scrutinized as well.

Homogeneity and the burgeoning population

Some of the members of March Street Baptist Church found that they could not submit to Alexander Stewart's leadership by virtue of their own character. More specifically, it was likely the recent additions, who were drawn from the community's exploding population, that accelerated the church's plunge into a state of discord. As of March 6, 1834, the Town of York was incorporated as the City of Toronto and had a population of 9,252, more than double its population in 1831.[9]

With the influx of newcomers came socio-economic upheaval, which impacted both town and church. The most significant change was the rise of a middle class. Prior to the War of 1812, York was an insular outpost: "Outside influences were minimal; the town grew slowly in an inbred, stagnant, atmosphere."[10] Conversely, post-war York welcomed a people who were to challenge the ideas and supremacy of the town's upper class; they were "articulate,

---

8 Entry for May 14, 1835. "Rev. William Proudfoot Diaries."

9 Edith Firth, ed. *The town of York, 1815-1834* (Toronto: University of Toronto Press/Champlain Society, 1966), lxxxii.

10 Firth, *The town of York,* lxxxii.

practical, [and] keenly aware of the world beyond their immediate surroundings."[11] However, this challenge was not united in its attack. New ideologies were as diverse as the immigrants themselves. There existed seemingly insurmountable differences between Highland and Lowland Scot, Ulsterman and Catholic Irish, Yorkshireman and man of Kent. Thus, competing viewpoints jockeyed for position as Old Country, imperial, and North American influences clashed, creating the distinctive character of Toronto.[12]

In religious matters, dissimilarities surfaced as "divergencies of custom which made conflict inevitable."[13] For instance, in the Secessionist Presbyterian Church, William Lyon Mackenzie often complained of James Harris' use of unfamiliar psalm tunes. Mackenzie preferred the *Scottish Psalter* instead of Isaac Watt's version of the Psalms and ensured the public was aware of his dissatisfaction using his *Colonial Advocate* as a voice.[14] Likewise, Alexander Stewart's church was not immune to strong differences of opinion. In speaking of the difficulties of the March Street Church, Rev. Robert Alexander Fyfe echoed this sentiment at length:

> Another obstacle to her progress, was encountered in the want of homogeneity, among a considerable portion of her members. Without reflecting on the character of a single individual, it cannot have escaped the notice of the observant that in a new country, where immigrants from all points of the compass are thrown together, even good men of the "same faith," are often very illy adapted to work together. Men of strong individuality, with set habits, made angular sometimes, by the peculiarities of some able ministers under whom they were trained in the old world,

---

11 Firth, *The town of York*, lxxxiv.
12 Firth, *The town of York*, lxxxv, lxxxvii.
13 Firth, *The town of York*, lii.
14 "Service in Secessionist Presbyterian Church." *Colonial Advocate* (Toronto: December 22, 1825).

WILLIAM LYON MACKENZIE
(1795-1861)

are generally more anxious to lead than to follow. Half a dozen such in any church, would be likely to make severe friction in its working; and the smaller the Church the worse would this state of things be. Each one would think, when the work was not done as he had been accustomed to see it done, that there must be something very wrong, and his conscience could not sanction wrong. O that conscience, what a singular instrument it is! And practically it often happens that such men will do nothing, because they cannot have precisely their own way. Their principles are so strong and sharply defined, that they constantly stand in the way of their practice. If they were not men of such sterling principle, they might do something for God and their fellow men, but as it is they have too much principle to have much practice! A man has made great progress when he has learned to co-operate heartily with his brethren, with the full approbation of his whole nature. It requires a many sided and self-forgetting person, to see that it is rarely of much importance how a thing is done, so that it really is well done; and that in all organizations it is generally better to co-operate with our brethren in a less perfect scheme, than to stand alone admiring the most perfect. Opinions regulate the ways and modes of doing things, principles rarely do. Such people as I have in mind, have a very imperfect idea of the true design of the gospel. That is chiefly remedial, and its loving spirit should be wrapped around all we touch and do. A few such members as I have sketched would soon influence a church, and without intending it, make her feel that work for God and for perishing men is not the greatest thing, that *building up* is not the main idea, but *building up in their way*. Such principles introduced among the members of any organization infallibly lead to disintegration. I believe no denomination in this country is yet wholly free from spiritual stones so peculiarly cut, that no other stone can be laid beside them. The state of things was much harder to manage twenty-five years ago. When a Church becomes large and strong, a few such stones do no great harm; they can be laid upon the top of the wall to keep over-forward folks from climbing over.[15]

---

15 Robert Alexander Fyfe, *A forty years survey from the Bond Street pulpit* (Toronto: Dudley & Burns, Printers, 1876), 13-14. One of March Street's "peculiarly cut stones" is sufficient to illustrate the personalities Pastor Stewart had to nurture. James Beaty (1798-1892) was one of the early members of the Baptist church in York reorganized in 1829. He left the church in 1836 (split over Calvinism) and became prominent in founding the first Disciples congregation in the city. Joseph Ash, the Disciples of Christ historian, elaborated on this man's temperament:

...Jas. Beaty sen., is, and has been, a very peculiar man. He was greatly devoted to "the Word of God," and desired to bring everything to that standard. Early in life he contracted a great dislike to that class of men who delight in being a separate class of men from their brethren, and call themselves clergy, and their brethren, laity. He saw so much of their "lording it over God's heritage," and despising the poor that he took strong grounds against it. Having such an aversion to "the Kingdom of the clergy," among the sects, he became very jealous of any proceeding, action, or teaching among ourselves, that even squinted that way. Sometimes many of our own brethren thought he laced too tight, and stood too straight on the subject... James sen. was a very prosperous business man, and raised to high distinction in the city, held high offices even to the House of Commons, at the will of the people. All this popularity even invitations to Governors' dinners did not spoil him for he would not go...

On a certain occasion he was driving a gentleman from the United States through the city wonders. He drove past a Theological Institute, when the gentleman admired the building and enquired what it was for? Oh! said Mr. Beaty, that is a factory. Indeed, said his companion, that is a remarkably fine building for a factory, and tell me what do they manufacture there? Oh, said Mr. Beaty, they manufacture Priests there. They put in the raw material, and run them through and they come out finished Priests all ready for the market, like putting rags into a paper mill they go on from one mill to another till they come out clear white paper. A good old fashioned yankee laugh ended that, but left a lasting impression on his mind.

On another occasion 10 or 12 gentlemen of the city accidentally gathered on the corner of King Street and the Leader Lane. Among the subjects talked and indeed, the principal one was about the "Armstrong Gun." At that

In addition to the challenge of leading these "odd" stones of the church, Alexander and the Baptists of Toronto were hindered in their progress by March Street itself.

March Street: a "byword"

Rev. Stewart and the society of Baptists had envisioned that their choice of March Street as a location for their chapel not only would provide them with a place of worship but would attract newcomers into their fold. Unfortunately, March Street became a byword for everything that was vile. No one could have predicted

> time the "Armstrong Gun" was the most formidable weapon of warfare known, they were jubilant over it, and said through that weapon "Great Britain" could hold her prestage by land and sea. They thought a monument should be erected to the memory of Mr. Armstrong. Mr. Beaty listened to them for some time in silence. At length he said, gentlemen, you have landed Mr. Armstrong and the "Armstrong Gun" as the most formidable weapon known to kill and slay human beings; but I can tell you of one more formidable than that. It kills more men, makes more destitute widows and orphans, brings more poverty and wretchedness, it fills more prisons, causes more murders and loads down the nation with more taxes than any other weapon can do. Look down yonder and see a Gooderham & Worts Distillery. It is far more destructive than the "Armstrong Gun" can be, and if a monument is to be erected to the one that causes the greatest woe and destruction of life and property let us erect one to the memory of Gooderham & Worts. *Mr. Worts was there but was silent.*
>
> ...Mr. Beaty was in his office (the *Leader* office) a Presbyterian minister presented and introduced himself as a Presbyterian Missionary to Hindoostan and returned on a visit to friends and desired to deliver a lecture on Mohomedanism and desire a little puffing notice in the Daily *Leader*. After considerable pleasant talk Mr. Beaty said "the Mohomedan's believe in the Bible? Oh, yes, said the Minister, they believe in the Bible but allow me to illustrate. They put the Coran on top of the Bible and read everything through that and thus make everything in the Bible correspond with the Coran. Oh, I see, said Mr. Beaty. Well, I don't see very much difference between you and all the sects and the Hindoos for as they read the Bible through the Coran so do you; you place your Creed on the Bible and read it through the Creed and make the Bible read like the Creed. I don't see much difference between you." The Minister vanished. (Joseph Ash, "History of the rise and progress of our cause in Canada." *Christian Worker*, Reminiscences No. 7, July 1883.)

that March Street would have become one of the worst avenues in the town. However, subsequent to the erection of the Baptist meeting house, "[m]iserable houses sprang up all around it; and what was still worse, many of them were inhabited by the most vicious, and miserable kind of people," stated Robert Alexander Fyfe.[16] Often, on Sunday evenings, a policeman was secured to patrol the sidewalk in front of the church so as to keep down the noise that the children and others would make in the neighbourhood. Thus, the advance of the Baptist cause was hindered by these conditions, compounding the other problems of the church.

Doctrinal issues

Some have suggested that, "when the church which had been founded in Toronto in 1829 was shattered in the mid-1830s, it was almost certainly because of Pastor Stewart's defection to Campbellism."[17] While differences in doctrine may have played a part in creating factions within the church, the idea that Stewart "threw off" the Baptist principles he cherished is baseless. In fact, the early historian for the Campbellites or Disciples of Christ, Joseph Ash, clearly recorded on which side of the divide Stewart stood:

> The origin and first name the first church bore, I could never get clearly. From the best information I could get, it appears James Beaty, sen., Peter Rutherford, Wm. McMaster, and others met with Alex. Stewart, a Scotch Baptist preacher, for some time. Finally there was a rupture among them on Calvinism, Stewart was a Calvinist, Beaty, Rutherford, and some others went by themselves, and

---

16 Fyfe, *A forty years survey,* 12. Dr. Fyfe was later instrumental in moving the Baptists of March Street to Bond Street in 1848: "For sixteen long years the outward condition of the Baptists of this city might be compared to that of those unhappy criminals, who were, by their Tuscan tyrants, tied hand to hand and face to face, with the rotting dead."

17 Theo T. Gibson, *Robert Alexander Fyfe: his contemporaries and his influence* (Burlington: Welch Publishing Co., 1988), 341.

worshipped in the house of Geo. Armstrong. This occurred about the year 1836... Those who followed Stewart, McMaster was one of them *who finally went with the regular Baptists.*[18]

However, it should be noted that Campbellism *did* draw heavily from Baptist works during this period, including some of the congregations Alexander had founded and ministered to north of Toronto. Thus, Stewart's uncompromising stand with the Regular Baptists likely fed division and alienated those in the congregation who were sympathetic to Alexander Campbell's so called "enlightened" message.

By the mid 1830s, Toronto was a city undergoing a tremendous amount of change. Likewise, the composition of the membership of March Street Baptist Church was also experiencing change. Conversely, Alexander Stewart was a minister of the gospel who remained unchanged. He was consistent in his practice and perhaps more decided in his beliefs. He simply did not have the time or the energy to move the Baptists to a better location; nor did he possess the gifts necessary to promote an atmosphere of forbearance, melding the divergent personalities and perspectives within his church. In times such as this, a pastor often looks to his own congregation to supply those leadership skills lacking in himself. At the centre of the March Street dilemma, two men stand out in addition to Stewart, but only one had the ability to unite the church. Further, both men contributed to altering the course of Toronto's Baptist history and the life story of her first president.

---

18 Ash, "Rise and progress." *Christian Worker*, Reminiscences No. 7, July 1883. Author's italics.

Chapter 16

Maxwell, Caldicott, and the schism of 1836

Thomas Ford Caldicott was endowed with gifts that enabled him to bring together the opposing personalities within March Street Baptist Church. He was regarded highly by Pastor Stewart, and he was universally beloved and esteemed by the congregation. In short, he possessed those unifying talents that Alexander did not possess. Nevertheless, this would not be enough to spare the Baptists from a future split. For, another man would enter the scene and disrupt the fragile oneness of the church.

The arrival of John Eglinton Maxwell

John Eglinton Maxwell (b.1803), a Baptist preacher and teacher from Edinburgh, arrived in Toronto on July 28, 1834.[1] In many ways his coming marks a downturn in the history of the March Street church. Initially, he threw his support behind Stewart's ministry.

---

1 Entry for July 28, 1834. "John Eglinton Maxwell Diary." (Baldwin Room, Toronto Reference Library, Toronto).

His gift for preaching was recognized by Stewart and, like Paterson, Parson and Caldicott before him, he was given opportunities to exercise that gift. In fact, his first engagement occurred only two weeks after he settled in the community.[2] Towards the end of August, Maxwell travelled down the lake, visited Brother Wenham in Brockville, and scouted prospects for preaching in the area. However, he returned to Toronto on September 9 "on account of ill health" and likely was disheartened at the lack of opportunity in that district.[3] It was a decision that would have a profound impact on the church.

Is Christ divided?

In the fall of 1834, a close relationship developed between John Maxwell and Thomas Caldicott. Both were teachers, and Maxwell became an instructor at Caldicott's Commercial and Classical Academy on Colborne Street. It was about this time that Maxwell made Caldicott privy to his plan for furthering the gospel in Toronto and its environs. His idea was quite Scotch Baptist in its nature. Simply put, he wanted to institute a formal preaching rotation in a few places around the city—including March Street Baptist Church. The schedule would be drafted and circulated among the people six months in advance, and would show the place and time when each individual would preach. Caldicott favoured Maxwell's proposal, and Maxwell was then obliged to present his ideas to March Street's "elder statesman," Alexander Stewart.

On the evening of Friday, December 19, 1834, John Maxwell met with Pastor Stewart to convince him of the merits of his proposition. Thomas Caldicott, Timothy Parson and Peter Paterson were also present at the meeting in Stewart's home. The plan was offered for consideration and was quickly *rejected outright* by Stewart. Alexander had become a firm *Scottish* Baptist and in no way did he want to accept a proposal that would promote a return

---

2 Entry for August 10, 1834. "John Eglinton Maxwell Diary."
3 Entry for September 9, 1834. "John Eglinton Maxwell Diary."

to the polity of the *Scotch* Baptists. Further, he questioned the merits of the plan, perhaps reflecting on the apostle Paul's exhortation to the Corinthians: "Now I say this, that each of you says, 'I am of Paul', or 'I am of Apollos', or 'I am of Cephas', or 'I am of Christ.' Is Christ divided? Was Paul crucified for you? Or were you baptized in the name of Paul?" (1 Corinthians 1: 12-13, NKJV). More specifically, Maxwell recorded the thrust of Stewart's argument:

> Mr. Stewart objected to the plan—The reasons he gave were *1st* That should the people know who was to preach at any given time, they might be induced to come at one time when a preacher was to engage whom they favoured, and might forbear coming when one came whom they disliked; he thought this should not be encouraged; but that people should come whoever preached; also, that they were not competent judges. *2nd* That such a plan was calculated to call forth unhappy feelings among ourselves, one finding himself in the shade while he saw the people running after another; he thought it would do more harm than good.[4]

The young Maxwell could be just as stubborn as Stewart and could not accept this rejection. Consequently, he replied sharply, in response to Alexander's "narrow-mindedness":

> To these statements I replied, that I thought it the duty of every Christian to go and hear a man by whom they were edified, instead of one under whose ministry the precious time was wasted. I suppose a preacher well instructed in the mysteries of the kingdom of God, who had ample stores of knowledge, both human and divine at his command, who had a correct understanding of the great truths

---

4 Entry for December 19, 1834. "John Eglinton Maxwell Diary."

of the scriptures, who also had acquired a great share of sound Christian experience, from having been in these circumstances... and who in his preaching could bring all his speculative and experimental knowledge to bear upon the intellect and moral powers of his audience could in his preaching open up to the perceptive powers new fields of vision and give correct views of the Divine character. Paint out some feature of that character in the administration of providence and grace which I had not previously known or but imperfectly understood or had forgotten, by which my own knowledge was enlarged or corrected, my darkness removed or prejudices dispelled, my faith confirmed—my hope revived, my joy increased, my zeal fired, my purposes of good determination strengthened, my unhallowed passions subdued, my bad habits corrected, that should these be effected or any of these by attending one minister, I should think it my duty to attend him in preference to another.

If, on the other hand, one preached who was utterly unfitted for the task, who instead of making things better made them worse, gave wrong views of scripture truth, from his ignorance misapplied them, or trifled away the precious time from his scanty ill furnished mind—or from being a novice in the Kingdom of Christ, or from the multitude of prejudices mangling and destroying the subject he takes in hand, I am warranted in not supporting him.

I also mentioned that when preachers found themselves deserted, it was to them a hint to improve. Dr. Chalmers, I mentioned, was at one time not cared for as a preacher, but when grace irradiated his mind he set to study in good earnest... then the people ran to hear him because he could then inform their understandings and warm their hearts. These were the arguments I addressed in reference to what Mr. Stewart had said..."[5]

Heated words indeed! With Paterson and Caldicott in agreement with Maxwell's proposal, it was now Timothy Parson's turn to add a conciliatory note to the meeting. In his attempt to bridge the gap, he offered this compromise: "Mr. Parson then said that while people liked one and not another might it not keep them away altogether? He proposed that we should know a week and two days before we preached."[6] Blessed are the peacemakers! "With this arrangement Mr Stewart complied; wishing that our plans should only be known to ourselves, and not to the people."[7] Unfortunately, Maxwell would not accept any change to his plan. Wishing to extend one last "olive branch," Stewart asked Maxwell if he would preach on the ensuing Sabbath. The offer was declined by Maxwell "until a proper arrangement should be made."[8] The meeting disbanded without anything definitely being done except perhaps fuelling the fires of discontent.

Alexander Stewart never did acquiesce to Maxwell's plan, nor did Maxwell ever accept Parson's compromise. In addition, there is some evidence to suggest that the relationship between Stewart and Maxwell became severely strained following their Friday encounter. One instance witnessed Stewart accusing Maxwell of undermining his ministry by attacking his doctrine. John Maxwell called upon the pastor, on a Sunday afternoon, and gave a veiled response to Stewart's charge: "I defined my views of knowledge as consisting of two kinds Intellectual and perceptive and experimental."[9] Furthermore, other differences arose that widened the rift between these two men.

---

5 Entry for December 19, 1834. "John Eglinton Maxwell Diary." The "Dr. Chalmers" mentioned is Dr. Thomas Chalmers (1780-1847), the great mathematician, preacher and theologian, who led a group in the founding of the Free Church in Scotland in 1843.
  6 Entry for December 19, 1834. "John Eglinton Maxwell Diary."
  7 Entry for December 19, 1834. "John Eglinton Maxwell Diary."
  8 Entry for December 19, 1834. "John Eglinton Maxwell Diary."
  9 Entry for December 21, 1834. "John Eglinton Maxwell Diary."

Matters of association

Whereas Stewart advocated Scottish Baptist principles in the organization of his own church, the opposite was true when he considered affiliation with the larger Baptist family in the province. Like the church in Breadalbane, March Street followed the example of the Haldanes in Scotland, in that the "church emphasized the independence of the local congregation. Little stress was laid on the importance of an ordained ministry or on the desirability of the church being recognized by the Baptist Body in Upper Canada through the calling of a council."[10] While, it is true that Stewart did have fellowship with other Baptist ministers and churches, he did not see the need to formalize that relationship. In fact, it has been recorded that Stewart and his church refused to co-operate with one of the associations active in Ontario in 1836, although the context of that refusal is not known.[11] Strange as it may seem, Maxwell endorsed working with the association. He surmised that the church's prospects would be enhanced if it entered into agreement with other churches of like faith and practice.[12] Without commenting on the merits of either Stewart's or Maxwell's viewpoint, it is sufficient to state that denominational issues must have proved a further source of contention between them.

Johanna Carfrae Paterson

In the early months of 1835, a rumour began to spread concerning one of March Street's licentiate preachers. It seems the story con-

---

10 Stuart Ivison and Fred Rosser, eds. *The Baptists in Upper and Lower Canada before 1820* (Toronto: University of Toronto Press, 1956), 94.

11 Albert Henry Newman, "Sketch of the Baptists of Ontario and Quebec to 1851." In *The Baptist Year Book for Ontario and Quebec* (1900), 89.

12 "John Eglinton Maxwell Letterbooks." (Baldwin Room, Toronto Reference Library). In a letter to a Pastor James Mitchell written on May 9, 1838, Maxwell encouraged them to join a larger fellowship: "I think it would be well for you to join an Association; you would have much more friendship thrown around you and your little church."

cerned a relationship that had developed between Thomas Ford Caldicott and Johanna Carfrae Paterson (1795-1846), the daughter of Thomas Carfrae, Sr., and future wife of John Eglinton Maxwell.[13] Elder Stewart and Timothy Parson were empowered by the church to investigate the matter. Apparently, John Maxwell had some knowledge of the situation, and thus Stewart and Parson called upon Maxwell twice:

> Mar 27
> Mr. Stewart called and spoke of Mr. Caldicott and Mrs. Paterson. Called for Mrs. Paterson and took tea… found Mrs. Paterson very unwell from same base reports circulating through Toronto about her. I mentioned a little story I had heard about her from Mr. Reid's people, for which felt sorry afterwards…
> Mar 28
> …Mr. Stewart and Parson called. I was questioned as to the story—was severely handled about it…[14]

The ordeal was a delicate one because it involved three individuals who were well known in Baptist society. Stewart's apparent heavy-handedness in the matter seems to have left a bitter taste in John Maxwell's mouth, complicating the already tenuous relationship between them. It seems that this matter may have precipitated the exit of March Street's most unifying member.

The departure of Thomas Ford Caldicott

"T.F. Caldecott is supposed to have left the city during the year 1833, about which time commenced the difficulties which led to

---

13 Thomas Ford Caldicott was unmarried at the time. The context and details of Caldicott's questionable relationship with Johanna Paterson are unknown.

14 Entries for March 27 and 28, 1835. "John Eglinton Maxwell Diary." (Note: The "Mr. Reid" mentioned is likely Hugh Reid, who came into the membership of March Street Baptist Church around 1835.)

the resignation of Mr. Stewart."[15] While the 1833 date is erroneous, the substance of this statement cannot go unnoticed. Caldicott was called to the Baptist church in Cheltenham, Chinguacousy Township, late in 1835.[16] Whether he left March Street Baptist Church, solely because of his call to preach the gospel full-time, or whether he wanted to leave the city, in part, to diffuse the "rumour mill" and thereby protect the reputation of Johanna Paterson, may never be known. In any event, his departure dealt a crushing blow to the congregation, and upset the balance of unity.

Maxwell and Caldicott were talented individuals and were viewed by Stewart as welcome additions to his congregation. In regards to their character, each left their mark on the church in March Street. Maxwell was a young, opinionated man, whereas Caldicott exhibited a mature, conciliatory presence. Together, their opposing dispositions seemed to offset and compliment each other, maintaining a oneness in the Baptist body; when they separated, the balance in the church was disrupted, the slide towards discord was accelerated, and the potential for a great separation in the church was realized.

The schism of 1836

The life of March Street Baptist Church and the life of her undershepherd, Alexander Stewart, reached a low point in 1836. To state the matter plainly, Robert Alexander Fyfe reflected that some of the brethren became "too pious" to walk with their fellow believers any longer, and consequently impeded the progress and life of the church:

> Or to state the thought differently; they lost their sympathy for humanity, through the professed greatness of their love

---

15 *Jarvis Street Baptist Church: directory and historical sketch* (Toronto: Dudley & Burns, 1897), 53.

16 John Carter, "Reminiscences of the Baptists of Toronto." *The Canadian Baptist*, April 22, 1885.

for Christ. St. Augustine says, if one reached up to kiss the Saviour's lips, and in doing so, he should lacerate and tear the Saviour's bare feet, with the spikes and nails of his shoes, he would be asked why do you wound and pain my feet, in your endeavors to kiss my lips? So he asks, why do you trample upon, and wound my people, through your professed great love for me? Such people set up to be Angels before their wings are grown.[17]

In short, division would rock the church in the spring of 1836. Moreover, a second setback would come soon after, and decimate the church altogether: the departure of her pastor from active ministry.

Two Baptist churches

John Eglinton Maxwell could no longer, in good conscience, walk together with Stewart and the people of March Street—nor could he exit quietly. He succeeded in attracting a large number of the church's membership to his banner, and set up a new Baptist fellowship in the city of Toronto.[18] John Carter, who left with his mother, summarized this sad sequence of events: "considerable hard feeling was aroused, a large number of members withdrew and organized as a separate church."[19] Ironically, the new church procured the use of the Masonic Hall in Market Lane as their meeting place. In addition to the Carters, only one other seceding family can be ascertained with certainty. The Tost family, who had been "virtually baptized" in 1832, also left for the new church. In fact, Henry Tost became the new Society's first deacon.[20] The likes of

---

17 Robert Alexander Fyfe, *A forty years survey from the Bond Street pulpit* (Toronto: Dudley & Burns, 1876), 14-15.

18 *Canadian Baptist Magazine & Missionary Register*, Vol. 1 (June 1837-May 1838), 165. The December 1837 issue indicates that Maxwell's congregation had nineteen members.

19 Carter, "Reminiscences of the Baptists of Toronto."

20 *The City of Toronto and the Home District commercial directory and register with almanack and calendar for 1837* (Toronto, UC: Thomas Dalton, Printer), 30.

Peter Paterson, William McMaster (1811-1887) and Robert Cathcart (1799-1863) were among those who remained loyal to Stewart.[21] Furthermore, the Baptists of March Street were also reduced in number by those who departed and would eventually form Toronto's first Church of Christ Disciples.[22] Hence, by the summer of 1836, there were two Baptist churches in Toronto—both of them were weak and weary from months of infighting, and both needing desperately to refocus their efforts outward and reach the lost in their appointed mission field.

Stewart's resignation

The weeks and months that followed the split in March Street must have been terribly discouraging to the man who was instrumental in building the first Baptist work in Toronto. Despite the fact that services continued, the atmosphere among those who remained did not improve. On this point, John Carter agreed and elaborated: "the March Street church met as usual, but, alas, there was a lack of harmony among the members. Elder Stewart had been guilty of some indiscretions, and the church was obliged to administer discipline in his case and depose him."[23] Whether Alexander was removed or resigned, as some other sources indicate, is not known.[24] In either case, his departure did not remedy the continuing contention in March Street Church. On the contrary, without a leader, the congregation continued to flounder. Sadly, "the church very soon became extinct and the meeting house empty."[25]

---

21 Carter, "Reminiscences of the Baptists of Toronto." (Note: Carter indicated that the new church had no wealthy members.)

22 Joseph Ash, "History of the rise and progress of our cause in Canada." *Christian Worker*, Reminiscences No. 7, July 1883. Ash indicates that William McMaster followed Stewart, while James Beaty and Peter Rutherford and some others, went by themselves and worshipped in the house of George Armstrong.

23 Carter, "Reminiscences of the Baptists of Toronto."

24 Fyfe, *A forty years survey*, 17. Fyfe states: "The first pastor, the Rev. A. Stewart, seems to have met with some difficulties as pastor, and he resigned his office in 1836…"

25 Carter, "Reminiscences of the Baptists of Toronto."

Although there were many factors that contributed to the collapse of March Street Baptist Church, it is not imprudent to state that as the strength of her leader waned, so too did the strength and resolve of the congregation itself. For the most part, Alexander Stewart was a tired man. He no longer had the energy necessary to shepherd the church. Wisely, he left the eldership of the church, and concentrated his efforts on his other missionary interests: the Bible Society and ministering to individual needs. At the same time, he probably watched and prayed for the Lord to resurrect March Street, and raise up another pastor to lead her.

Section 9

A persevering saint 1837-1840

Chapter 17

Observing Toronto's Baptists

Alexander Stewart was no longer an active leader in Toronto's Baptist affairs. Nevertheless, he still took a keen interest in the advance of any Baptist work in the city. In regards to the March Street Church, although the chapel was closed, it was certainly his wish to see services resumed in that house of worship. He was not alone in this hope. Indeed, the fact that the trustees never disposed of the meeting house testifies of their resolve to resurrect a Baptist witness there. The building was rented out for a time, and thus the Baptists never really lost their identity.[1] In addition, for those who remained faithful to March Street, this was a period when they would wait on the Lord for clear guidance. A prayer meeting was sustained, "mostly at the house of one of the brethren then residing near Knox Church on Queen Street West."[2] Of course, there was another Baptist church

---

1 *Jarvis Street Baptist Church: directory and historical sketch* (Toronto: Dudley & Burns, 1897), 53.
2 *Jarvis Street Baptist Church: directory and historical sketch*, 53.

in the city under John Eglinton Maxwell, and Alexander Stewart observed the progress of this work as well. Shortly, it became readily apparent to Stewart, that God was preparing the entire mission field of Toronto for a reunification of the Baptists.

The rise and fall of Maxwell's church

John Maxwell's church struggled for three years following its birth in the spring of 1836. Perhaps, some of her difficulties arose from the want of a permanent church home. At the first, the congregation gathered at Market Lane Hall, but by the fall they had moved to a school house on King Street West. Within a few months, they had relocated again, this time to a house on Peter Street, near Lot Street. Their travels did not stop there. For, in the early months of 1837, they moved a fourth time...into March Street chapel itself! John Carter explained this odd set of circumstances: "Strange as it may seem, the first Baptist church, the seceding church, after preliminary matters had been arranged, took possession as tenants of the March Street meeting-house."[3] The *Toronto Directory* for 1837 corroborates Carter's statement: "The Baptist Church in the City of Toronto is situated in March street east, and has services every Sunday at 11 in the morning, 3 in the afternoon, and at 6 in the evening. J E Maxwell, Pastor, H Toast, Deacon."[4]

However, their time in March Street would be short-lived. "Some of the members and friends of the defunct church were desirous of again holding services in March Street"[5]—thus, they received notice to quit the premises. Finally, through the generosity of Johanna Carfrae Paterson, a lot and building was provided for the church on Lot Street, opposite College Avenue, in the fall of 1837. "Here considerable prosperity was granted by the Master to the church,"

---

3 John Carter, "Reminiscences of the Baptists of Toronto." *The Canadian Baptist*, April 22, 1885.

4 *The City of Toronto and the Home District commercial directory and register with almanack and calendar for 1837* (Toronto, UC: Thomas Dalton, Printer), 30.

5 Carter, "Reminiscences of the Baptists of Toronto."

wrote John Carter.[6] Unfortunately, that prosperity would not last, for the congregation was not numerically strong, nor did it possess the financial means to support its pastor.[7] Maxwell supplemented his income through teaching and ultimately decided to leave the church. In a letter to a fellow instructor in Edinburgh, Maxwell described his disappointment and subsequent course of action:

> In October '36 I had a very pressing invitation to come to the States and take the charge of a church with the offer of a competent salary of which I did not then accept. Again in July '38 I had another invitation. The church in Toronto was small. I had already sacrificed much in being there so long and must have continued to do so had I remained with little prospect of doing much good. I accepted of the second invitation.[8]

The call was to a Baptist church in Clyde, Wayne County, New York. Thereafter, the church in Toronto continued for a period of half a year, and at last agreed to disband in the summer of 1839.[9] The Maxwells eventually sold their interests in the property on Lot Street.

Tapscott, Bosworth, and reviving March Street

The prayer meetings held by the friends of March Street led to a reopening of the meeting house in the summer of 1837. The trustees engaged Rev. Samuel Tapscott (1804-1888), an agent for

---

6 Carter, "Reminiscences of the Baptists of Toronto."
7 Carter, "Reminiscences of the Baptists of Toronto."
8 Letter to Mr. James Johnston, Teacher in Edinburgh, June 18, 1840. "John Eglinton Maxwell Letterbooks." (Baldwin Room, Toronto Reference Library).
9 That the church agreed to disband by the summer is clear from a letter Maxwell wrote on July 3, 1839: "To Mr William Osborne… If you lease the house in Lot Street for a School I wish you to allow Mr Samuel George, Tailor in King St, and Mr Henry Tost Blacksmith in Lot Street to have still the use of it for a Sabbath School as they have promised to raise a little by way of rent and will pay it to you…" (See "John Eglinton Maxwell Letterbooks.") It is apparent that the building was no longer used for regular church meetings.

the *Canadian Baptist Magazine and Missionary Register*, to fill the pulpit. This he did effectively for almost six months.[10] About the time of the Mackenzie Rebellion, he left the city and settled at Colborne.[11] However, his zeal for the lost and for unity spilled over into the congregation and left a deep and lasting impression. Although, the chapel on March Street would close its doors and be rented out again, the Baptist reunification "fire" that was "stoked" under his ministry would not die out.[12] Indeed, another minister of the gospel would propel the Baptists into familial relationship once again.

In August 1838, Tapscott reported on the state of the Baptists in Toronto and of the March Street chapel. He commented, "It is exceedingly desirable that a suitable minister should occupy this important station."[13] At this time, many of the Baptists, including Stewart, were attending the services of Congregationalist minister John Roaf (1801-1862).[14] Thus, in response to Tapscott's call, the Rev. Newton Bosworth (1776-1848) and his family left the Baptist church in Montreal, "desirous of resuscitating the Baptist cause in Toronto."[15] Upon his arrival, Bosworth held a weekly prayer meet-

---

10 Carter recorded that Tapscott's ministry lasted "about a year." However, given the chronology and several moves of Maxwell's church, the period must have been much shorter than that. (See Carter, "Reminiscences of the Baptists of Toronto.")

11 Frederick Tracy, "Samuel Tapscott." *McMaster University Monthly* (Toronto: Dudley & Burns Printers, 1897), 341. The Mackenzie Rebellion refers, of course, to William Lyon Mackenzie's attempt to overthrow the administration and establish democratic government based on the American plan. The fiery critic of the Family Compact, and 800 followers, marched on Toronto in early December 1837. This motley radical army was quickly dispersed by the local militia. Subsequently, Mackenzie fled to the United States.

12 The building was rented for a time to a congregation of black Baptists, led by Elder Washington Christian. This church was founded by escaped slaves around 1826, and exists to this day as First Baptist Church, Toronto. (See *Jarvis Street Baptist Church: directory and historical sketch*, 53.)

13 Albert Henry Newman, "Sketch of the Baptists of Ontario and Quebec to 1851." *The Baptist Year Book for Ontario and Quebec* (1900), 89.

14 John Roaf came to Toronto in 1838 and became minister of a small Congregationalist body.

15 Carter, "Reminiscences of the Baptists of Toronto."

SAMUEL TAPSCOTT
(1804-1888)

ing once a week for the purpose of gathering the scattered Baptists of Toronto. His actions met with immediate success. John Carter recounted: "The prayer meetings were well attended, Mr. Bosworth generally presided. His opening addresses were always good... The Lord himself was always there, and those meetings were not held in vain."[16] Not only did these meetings serve to unite the Baptists in their cause, but many were convicted of their sins and of their need for a Saviour, Jesus Christ. On Sunday, December 8, 1839, seventeen people gave evidence of the "new birth" as they were baptized in Lake Ontario, at the foot of Bay Street.[17] The climax of this reunification came when six leading members of the March Street congregation made application to the Colonial Baptist Missionary of London England, for the purpose of securing a missionary pastor. After reciting the prospects and hopes of earlier days, the letter goes on to state that

> ...these encouraging prospects were blighted by laborers who were defective in character or talents, and therefore failed to bring in and keep united the elements of which a Church of Christ is composed; the members one after another retired to other denominations or formed themselves into lesser divisions, either with or without a ministry; these lesser divisions, however, soon dwindled away to a mere nominal existence, and the difficulties which but recently stood in the way to render the reoccupancy of the station in some measure painful or embarrassing to the Christian laborer, no longer exist.[18]

---

16 Carter, "Reminiscences of the Baptists of Toronto."

17 *Canadian Baptist Magazine & Missionary Register*, Vol. 3 (July 1839-June 1840), 162.

18 Robert Alexander Fyfe, *A forty years survey from the Bond Street pulpit* (Toronto: Dudley & Burns, 1876), 17-18.

Subsequently, the letter was sent, and the members of March Street would wait and anticipate a new beginning.

Three years had passed since Alexander Stewart had withdrawn from the eldership of March Street Baptist Church. He was not idle while he observed how the Toronto Baptist story was unfolding. Indeed, even in the twilight of his earthly journey he gave evidence of his willingness to serve the Lord and to minister to others. In the strength of the Lord, he was a persevering saint.

Chapter 18

The death of a saint

Alexander Stewart was growing old. Despite this fact, he was not the type of man that would sit back and resign himself to the inevitable. Alexander understood the importance of redeeming the time God had given him. Therefore, he would not be idle. Although the final three years of his ministry would not be as public as overseeing the affairs of a church, his kingdom-building efforts would persist in at least two areas. First, he would focus on a "labour of love" that had begun in his native Scotland. Second, he would act as pastor and friend to those he saw in need.

Still active in the things of God

Alexander's involvement in the Toronto Auxiliary Bible Society continued unabated till the day of his death. In 1837, he moved from the role of corresponding secretary and became one of the organization's vice presidents.[1] Lest one assumes that this new status was symbolic in nature, one only has to look at his correspondence to realize the opposite was true. For example, this letter, written to James Black on September 6, 1837, illustrates that he was truly a "hands-on" vice president. The missive itself concerned the preparation of the Scriptures for Upper Canada's aboriginal population. This description of Alexander's directions to Black, demonstrates his penchant for maintaining simplicity:

> He was co-operating with James Black about some of his Bible Society work, but took exception to the translation of the word "baptidso" in a gospel that James Black was printing for the Chippewa Indians. Alexander Stewart thought the King James version was sufficient for the Indians. It is likely that at the time of writing he had gone over to the Regular Baptists, who received a section of the early Toronto group after a split over Calvinistic teaching.[2]

The plainness of the spoken word had always been a hallmark of Stewart's ministry. In Scotland, he was a common man and preached the gospel in the language of the common people. The same was true in Canada. Alexander exclaimed,

> As to language, sound plain English is all that is necessary, yea this is best for common hearers in this country.—They have no need of scraps of latin quotations, a translation would suit better. Neither do they need what the lovers of the marvelous call learned words, for they only display the preacher, but give no edification to the hearers. No man

---

1 *The ninth report of the City of Toronto Auxiliary Bible Society: for 1837* (Toronto: Christian Guardian, 1838), iii.

2 Reuben Butchart, *Old Everton and the Pioneer Movement amongst the Disciples of Christ in Eramosa Township, Upper Canada, from 1830* (Toronto: Church of Christ Disciples, 1941), 6-7.

can benefit by unknown words. The speaker who uses unintelligible words speaketh to the air.³

While Alexander Stewart's work with the Bible Society took up much of his time, he also availed himself of pastoral opportunities, and displayed a fervent love for the people of God.

The Rebellion of 1837 provided Stewart with a unique setting in which to minister. More specifically, he was given the chance to defend the good name of a prominent Baptist family, before the courts of the land. When William Bentley was charged with sedition on December 17, 1837, Stewart could not remain silent. As an aside, the Bentleys were no strangers to charges of disloyalty. Elijah Bentley, a cousin of William and founder of the Baptist cause in Markham Township in 1803, was likewise charged with sedition after preaching a sermon in May 1813, that gave expression to pro-American sentiments.⁴ Now it was William Bentley's turn, and Stewart rose to the family's defense and "intervened on their behalf at that time when he became convinced that some of them were being unjustly punished, so that Elijah Bentley's services to the Baptist cause in an earlier day did not go entirely unrequited."⁵ As a consequence of Alexander's action, Mr. Bentley "was discharged by commission after examination December 26, 1837."⁶ With this minor battle won, Alexander Stewart would engage the "last enemy."

---

3 Alexander Stewart, *Two essays: the first, on the gospel; the second, on the kingdom of Christ; and a sermon on baptism* (York: Colonial Advocate, Wm. Lyon Mackenzie, Printer, 1827), 61.

4 Stuart Ivison and Fred Rosser, eds., *The Baptists in Upper and Lower Canada before 1820* (Toronto: University of Toronto Press, 1956), 56. Elijah Bentley was found guilty and sentenced to jail for six months. He was also bound to keep the peace for five years.

5 Ivison & Rosser, *The Baptists in Upper and Lower Canada*, 126.

6 *Rebels arrested in Upper Canada 1837-1838* (Toronto: Ontario Genealogical Society, 1987), 9.

"*Absent from the body, present with the Lord!*"

On Saturday, April 4, 1840, Alexander presided at the marriage of George Redrelle and Catharine Busby.[7] It would be his last public pastoral act. His health must have deteriorated quickly subsequent to this event. With his wife Janet by his side, Alexander Stewart entered into the presence of his Saviour Jesus Christ, on Friday, June 21, 1840.[8] Both the *Christian Guardian* and the *Toronto Examiner*

---

7 See Alexander Stewart, "Marriage register, 1830-1840." (Louis Melzack Collection, Thomas Fisher Rare Book Library, University of Toronto, Toronto).

8 The observant reader will notice that nothing has been said regarding Alexander and Janet's youngest son, Alexander Jr. Unfortunately, little has been found regarding the circumstances surrounding Alexander Jr.'s life. It seems obvious that he returned with his parents to York in 1826. (See John Menzies, "Letter to Elder Archibald Cameron, January 12, 1841." Canadian Baptist Archives, McMaster University, 3). He was living when his father died in 1840. However, he was not involved in the disposal of his father's lands in Esquesing Township. The executors and executrix of the estate (Peter Paterson Sr., John McIntosh, James Menzies and Janet Stewart) sold the remaining 100 acres of Lot 7, Concession 11 Esquesing Township to Thomas Johnson on February 8, 1844. (See Instrument 459B, *Deeds of Esquesing Township, Halton County 1847-1855*, Public Archives of Ontario.) Interestingly, the "memorial" of the deed makes reference to Stewart's "Last Will and Testament." The will was likely never probated, as it dealt mainly with the disposition of his lands, making it near impossible to find.

The author loses track of Alexander Jr. after 1853 when he is mentioned in the will of his brother-in-law John McIntosh. McIntosh had given a bond to Alexander Stewart Sr. to hold his property at Yonge and Queen Streets in Toronto as a residence for the duration of "three lives": Alexander Sr., Janet and Alexander Jr. The will states that after Alexander Jr.'s death the property was to revert to Alexander's three surviving grandchildren: Catherine, John and Ann Jane McIntosh.

In conclusion, a comment made by Robert Fyfe regarding Janet Stewart, and the early Baptists of York, seems to suggest that she suffered greatly in terms of her family: "Though we do not find in the minutes the names of any females, either as constituent members or as attending the earlier meetings, yet we know there were, at least eight women, and some of them very mothers in Israel, like Mrs. Carter, and Mrs. Stewart, who were enrolled at the first organization of the Church. Mrs. Stewart, the wife of the first pastor, I well remember as one of the saints of the Lord, chastened and mellowed by suffering..." [Robert Alexander Fyfe, *A forty years survey from the Bond Street pulpit* (Toronto: Dudley & Burns, 1876), 10.] The context of the burden she had to bear *vis a vis* her surviving son Alexander Jr., be it a physical or

The death of a saint 231

ALEXANDER STEWART'S GRAVE
(NECROPOLIS CEMETARY, TORONTO)[9]

carried obituaries of this man of God, and it is appropriate, at this point, to allow them to "speak" of this man's life and work:

> DIED—In this city, on Friday last, the Rev. Alexander Stewart. He was the founder of the Bible Society in Upper Canada; and so as a mark of respect, the President, Secretaries, and Committee of that Institution formed a procession to his grave, where the Rev. Mr. Roaf delivered a suitable and impressive address (*Christian Guardian*, June 24, 1840).

> DIED—On Friday last, the Rev. Alexander Stewart, lately a Baptist clergyman in this city and formerly a missionary in the highlands of Scotland, his native country. He was one of the earliest, most laborious and most persevering officers of the Bible Society in this city, and since had an extensive connection with the most prominent friends of religion in the Province. He maintained the attachment of his acquaintances by strict fidelity and a ready benevolence, and will long exert posthumous influence both in the esteem of his late friends and in the religious principles of many to whom he was personally unknown (*Toronto Examiner*, June 24, 1840).

Alexander Stewart was buried in the Potter's Field, next to his son James and daughter Catherine, on June 21, 1840.[9] Those who

---

spiritual one, may never be known. Alexander Jr. died on March 26, 1885.

9 Elizabeth Hancocks, ed. *Potter's Field Cemetary 1826-1855; Otherwise Called the Stranger's Burying Ground* (Agincourt: Generation Press, 1983), 91. "Stewart, Alexander, b. Scotland, bd. 21 June 1840, 65y, Motification (sic). 1149." Janet, his wife, would die 8 years later: "Stewart, Mrs. Janet, b. Perthshire, Scotland, widow of the late Rev. Alexander, d. 23 July 1848, bd. 25 July, 78y, Old age. 3214." (Note: The bodies of the Stewart family were exhumed and were re-interred in Section P, Lots 1 & 7 of the Necropolis Cemetary in Toronto in 1856, after the Potter's Field was closed.)

REV. W.H. COOMBS SUBSCRIPTION LIST
(FOR THE BAPTIST CHAPEL IN MARCH STREET, OPENED JULY 5, 1840)[13]

attended the funeral procession, did not grieve as those who have no hope.[10] For, this was the death of a saint. Therefore, those who share Alexander's faith can say with joy: "We are confident, yes, well pleased rather to be absent from the body and to be present with the Lord" (2 Corinthians 5:8, NKJV). Amen and amen!

It is rather ironic that only two weeks after Alexander Stewart's burial, the doors of March Street Baptist Church opened never to close again.[11] The letter to the Colonial Baptist Missionary Society had been answered, and the Rev. William H. Coombs (1802-1892), of Taunton, England, was the chosen minister. He arrived in Toronto in July 1840 and immediately commenced his ministry. "He was a godly man, an efficient minister, and of good address," wrote John Carter. "Our March Street meeting-house was once more occupied by a Baptist congregation. All the meetings were enthusiastic.[12] Certainly Stewart would have been pleased to witness the Baptists united again. The subscription list itself illustrates that the Baptists of Toronto had put aside their differences, for the once opposing names of McMaster and Tost appear together on the record of supporters.[13] Unfortunately, there is no way of knowing whether or not Stewart was aware that a missionary pastor was being sent; however, the author is inclined to believe that he did. Hence, confident that his Lord had provided a successor to shepherd the Baptists of Toronto, Alexander Stewart "drew his feet up into bed and breathed his last, and was gathered to his people" (Genesis 49:33, NKJV).

---

10 1 Thessalonians 4:13.

11 "Finances in Sterling of Bond Street Baptist Church, 1840 to 1846." (Jarvis Street Baptist Church Archives, Toronto.) The subscription list for the support of William H. Coombs shows that the meeting house opened on Sunday July 5, 1840.

12 Carter, "Reminiscences of the Baptists of Toronto."

13 "Finances in Sterling of Bond Street Baptist Church, 1840 to 1846."

Conclusion

Alexander Stewart was a man committed to the proclamation of the gospel of Jesus Christ. His preaching, essay writing and hymns all testify of his love for his Lord and his desire to see Christ's kingdom extended. In many ways his lifework and ministry are not atypical of one who has answered the call of God. Truly, there have been many pastors in the 2,000 year history of the church of whom it can be said: "They were raised up in mercy to a perishing world; and if they did not succeed in drawing multitudes to their chapels, it must be ascribed, in a great measure, to the unbending principles which they ever maintained."[1] But what were some of the outstanding principles that Alexander maintained? And, after everything has been said and done, what legacy did Stewart leave for the church?

There is no question that Alexander Stewart was a product of Robert and James Haldane's teaching and example. However, the

---

1 Alexander Haldane, *The lives of Robert Haldane of Airthrey, and of his brother, James Alexander Haldane* (Edinburgh: The Banner of Truth Trust, 1990), 331.

student did not completely adhere to the mentors' pattern. In character and in practice, Alexander Stewart was a Baptist, through and through. Unlike James Alexander Haldane, Stewart made the ordinance of baptism a test of fellowship—that is, one could not be admitted to the Lord's Table or the membership of a local church unless one first gave public testimony of his faith through believer's baptism.[2] Dr. Robert Alexander Fyfe, the great Canadian Baptist of the nineteenth century, gave credit to Stewart and the people of March Street Baptist Church for laying this baptistic foundation:

> I find no evidence... that Scotch Baptist views were ever even proposed, to be embodied in the constitution of the church, whatever individual members may have held. Indeed the constitution of this church has ever been eminently sound and scriptural. None but converted members, were received to the ordinances and thus spiritual character always came first. Those only who were professedly regenerated by the Spirit of God, and who exercised faith in the Lord Jesus Christ could be received for baptism; and none but those who had been baptized on a profession of their faith could be received to the Lord's Supper. And in passing, I deliberately affirm, that it is this last mentioned position alone which gives us the logical right to organize a church separate from our pedo-baptist brethren. Let the Baptists give up close communion, and with this surrender they yield up their logical right to have a Baptist Church at all. This church was "close communion" from its foun-

---

2 On the other hand, James Haldane advocated open communion and membership: "Many have even the impression that he declined to have fellowship with any but Baptists; but this is a mistake. In the Tabernacle church, he acted, at various periods of his history, on the free communion principle, by admitting Paedobaptists to fellowship. Thus, while he firmly held his sentiments as a Baptist, he extended his love to all who loved the Lord Jesus Christ." [Robert Kinniburgh, ed. *Fathers of Independency in Scotland; or, Biographical sketches of early Scottish Congregational ministers. A.D. 1798–1851* (Edinburgh: A Fullarton & Co., 1851), 465.]

dation, and her strength and compactness this day are largely due to the consistent position which she has always held on this subject.³

Given the independent nature of Baptist churches, in general, one could argue that Alexander Stewart's promotion of Baptist distinctives went no further than his own church. However, March Street Baptist Church was no ordinary church.

More than any other Baptist church in Upper Canada, the March Street congregation had the potential to influence the direction of the denomination simply because the assembly met in the capital of the province. Despite the troubles and setbacks suffered in the mid-1830s, March Street (later Bond Street and then Jarvis Street) would become the most influential Baptist church in the Dominion of Canada.⁴ In hindsight, the labours and sacrifices of Alexander Stewart were not to no avail. For, unbeknownst to Alexander, he established the "mother" church that would give rise to many "daughter" Baptist works throughout Toronto. Thus, the paramount reason why Alexander Stewart's story should be told is precisely because he founded the *first* Baptist church in the city. This is his legacy.

I've often wondered what Alexander Stewart would like to have been remembered for? The answer to that question cannot be answered satisfactorily on this side of glory. However, the author is inclined to think that Alexander saw himself as a Christian who did his utmost to fulfil the mandate of the Great Commission.⁵ In conclusion then, let Alexander Stewart's own words reverberate in every Christian heart until our Lord returns:

---

3 Robert Alexander Fyfe, *A forty years survey from the Bond Street pulpit* (Toronto: Dudley & Burns, 1876), 16-17.

4 The congregation of March Street relocated to Bond Street in 1848, and then to Jarvis Street in 1875.

5 Matthew 28:18-20.

...I consider it my duty to use every means in my power to propagate the gospel of Christ—to point out the nature of his kingdom—and the ordinances he has set on foot in that kingdom. If any one be disposed to criticise my style or arrangement &c they may have their pains for their reward; and while my Lord and Master enables me I am ready to defend his kingdom with its doctrine and ordinances:—nor shall I desist from the combat because I have not a silver mounted sword to fight with. I know the sword of the spirit, and I shall not fail to wield it against every enemy, in the calm spirit of the gospel of peace.[6]

---

6 Alexander Stewart, *Two essays: the first, on the gospel; the second, on the kingdom of Christ; and a sermon on baptism* (York: Colonial Advocate, Wm. Lyon Mackenzie, Printer, 1827), preface.

Afterword

A Scotsman, a Baptist, an early inhabitant of what would become the bustling urban metropolis of Toronto, a pioneer of the future Jarvis Street Baptist Church—Alexander Stewart was all of these, and for anyone with similar links and convictions, this detailed account of his life by Pastor Tomlinson should be of deep interest. It has been so to me certainly.

Ever since I married my Scottish wife in Stanley Avenue Baptist Church in Hamilton—which had strong links to Jarvis Street Baptist Church for much of the twentieth century—I have been interested in Scottish Baptists and, because I was living in Ontario, their impact on this province. As I studied the influence of various first- or second-generation Scottish Baptists—men like William Fraser, John Gilmour, Robert Alexander Fyfe, or D.A. McGregor, and now, Alexander Stewart—I found that they played a key formative role in the community of nineteenth-century Ontario Baptists. The story of that role has yet to be fully told. But I am deeply thankful for this account by Pastor Tomlinson of one of these men, an important step in the realization of that larger project and a stimulus to others to hopefully become interested in the riches of Ontario Baptist history.

But Alexander Stewart's story is important in its own right. His life reveals what Baptists have always insisted on: that a personal relationship with God through the Lord Jesus Christ is the most valuable treasure a human being can possess and that through such a relationship God can do great things in the advance of his kingdom. Since Stewart laid the foundations for what is now Jarvis Street Baptist Church in the second decade of the nineteenth century, this church has played a central role in the Baptist cause in Toronto and Ontario. And for that, and Stewart's life, may God be praised and glorified!

Michael A.G. Haykin
Professor of Church History and Biblical Spirituality,
The Southern Baptist Theological Seminary, Louisville, Kentucky

Appendices

Appendix A

Roll of members, Perth Baptist church, 1812-1815

This is a partial roll of members of the Baptist church at Perth, Perthshire, Scotland.[1]

Anderson, D.
Anderson, John
Campbell, Ann
Campbell, Christian
Campbell, John
Campbell, Peter
Candie, William
Christal, Robert

---

1 Alexander Stewart, "Sermon Notes 1810"; "Notes on the Baptist church at Perth, Scotland, 1812-1815"; "Register of sermons preached chiefly at York, Upper Canada, 1827-1833"; "Marriage register, 1830-1840"; "Returns of subscribers for *Essays on the gospel and the kingdom of Christ*." (Louis Melzack Collection, Thomas Fisher Rare Book Library, University of Toronto, Toronto).

Cuthbert, M.
Hendrie, Hellen
Humes, Andrew
Laurie, George
Laurie, Mrs. George
Lothian, Christian (Mrs. John)
Lothian, John
McFarlane, John ★
McIntosh, Dougal
McIntyre, John
McNaughton, Betty (Mrs. Peter)
McNaughton, Peter
McNaughton, William
McPherson, James
McRobbie, John
Pullar, Hellen
Pullar, Isabel (Mrs. Robert)
Pullar, Robert
Robertson, George
Robertson, Elspeth
Scott, James
Scott, John
Scott, Robert
Stalker, John ★
Stalker, Ann (Mrs. John)
Stewart, Alexander ★
Stewart, Janet (Mrs. Alexander)
Stewart, William
Stot, Bell
Thomson, Andrew
Whittat, Robert
Young, John
Young, Mrs. John

★ held office in the church

Appendix B

Roll of members, York Baptist church, 1818-1820

This is a partial roll of members of the Baptist church at York, organized on October 25, 1818. Dates of admission are approximate.[1]

	Date of admission
Armstrong, James	1819
Birnie, John	1818
Collins, James	1819
Fyfe, Thomas	1819
Laidlaw, James	1819
Menzies, John	1818

---

1 Sources include: "Petition of James Smith, Alex Stewart, Thos Stephens & others." *Upper Canada Land Petitions 'S' Bundle Miscellaneous 1799-1842 RG 1, L 3,* Vol. 447a, #40, Public Archives of Ontario; Stewart, Alexander, "Letter from Alexander Stewart, Canada." *New Evangelical Magazine and Theological Review,* Vol. V (London: 1819); Stewart, Alexander, "Letter from Alexander Stewart, Canada." *New Evangelical Magazine and Theological Review,* Vol VI (London: 1820).

Menzies, Isabella	1818
Carfrae, Thomas Sr.	1818
Carfrae, Janet	1818
Smith, James	1819
Stephens, Thomas	1818
Stephens, Eleanor	1818
Stewart, Alexander	1818
Stewart, Janet	1818

Appendix C

Petition of James Smith, Alex Stewart, Thos Stephens

This petition was presented to Lieutenant Governor Maitland in 1819, requesting that land grants not be assigned by lot but rather that they be assigned together so that Alexander Stewart, James Smith and Thomas Stephens could all be located in one area—for the purposes of meeting together and attending to the ordinances. (See chapter 9.) There are three parts to the petition.[1]

I. Unto his Excellency Major General Sir Peregrine Maitland K. C.B. Lieutenant Governor and Commander in Chief of His Majesty's Province of Upper Canada.

In Council

The petition of the under mentioned persons humbly sheweth

---

1 Taken from *Upper Canada Land Petitions 'S' Bundle Miscellaneous 1799-1842* RG 1, L 3, Vol. 447a, #40, Public Archives of Ontario.

That your petitioners, His Majesty's loyal and dutiful subjects, are of that religious denomination known in Scotland by the name of Baptists. That on removing from their native countries into this province they were happy to meet so as to join together to attend to the ordinances of the Lord Jesus Christ as they understand them from the Scriptures of Truth.

That it is the earnest desire of your petitioners that they may enjoy their present privilege of assembling themselves together on the first day of the week to attend to what they consider the will of Christ desiring the remainder of their short pilgrimage here before and that can only be obtained by your Excellency's granting them the location of their lands together or in one place.

That your petitioners have heard that the Township of Toronto for a location in which most of your petitioners have waited a considerable time, is to be given out by lot and that if blocks of land are to be given by lot in that Township, your petitioners wish to be included for that portion of lands which your Excellency in Council has been pleased to grant to them individually.

That the only possible objection your petitioners can have to take their chance of individual lots is that strong desire to be together and that this is the sole cause of their present petition.

That your petitioners though they prefer their lands to the west of the Credit River or on the Tobico River, leave it with your Excellency in Council to point out that part of the Township that shall seem to you most proper, only they wish their lands together and of course as they are entire strangers to living in the woods, as near a road as possible. Although your petitioners know of several persons of their own minds being on their way to this place and have formerly expressed their wish that these also might locate beside them they leave this for your Excellency's after consideration.

Your petitioners beg leave only to add that as some of their number have a little money and could direct machinery they would wish to be near a river and that several of them are disposed to take a lease of some reserved lots.

May it therefore please your Excellency in council to take the request of your petitioners into your most serious consideration and to give such answer as to your Excellency shall seem meet. And the prayer of your petitioners is that your Excellency may be preserved many years for a blessing to this province.

Signed in behalf of the under mentioned persons
James Smith
Alexander Stewart

Names of petitioners with the quantity of lands granted to each:

Thomas Carfrae	300 acres
Thomas Stephens	300 acres
James Smith	300 acres
William Smith, his son	100 acres
John Armstrong	200 acres
Alexr Stewart	200 acres
John Menzies	100 acres
John Robertson, his brother in law	100 acres
James Collins	100 acres
Total	1700 acres

York 20 April 1819

II. To His Excellency Major General Sir Peregrine Maitland Lieutenant Governor and commander in chief of his Majesty's

Province of Upper Canada.

The petition of the undersigned and under mentioned humbly sheweth that the persons under mentioned His Majesty's loyal and dutiful subjects are of that denomination known in Britain by the name of Baptists. That in removing from their native countries they are happy to meet here to unite in attending to the ordinances of the Lord Jesus Christ according as they understand them from the Scriptures of truth.

That they now accordingly meet in this Town every first day of the week for the purpose of attending to the ordinances of Christ and of preaching the Gospel to their fellow sinners. That the circular letter sent herewith for your Excellency's inspection fully explains the views and practice of your petitioners being from a Church with which your petitioners hold full fellowship in the Gospel and the ordinances of Christ.

That it is the earnest desire of your petitioners that they may continue to enjoy their present privileges of assembling themselves together on the first day of the week for these purposes and that these privileges cannot be enjoyed unless they obtain the location of their lands in one place.

Your petitioners are not aware that any complaint of disloyalty has been laid against them though they know it is a general charge brought against all those who do not submit to the authority of men in religious matters but they beg leave to assure your Excellency that they consider themselves bound by the authority of Jehovah to submit to the Powers that be to obey Magistrates, to give honour & tribute to whom they are due and that it is a part of their religious worship to pray for the King and all that are in authority under him and that they can have no religious fellowship with those who do not obey the laws of the country.

So your petitioners know that several of their persuasion are on their way to this place who wish to locate beside them they beg your Excellency's attention to a communication from the British Consul in New York on this subject.[2]

Your petitioners are desirous of Locating in the Township of Toronto just now surveyed on the River Credit. If your Excellency has not otherways disposed of the west half of the fourth together with fifth and sixth concessions to the west of that River your petitioners would prefer that place but should that be disposed of they would prefer the Land close to the Credit on the east side.

Your petitioners beg leave to add that as some of their number have a little money they will be able to erect Mills on that River and that it is their intention to lease some Reserves. Those who sign this petition will give any explanation your Excellency may require.

May it therefore please your Excellency to consider the above to give such answer as to your Excellency may seem meet. And our prayer to God is that your Excellency may be preserved many years for a shield to us His people a terror to those who do evil & a praise to such as do well.

Signed in behalf of the under mentioned
Thos Stephens
Alexr Stewart
James Smith

Names of persons & quantity of lands granted each:

Thomas Carfrae   three hundred acres

---

2 The British Consul in New York City was James Buchanan (1772-1851), a member of the "Haldane Church" under the eldership of William Ovington and Henry Errett, and a friend of Thomas Stephens.

Thoms Stephens	three hundred acres
James Smith	three hundred acres
Wm Smith his son	one hundred acres
James Armstrong	two hundred acres
Alexr Stewart	two hundred acres
John Menzies	one hundred acres
John Robertson	one hundred acres
James Collins	one hundred acres

W Smith & J Robertson are not members but wish to be near their friends.

P.S. The quantity of land granted your petitioners is seventeen hundred acres this with what we deemed necessary for the accomod of the Twenty Families to be forwarding the British Consul may amount to Five thousand.

York April 14th 1819

III. THE CHURCH PROFESSING OBEDIENCE TO THE FAITH OF JESUS CHRIST, Assembling together in New York;

To the Churches of Christ, scattered over the earth, to whom this communication may come—Grace, mercy, and peace, be multiplied from God the Father, by the Holy Spirit, through our Lord Jesus Christ:

DEARLY BELOVED,
Participating in the attention that has been, of late years, excited among the disciples of the Lord Jesus to the consideration of the Holy Scriptures, and the obedience therein exhibited, as connected with the belief of the Gospel;—We have been led, by the mercy of God, to separate from various religious connections and denomi-

nations, and to come together into one body, that, in the fear and reverence of his authority, we might walk as a Church of Christ in this city, continuing in the Apostles' doctrine and fellowship, and breaking of bread, and prayers; strengthening each other in our most holy faith, and manifesting our love towards each other as brethren for whom Christ died. It is more than seven years since we began to enjoy these blessings, and though we were some time together before we were, as a Church, fully set in order with both Elders and Deacons; yet, as the disciples and subjects of Jesus, our Lord and King, deriving all our privileges and advantages from Him, as the Head of the Church, we deemed it our duty to attend to all the institutions of his kingdom. But it is cause of great thankfulness, that the Lord has raised among us Elders and Deacons, possessing, in degree, the qualifications required by the Holy Spirit, in Paul's epistles to Timothy and Titus; and having attained to this privilege, we are cheered with the information, that there are, in other parts of the earth, many churches "of like precious faith with the Apostles"—founding their hope of eternal life, upon the faithful testimony concerning the atonement—who having renounced the hidden things of dishonesty, are not walking in craftiness, and hypocrisy, nor handling the word of God deceitfully; but by manifestation of the truth, are commending themselves to every man's conscience in the sight of God.

Remembering, dearly beloved, that the first churches of Christ in Judea, are set before us as a pattern; and that amongst them there was not only a unity in the faith, but a friendly and affectionate intercourse—according to the prayer of Jesus (John, 17);—we deem it the duty and the high honor of the churches of the Lord Jesus, after the lapse of so many ages of division and distraction, to lay aside all the questions and strifes of words created by the wisdom of man, and with one heart, to endeavor to restore and promote the unity and prosperity of his kingdom.

With the view of assisting in this good work, dearly beloved brethren, we address this epistle to you; having reason to believe, that your love to the Lord Jesus has led you, also, to cease from all human institutions and expedients in the worship of Him, whose fear is not to be regulated by the precepts of man, and to maintain a walk and conversation becoming the gospel, both towards each other and towards all men. To you, therefore, and to all such, we make a tender of our love and esteem; and desire an epistolary intercourse for the promotion of mutual love, and of mutual acquaintance with each other's views, in all things belonging to the kingdom of our Lord Jesus Christ. And our prayer to God is, that by these means, both you and we, may be enabled to contribute somewhat to the restoration, amongst the true disciples of Jesus, of a uniform adherence to the apostolic practice, whereby they may exhibit the harmony and beauty of His religion, when relieved from the false views, and worldly maxims, by which its purity has been defiled, and its glory obscured.

That you may be better informed concerning those who thus address you, we have deemed it requisite to give the following brief sketch of our public worship—soliciting, at the same time, that wherein you may differ from us in any matter, faithfulness will dispose you to refer us to apostolic practice, plain and intelligible to the capacity of the plain and simple followers of the Lamb—*as we have not much of this world's learning*, and are disposed to admit that alone as obligatory, which can be clearly adduced from the New-Testament, without the aid of sophistry or allusion to the practices of man. And we trust, it may be given us from above, to receive with meekness whatever of this nature your love and concern for our welfare, may dispose you to communicate.

The order, which we derive from the law of Christ, is as follows:

We require, that all whom we receive into fellowship, should believe in their heart, and confess with their mouth, that *Jesus is the Christ*; that he died for our sins, according to the scriptures: and that upon such confession, and such alone—they should be baptized.

We hold it to be the duty, and privilege of the disciples of Jesus to come together into one place, on every first day of the week—rejoicing in the recollections which that day revives—whereon the Lord Jesus destroyed the power both of hell and death, by his resurrection from the dead—and gave sure hope to his people of being raised also. When thus assembled, we proceed to attend to all the ordinances which we can discover to be enjoined by the practice of the first churches, and the commandments of the Lord and his Apostles.

1st. Our Elders presiding, and the brethren all together, (having no fellowship in sacred things with those who confess and obey not the faith)—in obedience to the command 1 Tim. ii. 1, &c. We commence our public worship by kneeling down and offering supplications, prayers, &c. directed in that passage—the Elders by themselves, or one of the brethren selected by them as competent, speaking as the mouth of the body.

2d. One of the Elders selects a suitable Hymn or Psalm, expressive of praise; in the singing of which all the Members stand up and join.

3d. A portion of the word of God is read by one of the Elders relative to the subject or institution of the Lord's Supper: upon which, thanks are given, by one of the Elders or brethren, for the Bread;—and after the breaking of Bread—thanks for the Cup;—and after the taking of the Cup—a suitable Hymn or Psalm is sung.

4th. A passage relative to the fellowship or contribution for the poor saints is read;—then prayer for suitable dispositions, and thanksgiving for ability, and privilege to contribute in this way. The collection for the saints follows.

5th. Previous to reading the Holy Scriptures—prayer for the Holy Spirit to open the understanding of all present, to understand and receive the sacred word. The reading consists of a chapter in the Law—one in the Prophets—and one in the New-Testament. After each, a pause is made to allow opportunity to any of the brethren, to make remarks by way of illustration as the subject might require.

6th. Exhortation from the word of God, by the Elders of the Brethren.

7th. Praise

8th. Prayer, and separate.

In the evening, the church assembles for worship—after which the Elders in their turn, and some other of the brethren, approved by the Church, declare the gospel to those without.

A Love feast is also attended to—and a meeting on a week evening—but those not appearing to be of the same strict obligation with the duties of the Lord's day, are sometimes made to give way to circumstances.

The Kiss of Charity, the Washing of Feet, and the entertainment of the disciples, being things the performance of which, arises from special occasions exemplified in the New-Testament—we deem of importance to be attended to on such occasions.

Discipline, is also a duty which will sometimes fall to the lot of disciples on the Lord's day.

It may be necessary to observe that our Elders labour at their respective callings, for their support, and are not burdensome to the church, but in case of need, or that the duties of their office render aid necessary, the church deem it their duty and privilege to communicate liberally to them, as "the Labourer is worthy of his hire."

As to our intercourse with the world, we require strict uprightness in walk and in dealing, sobriety in spirit and behaviour—kindness towards all, even enemies—no evil speaking of any—but zeal for every good work—whether it respect the bodies or souls of men. In a word—that righteousness of character before all men, which the word enjoins as the evidence of being in Christ—and as the recommendation of his religion to mankind.—We believe also that according to the word of God, Christians should be subject to "the powers that be" in every nation—unless where any of their commands, might require a breach of the Law of Christ. Consequently, that disciples should have no lot, or part in any combinations for the overthrow or disturbance of Governments—it being injurious to the cause of Jesus our Lord, that any of his people should suffer justly in this world as evil doers. 1 Pet. 2

In our relationship to each other as Christians, we are all brethren, having no distinction in the church, except what gifts necessarily create—but we do not therefore seek to abolish, nor interfere with those earthly distinctions which our respective stations in the world may require, unless where, and so far as these might clash with the authority of the divine word.

We view it as our duty, to be subject to, and to forbear each other, to please our brethren, and not wound their weak conscience, but to deny ourselves, and in all things seek the peace and comfort of the Church, where such compliance would not countenance error. We esteem it also to be our duty to love our brethren, in deed, as well as in word; holding our substance (which we have as the stewards of God,) in readiness to supply their necessities: showing, by our willingness to contribute, that we walk by faith and not by sight, and are laying up our treasure where no moth can corrupt, nor thief break through and steal.

The questions and disputations that generally prevail among professing christians, have no place among us: their reasonings and speculations occupy no part of our time. The knowledge of the simple truth, declared by the Lord Jesus and his Apostles—and the practical godliness arising from that knowledge, are the things whereon we desire to bestow our attention.

It should not be omitted, that in all our measures and decisions, unanimity, and not majority is deemed the scriptural rule.

There are scattered over this continent, a few small societies who have conformed in part to the simplicity of the Apostolic faith and practice. We also address to such a similar epistle, and should you favor us with your correspondence, we purpose, if the Lord will, to make known the result of this our communication, to all whom we shall have reason to esteem disciples of the Lord Jesus.

The date of your coming together—the number of members—whether you have Elders and Deacons—together with any additional information, will be very acceptable to the Church that thus addresses you.

Now may He, who was dead, and is alive, and lives—over all, God blessed forever, preserve you blameless—to Him be glory both now and for ever. Amen.

The answer in duplicate, you will please forward to

NEW-YORK, March 1, 1818
Approved and adopted by the Church, and Signed in their behalf, by

WM. OVINGTON, HENRY ERRETT, *Elders.*
JONATHAN HATFIELD, JAMES SAUNDERS,
BENJ. HENDRICKSON, *Deacons.*

Appendix D

A sermon on baptism, by Alexander Stewart

This sermon was preached in 1825, in the Township of Chinguacousy, at the baptism of a professed believer.[1] This is part of the only printed record known to exist of Stewart's theological thought. It first ran in the Colonial Advocate in 1827 and then was published in book form under the title, Two essays: the first, on the gospel; the second, on the kingdom of Christ; and a sermon on baptism. *(See chapter 12.)*

Colossians 2:12
"Buried with him in baptism, wherein also ye are risen with him through the faith of the operation of God, who hath raised him from the dead."

---

1 Alexander Stewart, *Two essays: the first, on the gospel; the second, on the kingdom of Christ; and a sermon on baptism* (York: Colonial Advocate, Wm. Lyon Mackenzie, Printer, 1827). (Note: Minor edits have been made to the punctuation and spelling in the text.)

The Scriptures are given us by the inspiration of God, the Spirit. Whatever he reveals, we are bound to believe, and whatever he commands, we are bound to obey. The Spirit of God does not amuse our minds with non-essentials, as some would have us to believe; but gives us important doctrines to believe, and important ordinances to obey. The ordinance of baptism is none of the least important. It is not only a positive institution, but in this institution, or ordinance, we have very important truths figuratively held forth to our view. The consideration of this ordinance with its figurative or spiritual meaning shall form the following discourse:

I shall consider the subject under the following heads.

I. Baptism is an ordinance of Christ.
II. This ordinance is figurative.
III. Baptism is a profession of faith in Christ.
IV. Baptism is a binding duty on believers.
V. There is but one baptism.
VI. It is a profession of our having taken Christ's yoke upon us.

I. *Baptism is an ordinance of Christ*

The word baptism is a New Testament word, and holds forth a New Testament ordinance, or institution. Though there were divers baptisms, as the Greek term means (Hebrews 9:10), under the old, or Jewish dispensation (Numbers 19:7,19), they were carnal ordinances, imposed upon a carnal people, purifying ceremonial uncleanesses—and only shadows of good things to come (Hebrews 9:9-10). The New Testament baptism is an institution of Christ, given to a new creation of men, holding forth the most important doctrines of the gospel, *viz.*— the death and resurrection of Christ as the substitute for sinners—and the believer's death unto sin, and resurrection to newness of life, through faith in Christ Jesus.

This ordinance began with John the Baptist (Matthew 3:6; Mark 1:4; Luke 3:2-21; John 3:23-36), was continued by Christ (John

4:1-2), and by him instituted as a standing ordinance in his church to the end (Matthhew 28:19; Mark 16:16). Some disputes have arisen about a supposed difference between the baptism of John and the baptism of Christ; and it has been said that Paul rebaptized John's disciples (Acts 19:3-5): this is a mistake. Paul is here declaring John's doctrine and practice. John baptized into the faith of Christ as just at hand, & declared salvation through faith in him (John 3:36), and therefore this was enough. Those disciples had been baptized into the faith of the character of Christ. In Christ's commission to his apostles (Matthew 28:19), he commands those of all nations who should become disciples to be baptized. Here then we have a plain account of the institution: let us see what the institution itself consists of.

1st. Baptism is an immersion in water.
This appears, *first,* from the meaning of the word baptism. The word is a Greek word, adopted into our language without translating it, with a varied termination. The Greek words are *bapto* and *baptismo,* and in all the Lexicons I have seen—as, Schrevelli, Parkhurst, Ewing, More &c.—they are translated, dip, plunge, immerse, but never sprinkle, or pour. I shall here quote two eminent paedobaptist critics on the meaning of the term—Dr. McKnight of Edinburgh and Dr. Campbell of Aberdeen. Dr. McKnight says, in his *Harmony of the Gospels* (vol. 1. p.58), speaking of John the baptist: "he was sirnamed the baptist, from his baptising, or washing, his disciples." Again, on Luke 3:3-16 (p.69) he has these words as if expressed by John: "I am sent from God, and the message I bring is, that all ranks and orders of persons must *repent.* Withal, to impress this doctrine the more deeply upon their minds, I address their senses by *washing* all my disciples (in) with water." So far Dr. McKnight. Dr. Campbell translates Mark 7:3-4, as follows: "for the Pharisees, and indeed all the Jews, observing the tradition of the elders, eat not until they have washed their hands, by pouring a little water upon then: and if they be come from the market, by dipping them."

In his note on the above he says, "for illustrating this passage let it be observed, 1st. that the two verbs rendered wash in the English translation, are different in the original. The first is *nipsontai* properly translated *wash*; the second denotes to *plunge* to *dip*." The Jews thought themselves more defiled when they went to the market than at ordinary times. Again Dr. Campbell says (diss. 8, p.2), "for this reason, I should think the word immersion a better name than baptism." In a note on Matthew 3:11 he says, "the word *baptizein*, both in sacred authors and in classical, signifies, to dip, to plunge, to immerse." Here then we have the view of two of the first-rate critics of our day of the meaning of the word baptism — critics the more to be regarded as they were paedobaptists. If we are then, in our explanations of Scripture, to abide by the plain meaning of words we must conclude, that the baptism instituted by Christ, *is immersion in water*.

This appears, *secondly*, from the examples of baptism recorded in the New Testament. In Mark 1:9-10 we are told, "that Jesus came from Nazareth to Galilee and was baptized of John in Jordon, and straightway coming up out of the water" &c. Dr. Campbell [translates that as:] "as soon as he arose out of the water." How natural this account. John immersed Jesus in the river Jordan; and he arose, or came up out of the water, and the heavens opened and the Spirit of God descended, &c. We are told (John 3:23) that Jesus began to baptize, that is by his disciples (John 4:2), and that John was baptizing in Ænon, near to Salim, because there was *much water* there. After all the quibbles of paedobaptists upon this passage, any common reader, and for such the New Testament was written, must infer that much water was necessary. Any common well would supply water to sprinkle thousands, but *much* water was necessary to immerse the whole body. The only other passage I shall bring forward is Acts 8:38-39: "and he (the eunuch) commanded the chariot to stand still and they went down both into the water, both Philip and the eunuch; and he baptized him. And when they were come up out of the water" &c. What a natural, exact account! Philip and the eunuch went into the water, and Philip according to the eunuch's own request (Acts 8:36) immersed him. Could Philip have dispensed with immersion, and substituted sprinkling he would have surely done it in this case, as the person to be baptized was a great man, and neither he nor Philip could have clothes suitable for such an ordinance. But the command of Christ was positive—"Go and convert, or disciple, all nations, immersing them in the name of the Father, of the Son, and of the Holy Ghost." Philip understood the command and acted accordingly. The Holy Ghost seems to have given this account the more full that none in after ages might plead ignorance. After reading such plain language, how can professed disciples of Jesus, reject or neglect this ordinance? O, the darkness of the human mind!

2nd. The next thing to be considered is, who are the proper subjects *of this ordinance.*
It is plain from the Scriptures that *believers only* are fit subjects of baptism. This is seen, first from the words of institution, which we have in Matthew 28:19-20 and in Mark 16:15-16. The first of these passages reads thus in our common Bibles, "Go ye therefore, and teach all nations, baptizing them in the name of the Father, and of the Son, and of the Holy Ghost." The margin reads, "making disciples, or christians, of all nations." Dr. Campbell [translates that as:] "convert all nations." All comes to the same point, but the word means to disciple. The next passage is Mark 16:15-16: "And he said unto them, go ye unto all the world, and preach the gospel to every creature; he that believeth and is baptized shall be saved, but he that believeth not shall be damned"—here is a plain command to baptize believers only. Dr. McKnight, having brought forward both these passages together, adds, "Withal those who believed in consequence of their preaching, he appointed to be received into his church by the rite of baptism, and be taught all the precepts he had enjoined them." Dr. Campbell says on Matthew 28:19-20: "there are manifestly three things which our Lord here distinctly

enjoins his apostles to execute with regard to the nations, to wit, to convert them to the faith, to initiate the converts into the church by baptism, and to instruct the baptized in all the duties of the christian life." I do not bring forward the above authorities because they make these passages plainer, for that is impossible, but because these men, as critics on the language, and at the same time paedobaptists, have been under the necessity of giving a fair scriptural view of the text. Let those who contend for infant baptism point out any such passage and we will believe them. Our statutes say that all males above sixteen years of age, shall work on the highways — who would infer from this that infants must be militiamen, and work on the roads merely because the statute does not expressly forbid their doing so? Yet such is the absurd reasoning used respecting the subjects of baptism.

Secondly, that *believers only* ought to be baptized is evident from the uniform practice of the apostles. Even John the Baptist refused baptism to those whose conduct did not evidence their repentance towards God and faith towards our Lord Jesus Christ. Their fleshly relation (which is contended for in the case of infants) was of no avail. A new dispensation, and new ordinances required new men (Matthew 3:7-11; Luke 3: 7-10,17). Christ baptized only those who became disciples (John 4:1). Peter baptized only those who gladly received the word (Acts 2:41), after having declared to them the necessity of repentance as a thing previous to baptism (Acts 2:38). Philip baptized the Samaritans on a profession of their faith in the gospel he had preached (Acts 8:12,16). Yea Simon the sorcerer was baptized when he professed the faith. When the Ethiopian eunuch said, "See, here is water; what doth hinder me to be baptized?" Philip's answer was, "If thou believest with all thine heart thou mayest." Then, upon the profession of his faith, Philip baptized him. It is perfectly plain from these examples, that a profession of unfeigned faith in the gospel of Christ, and a corresponding conduct, only entitles to baptism. Moreover, it was when Peter saw the effects of the Holy Ghost on the family and friends of Cornelius, that he commanded them to be baptized (Acts 10:47-48). It was when the Lord opened the heart of Lydia to receive the gospel preached by Paul, that she was baptized (Acts 16:14-15). Yes, say some, but her household were baptized, and they are not said to have believed. Are they said *not* to have believed? Why should we restrict the grace of God in Lydia's more than in other houses? The household of the nobleman (John 4:53); Cornelius (Acts 10:2); the jailer of Philippi (Acts 16:34); Crispus (Acts 18:8); Aristobulus (Romans 16:10); Narcissus (Romans 16:11); Onesiphorus (2 Timothy 4:19); Stephanas (1 Corinthians 1:16; 16:15); were evidently believers: and why not the family of Lydia?—If we have the proof of the faith of eight families, and a ninth not mentioned, and that the family of a widow, of which there is no proof that ever she had children—can we conclude that her household were infants and that they were baptized, contrary to the command of Christ and to every other example of Scripture? Her household were *brethren* (Acts 16:40). The jailer and his house were baptized when they believed the gospel (Acts 16:29-35). Here Paul declares the jailer and his house should be saved if they believed in Christ. He preached the gospel to all the household—the jailer and his house believed, and rejoiced in God: This was the man and the household that Paul baptized. Nothing but the most obstinate blindness of mind, and the most stern prejudice, can lead any man to deny the faith of the jailer's household. All the prelates in England, joined by all the learned paedobaptists on earth, never can find infants in Lydia's or in the jailer's families, nor make their case an exemption from the general rule of baptizing believers only. Here then we have the strongest possible proof—proof arising from the plain commandment of Christ, & from the uniform practise of John the Baptist, of Christ, of his apostles, and the evangelist, without one case of a doubtful nature presenting itself to our view, that believers of the gospel *only* should be baptized. True, a profession of the faith only is required, but it is such a profession as includes the *knowledge of the truth*, or *gospel* and a corresponding conduct *from the commencement of that profession.* Faith without works is dead.[2]

A practise the reverse of this has been prevalent. Infant baptism was introduced, and by it believer baptism has been almost totally laid aside. Infant baptism began first about the third century. It arose from a wrong view of baptism itself and of the way of salvation. It was first contended that baptism was necessary to salvation — then that infants had as much need of salvation as others — and that, therefore, infants should be baptized. This is the origin of infant baptism. Now men plead for it on various grounds, widely differing from one another. Some call it regeneration, in direct opposition to the whole Word of God. With such it is not worth the pains to contend, if it be not for the good of others, as their views shew their complete ignorance of the gospel of Christ, and of all its effects. Some however, who give reason to hope that they have tasted that the Lord is gracious, hold this practice as an ordinance of Christ. They plead,

1st. The household of Lydia, and of the jailer, and say, that it is probable there were infants in them. Probability is no proof. Positive precept, or example must be brought forward to prove this subject, as it runs contrary to Christ's commandment, and to the example of the apostles. Inference however plausible, will never lay aside a command of Christ, nor establish a practice which he has not instituted — all such practices are will-worship.

2nd. Some say circumcision was the initiating ordinance under the old dispensation, and that infants were admitted to it; that baptism came in its place, and therefore infants ought to be baptized. Very plausible reasoning if true. Here however, two particular things must be proved. *First,* that baptism came in place of circumcision. To prove this it is contended that circumcision was a seal of the gospel covenant, for which Romans 4:11 is quoted. This text proves no such thing. Circumcision was a seal of the righteousness

---

2 James 2:20.

(justness) of Abraham's faith. A testimony to Abraham that what he believed was the true gospel (Romans 4:11), and a token that Jehovah was to be his God, and the God of his seed (Genesis 17:7,11). Instead of its being a seal of the gospel covenant it was a covenant (institution) of itself (Acts 7:3), instituted to certify Abram's faith and God's relation to him as the God of his seed; and a sign that the land of Canaan should be given him (Genesis 17). Again—baptism, say they, is said to be the circumcision of Christ (Colossians 2:11). It is not baptism, but the circumcision of the heart (Deuteronomy 10:16; 30:6; Jeremiah 4:4) that is here meant, by which the sins of the flesh are crucified. Therefore there is no proof that baptism has come in place of circumcision.

But though it were allowed, which I am not inclined to deny, that baptism, as well as circumcision, is an initiating ordinance—it remains to be proved, *secondly*, that the Old Testament and New Testament churches are the same. The reverse of this is plain. The people, and the ordinances thereof are quite different. The Jewish church was made up of the seed of Abraham according to the flesh, *holy* or *unholy*; but the New Testament church is made up of converted sinners—members of the body of Christ (Galatians 3:26-29). In Matthew 3:9-10, we are told that fleshly connection even with Abraham, the father of the faithful, is of no avail—that the axe is laid to the root of the trees—and that every tree, or professor, that has no fruit is rejected. In John 1:12-13, that parentage does not give a title to be members of the church of Christ, or sons of God. But that all such must be born again through faith. In 2 Corinthians 5:16-17, we are told that the apostles acknowledged no man after the flesh, i.e. for his fleshly relation; but that all those whom they acknowledge are new creatures. Yea they acknowledged Christ no longer as the son of Abraham, but as the son of God, and Lord of all. And lastly Paul tells us (Hebrews 8:9 &c) that the old church, with all its ordinances, is done away, and a church established, whose members *all know the Lord*, from the least of them to the greatest. It is plain from the above passages, and many others that might be quoted, that the New Testament church is made up of *believers only*, and that to them only belong the ordinances of Christ. All baptized persons have a right to membership, and to the Lord's Supper, indeed to all church privileges. There may be unworthy members in a church of Christ; such was the case in the apostolic churches; but the wholesome discipline of Christ, will bring them to repentance, or put them away (Matthew 18:18-20).

3rd. Next we are told that the children of godly parents are holy (witness the families of Abraham and David), as the apostles state (1 Corinthians 7:14). This holiness is neither of heart nor of life—and we know of no other. It is no more than legitimacy the apostle has in view. Holiness signifies *being devoted to God*—when any prove themselves so, they have a right to baptism. No man may forbid water.

4th. The long practice of infant baptism is brought forward. It is very true, the practice began, as I noticed before, upwards of fifteen-hundred years ago; but it did not begin with the apostles of Christ. It began with the *corruption* of the gospel, and has been its constant attendant. Men have long lived in sin—will this prove sin a duty? I know of no greater sin than supplanting an ordinance of Christ by an ordinance of man's making. Men have long despised Christ's ordinances—will this prove a warrant for rejecting these ordinances? More than two thirds of the human race reject the Scriptures—is this a reason for our neglecting them? If we call ourselves Christians, let us drop the systems of men, and let us hold fast the doctrine and practice of the apostles of Christ. To them Christ committed the keys of the kingdom of heaven (Matthew 16:9; 13:13; John 20:22-23), and all that are of God hear them (1 John 4:6). One sentence from an apostle of Christ is of more weight than all the councils of popes and prelates, and priests that ever were held in the world—yes, and a plain man, taught by the Spirit of God, understands the Word of God better than them all. The wisdom of this world can never find out the will of God. The teaching of the Spirit *only* leads a sinner into the knowledge of the truth of God (1 Corinthians 2:9-16).

The other reasonings, in favour of infant baptism, are not worthy of notice. They are carnal reasonings of the human heart. The above are the chief grounds I ever knew held by believers. Early education, and the reasonings of interested men, have made an impression on some of the minds of the people of God by the above things; but I hope the day is now in its dawn, when all God's children shall see his authority and ordinances alike. What a pity that the people of God should stand at a distance from the ordinances of Christ, and from one another, while the Scriptures are so urgent for their obeying Christ, and loving one another (Romans 16:26; 2 Corinthians 10:5; 1 Peter 1:2; Romans 6:17; Romans 2:8; 2 Thessalonains 1:8; 1 Peter 4:17; 1 John 4:7,16; John 13:35; Romans 12:9; Galatians 5:6; 1 John 3:10; 3:14; 5:1). It is perfectly evident these passages pointedly condemn the practice of many professors. Many professors can scarcely shew common civility to a Baptist, though their own consciences tell them these are godly people—and many Baptists act the same to other professors. Let these read the above portions of the Word of God.

II. *This ordinance is figurative*

1st. It represents Christ's burial, which includes his death, and the believer's death and burial to sin through faith in him. Our text says, the Colossians were buried with him by baptism, and that in the same rite, they were raised with him through the faith of the operation of God. Paul says to the Romans, not only that they were buried with him by baptism, but that they were also raised with him to newness of life—moreover, that their old man was crucified with him, so as the body (or power) of sin was destroyed —that they might not henceforth serve sin (Romans 6:4-7). The people of God are *naturally* dead in trespasses and sin, like other men (Ephesians 2:1-3). They are alienated from the life of God through the ignorance that is in them as others (Ephesians 1:18). They are enemies to God as other (Colossians 1:21; Romans

8:7), carnally minded, and the servants of sin as others, &c. &c. (Romans 8:5-6; 6:16-17). But when they believe the gospel they are quickened thereby—yea, they are moulded into its doctrines. Their ignorance is dispelled, the power of sin is broke in their souls—and they become new creatures (see Romans throughout). This change is represented in a figure in baptism. The shedding of blood under the law, in circumcision, and in other rites, pointed out the shedding of the blood of Christ as an event that was to take place in Judea, and the ordinances of the New Testament point out the sufferings of Christ as past—the change and union of believers through faith in him—yea that purity of soul which is the common lot of Christians—and the glorious life that awaits them beyond death and the grave. As Christ died *for sin* so the believer dies *to sin* through faith in his name.

2nd. Baptism represents Christ's resurrection, and the believer's resurrection from the power and slavery of sin, to newness of life. What a striking figure to see a believer immersed in water, as a token of the burial of Christ—and arising out of the water, as a token of Christ's rising from the grave! As Jesus rose from the grave, so all his people leave their former lusts and passions and cleave unto the Lord with purpose of heart—have their fruit unto holiness, and the end everlasting life. While we are without the knowledge of Christ it is the motions of sin that regulate our conduct: but when we believe the gospel, we are led by the Spirit of God (Romans 7; 8:1). Some people suppose the difference made upon a man through the knowledge of the gospel is very small, particularly upon those who formerly lived a decent, if not a religious life. This is a great mistake. The difference to a bystander may appear little indeed, but it is great in itself, and great in the all-seeing eye of Jehovah. The unbeliever's conduct, however fair in the eyes of men, is in itself, and in God's sight *all wrong*: "Whatsoever is not of faith is sin" (Romans 14:23) and "Without faith it is impossible to please God" (Hebrews 11:6). All the motives and springs of action of an unbeliever are wrong. All his good actions, even his religious services, spring from base motives. Self-love governs his mind. But when he believes the gospel, his works become works of faith and labours of love. It is then he serves God. Formerly he served himself, sin, and Satan, but the anxious inquiry of his mind is now: "Lord, what wouldest thou have me to do?" All this change upon the beleiver's mind and conduct we have represented to us in baptism.

3rd. Nearly allied to the foregoing remarks, I observe—that it is a figure of the purification from sin. In 1 Peter 3:21, Peter says that baptism is a figure, not of the washing of the body in water so as to purify the flesh, but of the answer of a good conscience. We have this explained (2 Corinthians 1:12). The believer is purified *in heart* by faith (Acts 15:9) and the same faith purifies his conduct—so that he is manifested to have been made a partaker of the divine nature, by his having escaped the pollution that is in the world through lust (2 Peter 1:4). Thus, feeling the power of the truth, purifying his heart and life, he has the answer of a good conscience. Ananias commands Paul to arise and be baptized, washing away his sins (Acts 22:16). The water in baptism can never wash away sin, but baptism represents the purifying of the soul by the blood of Christ—and the believer in baptism professes to be thus washed in the blood of atonement. Baptism is then a figure of the purification of the soul and conduct of the believer, through faith in the blood of Christ.

4th. Baptism is a figure of the believer's being filled with the Holy Ghost. John tells his disciples, whom he baptized, that he baptized only with water, but that Christ would baptize them with the Holy Ghost (Matthew 3:11). Some contend for sprinkling, pouring, &c. from this figure—but surely a full immersion in water is a fitter representation of the whole soul's being filled with the Holy Spirit. The outward sign then is a fit representation of the inward blessing. The sign is all one, whether of a thing soon to be possessed, or of a thing possessed already. All the people of God are partakers of the Holy Spirit (Romans 8:9), and it is he that operates in enlightening their minds, and in subduing their nature through the truth.

5th. Baptism is a figure of the believer's resurrection to eternal life (Romans 6:5). Those that now profess their faith in him in baptism shall be at last planted in the likeness of his resurrection. They now rise to newness of life, but they shall then rise from the dead and enter upon everlasting glory. This hope is produced in their souls by faith in his resurrection (1 Peter 1:3). What a glorious hope! How worthy of our taking up the cross, and of obeying all Christ's commandments! Many in their zeal for the subjects and mode of baptism have, in their discussions of this subject, quite overlooked its figurative representations — but these should be our *chief* study. The ordinance becomes peculiarly sweet when we look at it in this point of view. We obey it as a command, but its figures fill our minds with comfort. Every subject fills the child of God with pleasure in which he beholds Christ.

III. Baptism is a profession of our faith in Christ

The common account of baptism is, that it is a sacrament, which signifies an oath whereby we bind ourselves to give over evil and to do good. We learn nothing of this from the Scriptures. What we learn from them is that it is an act of obedience to Christ, whereby we profess our faith in him. Paul says in 1 Corinthians 10:2 that the Israelites were baptized unto Moses in the cloud, and in the sea — meaning that they were initiated into the faith of the doctrine of Moses, by being immersed in the sea and cloud. This was a most decided profession of belief in what Moses spoke to them. Who would venture into the heart of the sea, while the water stood in heaps on each side of them, under a shadow of a thick and dark cloud, on any other principle than pure faith in the promised protection of God given by Moses? So the believer is baptized into Christ (Romans 6:8) — into the faith of his death and resurrection. What else but faith, unfeigned faith in the death of Christ as the only atonement could make a man forsake all — all his self-righteousness, all his good works, prayers, tears, and religious feelings and exercises, &c — and take up his cross and follow Jesus Christ? What but real faith in the promise of Christ, of everlasting life, would, or could, make a man become the butt of the enmity, malice, revenge, and persecutions of his relations, friends, and neighbours, and deny himself to every fleshly, and every worldly gratification? What but faith in, and love to the Lord Jesus Christ, as the only Saviour of the guilty, could make a man devote *himself* and his *all* to the service of God—and make him willing to suffer even unto death, not only for Christ himself, but also for his laws, and his ordinances, and his people? How true is it that faith purifieth the heart (Acts 15:9), overcometh the world (1 John 5:4), worketh by love (Galatians 5:6) and leads us to endure every trial and every affliction in this world (Hebrews 11). Baptism is a fair and open profession of this faith. It is the first ordinance of the gospel, an entrance upon a new life of constant dependence upon Jesus Christ, and of unfeigned submission to his will, and devotedness to his service (Hebrews 11:1-12:6).

IV. Baptism is a binding duty on believers

Whatever God commands, his people are bound to obey, if he has placed them in circumstances in which they can obey. There may be circumstances in which it is impossible to obey, such as deep distress. In such cases God will have mercy and not sacrifice. This is quite a different thing from abstaining from baptism for fear of persecution, want of convenience, &c. It has been asked how men can be immersed where there is no water, and that there are some places where water cannot be found. This is trifling with the will of God. Can it be seriously thought that any person would live in a place where there could not be so much water found as would cover his body? Would a man not travel one or two hundred miles for gain or at the command of his sovereign—and is it too hard if it be absolutely necessary, to travel that distance to obey Christ? Where is the man in Canada that could not reach a lake or river? "He who knoweth his master's will and doeth it not, shall be beaten with many stripes."[3] Many will tell us they cannot see this subject—take heed lest you get stripes for shutting your eyes on a plain precept. When Christ instituted the preaching of the gospel, he instituted the baptizing of all who should believe it. There is no exception made. If any would tell Peter or Paul that they believed the gospel, but could not submit to baptism, they would reject them—for it was thus the first Christians professed the faith. How would it sound with the apostles to tell them that one professed their faith in infancy, through fathers, or godfathers. What! profess faith before you had it? Profess faith by proxy? This would look to the apostles, *as rank will-worship.*

See the pointed command of Ananias to Paul: "Arise, and be baptized, why tarriest thou?" Why do ye linger in obeying God? Was it not your prayer on the way, "Lord, what wouldest thou have me to do?" Christ would have you, Saul of Tarsus—you, lately the violent persecutor—Christ would have you to profess your faith in him by baptism—arise, and obey his will. Manifest your faith in him. No argument can excuse the neglect of this pointed command. Peter in his address to those who were pricked in their hearts on the day of Pentecost, told them to *repent* and be *baptized*. It was no less their duty to be *baptized* than to *repent*. The one was necessary to believing the gospel (a change of mind), the other to their professing it. The same Lord commandeth both—and all who profess to know the gospel, must manifest their knowledge by obedience. How many cry like Saul, "Lord what wilt thou have me to do?" and yet lend a deaf ear to Peter's command. Astonishing, that a baptism, instituted by men in opposition to the baptism of Christ, as to mode and subjects—attended to in many cases by ungodly ministers, ungodly parents, and in *all ungodly children*—should be called the baptism of Christ, and should blind men's eyes on a plain commandment of the Lord Jesus!

Some will be apt to say that we make everything of baptism:

---

3 Luke 12:47, paraphrased.

No! We make it what it is: a pointed commandment of Jesus Christ, which must be attended to, or we risk his displeasure; but we place every one of his commandments on the same level. All must be attended to in their proper places. Those who believe must be baptized. They must join themselves to the people of God, love the brethren, obey all Christ's commandments and attend to all his ordinances. This is a true manifestation of Christianity. It is the character of God's people that they tremble at his Word; that they know Christ's voice, and follow him; that they hear and obey the apostles.

V. There is only one baptism

Some people, in order to throw dust in the eyes of their hearers, to keep them from seeing the truth upon this important subject, tell us there were many baptisms under the law — and that the mode, if not the subjects of the New Testament baptism, is of trifling moment. If the ordinance is attended to, it matters little in their view, whether it is in childhood or in old age; whether by sprinkling or by immersion — any resemblance of baptism is enough. There we have three or four distinct ordinances attended to, all under the name of Christian baptism. Yea some will acknowledge the primitive mode — and subjects — but tell us that times have altered, climates differ, &c. and that this warrants a different conduct in this respect. It is good if they do not apply the same reasoning to the faith of the gospel. Indeed some do so to regeneration, and to the influence of the Holy Spirit. It is as just to apply this reasoning to the faith as to baptism. The application overthrows Christ's authority as much in the one case as in the other. Such would do well to weigh the words of Samuel to Saul: "To obey is better than sacrifice and to hearken than the fat of rams. Rebellion is as the sin of witchcraft, and stubborness as iniquity and idolatry. Because thou hast rejected the word of the Lord, he hath also rejected thee from being king" (1 Samuel 15:22-23).

Paul says, in Ephesians 4:5, that there is *one Lord, one faith, one baptism*. There is one God and Father, our Creator, who has a right to command us as he pleases—*one Lord Jesus Christ*, the only Mediator between God and man, through whom the chief of sinners are offered a free and full salvation—and *one baptism*, by attending to which we shew our faith in the Lord Jesus Christ, and our obedience to his will. The verses that close the New Testament ought to have their full force upon our minds: "For I testify unto every man that heareth the words of the prophecy of this book, if any man shall add unto these things, God shall add *unto him* the plagues that are written in this book: and if any man shall take away from the words of the book of this prophecy, God shall take away his part out of the book of life, and out of the holy city, and *from* the things which are written in this book." (Revelation 22:18-19). What solemn language!

It is the character of antichrist to change laws and times (Daniel 7:25), and the people of God had better retire from Babylon, lest they partake of her plagues (Revelation 18:4). Christ ordained one baptism and the man who changes, rejects, or despises this ordinance is accountable to him. What Christian does not tremble at the idea of supporting antichrist? Yet all who support infant baptism are, however unwittingly, guilty of this crime.

VI. *It is a profession of our having taken Christ's yoke upon us*

Though baptism is neither a sacrament nor an oath, it is evidently a full profession of our having put on Christ's yoke, and enlisted under his banner; and we are bound by this profession to devote ourselves to his service. Paul says, "As many as have been baptized into Christ, have put on Christ" (Galatians 3:27). Put on his profession—engage in his service. Here we profess ourselves to be the purchase of Christ's blood and therefore profess our entire obligation to serve him with our bodies and spirits which are his. The obligations under which we are laid are great and many: "I beseech you therefore, brethren, by the mercies of God, that ye present your bodies a living sacrifice, holy, acceptable unto God, which is your reasonable service. And be not conformed to this world, but be ye transformed by the renewing of your mind, that ye may prove what is that good, and acceptable, and perfect will of God" (Romans 12:1-2; see also Colossians 3; Philippians 2:1-17).

Conclusion

1st. From what has been said you will see, that though baptism neither saves the soul, nor cleanses it from its pollution, yet it is of great importance as an ordinance of Christ, and also as *a figure* of that which purifies the soul from all its filthiness—and fits it for the heavenly kingdom. It is an outward figure of an inward grace, already possessed by the believer. It is a profession of faith in that blood which justifies the ungodly, and purifies the conscience from dead works to serve the living God. The outward ceremony brings the sinner no nearer to God than he was before—it neither purifies the heart nor the conscience—but is an act of obedience to Christ, in which the baptized professes to be a child of God, and servant of Christ.

2nd. From what we have said above it is plain, that it is the duty and the privilege of every child of God to be baptized. The duty arises from the commandment of Christ—and what a privilege, for a poor guilty sinner, formerly the enemy of God, to confess Jesus Christ as his Saviour, his Prophet, his Priest, his King, his elder Brother, his fellow Heir, and his everlasting portion! This he does in baptism.

3rd. Some will think we are keen to *make people Baptists*. This we deny. If this were the case we should not live five years among you, yea, seven years in Canada, without preaching on the subject. We never shrunk from giving our view on this or on any other subject when it came in our way—but we never till now selected the subject. We are not keen to make Baptists. We would not, on any consideration, baptize one in whom we had not the fullest confidence as a Christian. We are keen to get people converted to

God, and then we would urge such to be baptized, and to observe all things that Christ hath commanded. This is our faith in the Word of God, and thus have we acted for seventeen years. We are not among those that court controversy, but we shrink not from the fullest investigation of our faith and practice. We are very confident of having the right side of the question, and we know the more it is examined, controverted, and opposed, it will become the plainer. We wish every man and woman to be fully persuaded in their own minds.[4] Blind obedience is not acceptable to God. It is the duty of every hearer and reader, to "prove all things, and hold fast that which is good,"[5] to "try the spirits whether they are of God."[6] May the Lord open the eyes of sinners to see the gospel — and the eyes of believers to see his whole will as revealed in the Scriptures. If the above have either of these effects our labour will not be in vain; and, if otherwise, we are confident we have done a duty which we owed to God, and to his professed people.

---

4 Romans 14:5
5 1 Thessalonians 5:21.
6 1 John 4:1

Appendix E

Hymns written by Alexander Stewart

The following hymns were published alongside Stewart's essays on the gospel and baptism (see Appendix D).[1] Stewart's theological convictions and his own experience of the grace of God, both seem to have influenced his hymns. (See chapter 12.)

Increase of the church [2]

Shout, for the great redeemer reigns,
   Through distant lands his trumpets spread,
And sinners, freed from Satan's chains,
   Own him their Saviour and their head.

---

1 Alexander Stewart, *Two essays: the first, on the gospel; the second, on the kingdom of Christ; and a sermon on baptism* (York: Colonial Advocate, Wm. Lyon Mackenzie, Printer, 1827), 75-76.
2 Suggested tune: Truro L.M.

God's sons and daughters from afar,
    Daily at Zion's gates arrive;
Those who were dead in sin before,
    By sovereign grace are made alive.

The love of truth unites their souls,
    Hence they are one in Christ their head,
His face by faith they all behold,
    His holy paths they cheerful tread.

In Christ their King they all rejoice,
    His laws are written in their hearts;
They know their shepherd by his voice,
    And from his fold they ne'er depart.

O may his conquests still increase,
    And may his pow'r his foes subdue,
While angels celebrate his praise,
    And saints his growing glories show.

Loud Hallelujahs to the Lamb,
    From all below and all above,
In lofty songs exalt his name,
    In songs as lasting as his love.[3]

---

3 "Increase of the church" is actually an adaptation of Benjamin Beddome's (1717-1795) hymn "Increase of Christ's Kingdom." Beddome was an English Particular Baptist minister who served in Bourton-on-the-Water, Gloucestershire. Compare stanzas 1, 2, 5 and 6 [*Hymns Adapted for Public Worship or Family Devotion*, (London: Burton & Briggs and Button & Son, 1818)]:

Shout, for the blessed Jesus reigns,
    Through distant lands his triumphs spread;
And sinners freed from endless pains,
    Own him their Saviour and their head.

His sons and daughters from afar,

Spiritual temple completing [4]

Sing to the Lord above,
  Who deigns on earth to raise
A temple to his love,
  A monument of praise;
Ye saints around, through all its frame,
The builder's name harmonious sound.

Beneath his eye and care,
  This edifice shall rise,
Majestic strong and fair,
  And shine above the skies:
There shall he place the polish'd stone,
Ordain'd to crown this work of grace.

Daily at Zion's gates arrive;
  Those who were dead in sin before,
  By sovereign grace are made alive.

Oppressors bow beneath his feet,
  O'ercome by his victorious power;
Princes in humble posture wait,
  And scorners tremble and adore.

Gentiles and Jews shall him obey,
  Nations remote their offerings bring,
And unconstrained their homage pay
  To their exalted Lord and King.

Oh may his conquests still encrease,
  And every foe his arm subdue;
While angels celebrate his praise,
  And saints his growing glories shew.

Loud hallelujahs to the Lamb,
  From all below and all above;
In lofty songs exalt his name,
  In songs as lasting as his love.

4 Suggested tune: Darwal 6.6.6.6.8.8.

The Lamb triumphant over all his foes[5]

O 'tis a sound should fill the world!
   The sound of mercy through the lamb,
Lo, Satan from his seat is hurl'd,
   Unable to withstand Christ's name,
From heaven like light'ning see him fall,
   Struck by the arm that conquers all.

Lord give the word!—and wak'd by thee,
   Let many tongues thy vict'ry tell!
That helpless sinners now may see,
   That thou hast vanquish'd death and hell:
Sound, sound the joyful truth abroad,
   And draw poor sinners near to God.

---

5 Suggested tune: Melita 8.8.8.8.8.8.

Appendix F

Roll of members, York Baptist church, 1827-1840

This is a partial roll of members of the Baptist church at York (later March Street Baptist Church) reorganized in 1826. Dates of admission are approximate. Dates and reasons for dismissal are given if known.[1]

	Date of admission	Date of dismissal
Allum, Joshua	1831	1832 (discipline)
Beaty, James	1827	1836 (split)
Beaty, Sarah Ann	1827	1829 (death)
Brownlie, James	1830	
Caldicott, Thomas Ford★	1831	1835 (transfer)

---

1 Sources include: "John Eglinton Maxwell Diary." (Baldwin Room, Toronto Reference Library); "Minutes of the Baptist church at York, Upper Canada, 1829-1833." (Jarvis Street Baptist Church Archives, Toronto); Joseph Ash, "History of the rise and progress of our cause in Canada." *Christian Worker,* No. 21, Reminiscences, November 1882 to February 1884; Robert Alexander Fyfe, *A forty years survey from the Bond Street pulpit* (Toronto: Dudley & Burns, 1876); E.O. White, "The first Baptist church in Toronto." *The Canadian Baptist,* August 16, 1906.

Carter, Mrs. E	1828	1836 (split)
Cathcart, Robert [2]	1828	
Cathcart, Ann	1828	1836 (death)
Chadwick, Mr.	1827	
Clements, Thomas	1831	
Fels, Agnes	1831	
Fels, John N.	1831	
Ferguson, Catherine	1832	
Ferguson, Dugald	1832	
Gorham, Nelson	1831	
Hewitt, Elizabeth	1829	
Hewitt, William	1829	
Langley, Esther	1834(?)	
Langley, William	1830	
Lesslie, James	1832	
Maxwell, John Eglinton	1834	1836 (split)
McCord, Andrew Taylor	1829	
McMaster, William [3]	1833	
Mitchell, James (William) ★	1827	1830 (transfer)
Mitchell, Mrs. James	1827	1830 (transfer)
Moore, Mrs.	1831	1832 (discipline)
Mosley, Henry	1827	
Orr, James	1829	
Orr, Nancy	1832(?)	
Parson, Timothy	1828	
Parson, Agnes	1832(?)	
Paterson, Peter Sr. ★	1827	

---

2   Both Robert Cathcart and William McMaster were adherents. Cathcart was baptized late in 1840 according to John Carter: "Mr. Cathcart had long been identified with the Baptist cause in Toronto... The wonder was, why he had not long before this been baptized?" ("Reminiscences of the Baptists of Toronto." *The Canadian Baptist*, April 22, 1885.)

3   William McMaster came into membership "on experience" in May 1848 ("Bond Street Baptist Church Minute Book, 1845-1855." (Jarvis Street Baptist Church Archives, Toronto).

Paterson, David	1827	
Paterson, Sarah	1827	
Reid, Hugh	1835	
Reid, Mrs. Hugh	1835	
Robertson, Grace	1830	
Rutherford, Peter	1828	1836 (split)
Sinclair, Catherine	1832	
Stewart, Alexander Sr.★	1827	1840 (death)
Stewart, Alexander Jr.	1827	
Stewart, Janet	1827	
Stewart, John	1832	
Thomson, Alexander	1829	
Tost, Henry	1831	1836 (split)
Tost, Jane	1831	1836 (split)
Wales, Mrs.	1828	1830 (transfer)
Wales, Sarah	1828	1830 (transfer)
Wenham, Joseph ★	1827	1832 (transfer)
Wolverton, Jonathan	1832	
Yorston, Robert	1829	

★ held office in the church

Appendix G

The York Auxiliary Bible Society

Letter of appeal, 1830[1]

The Committee of the York Auxiliary Bible Society, in thus addressing you, in the first place consider it necessary to state that, in the month of February last, a Society was formed in this Town, for the purpose of distributing the Bible without "note or comment":—that since its commencement the sum of £120 has been collected and sent to England for the purpose of obtaining a supply of the sacred Scriptures; and that in the mean time, a small quantity has been obtained from the Bible Society in Montreal—so that our plan is fairly in operation.

The object of our present address is to excite and solicit you to adopt the same plan, and pursue the same end—desiring that you may realise the same or even greater success.

We deem it unnecessary, on the present occasion, to urge upon

---

1 This letter of appeal is taken from *Report of The York Auxiliary Bible Society* (York: Christian Guardian, 1830), 14-15.

your attention the many arguments which might be brought forward, proving the claim of the Scriptures to a Divine authority, and a Spiritual inspiration, anticipating your cordial and entire concurrence in these truths; and would therefore direct your attention to those obligations to duty which arise out of this belief.

It is a truth which will, on very little reflection, commend itself to your minds, that, we can scarcely be considered sincere in our profession of a benefit received or enjoyed, if we hesitate to recommend it to others; and it certainly is the first evidence of a generous mind, that it refuses to confine any good to itself, always deriving its greatest happiness, either in sharing it with, or communicating it to others.

Such is emphatically the case with regard to the effect which a right reception of the word of God will invariably produce in the mind of a sincere Christian; for it is a certain consequence, as also one evidence of our having received the truth in sincerity, that we desire to make others acquainted with its blessings and benefits; nay more than this, for christianity expanding the heart, will cause it to be the fervent object of our desire, and the sincere matter of our prayer, that the whole family of mankind might read, understand, and be converted:—a Christian cannot be content to enjoy the blessings of the Gospel alone.

The object before you is so free from all possible imputation, that we cannot hesitate to recommend it in the strongest manner; and as all Christians professedly derive their Religion from the Bible, we are not aware that any reason can be consistently given, why its distribution should not engage all the virtuous, and all the good, in every class of society.

We invite you, therefore, to assist in the circulation of this Sacred Book; because it is the only one which contains a revelation of God's mind and will to man—the only record of that wonderful exhibition of Divine Love which was displayed in our redemption —and the only guide through the duties and difficulties of this life, to that rest which is prepared, and remains to be enjoyed by the people of God forever. As it is our wish that the Scriptures should be placed in the hands of all who are able to read and understand them, our attention has already been directed to the state of the various Indian Tribes throughout the Province, and extending themselves far into the interior of the country.

You are aware, that a considerable number of these within the last five years, profess to have embraced the Christian Religion, and although their conversion has, in most cases, been extremely rapid, and in some, instantaneous; yet very few of them who have thus been brought to feel and acknowledge the power of Christianity, have gone back from their first profession.

Here is a field for your labours, which will engage and exhaust all the means your liberality or exertion can produce; while at the same time we doubt not that you will find many calls upon your christian munificence in your own immediate neighbourhood, which will justly claim your first attention.

Our object, you will perceive, is two-fold:—first, to make our friends and neighbours acquainted with the word of God;—and then, as means will afford, to translate and distribute it amongst the Indians.

In calling you to this duty, we do not invite you to an undertaking of doubtful result. We are only instruments in the hands of that God who has said, he will bless his own word, so that, while the performance is ours, the faithfulness of his promise is pledged for our success. Therefore, we go boldly forward, knowing there is a rich recompense of reward awaiting such a course of conduct; while we believe, that God will graciously accept this our work of Faith and labour of Love, as a service done to him.

Let us, therefore, experience your hearty and sincere co-operation, and thus prove that, the word of God is not only the study of our closets, but also the standard and rule of our conduct:—So Shall our light shine before men, to the glory of that God, whose we are, and whom we profess to serve.

Appendix H

Marriage register

Date	Place	Names[1]
Mar 10, 1830	Pickering	Abraham Knowels & Nancy Barclay
May 3, 1830	York	William Bishop & Hannah Ward
May 6, 1830	York	Albert Brewster & Lucy Parsons
Jun 24, 1830	York	Thomas Fenwick & Jane White
Jul 10, 1830	York	Charles M.H. Baty & Mary Hellewell
Jan 11, 1831	Trafalgar	Ralph Thomson & Mary Anne Leach
Jan 30, 1831	Newmarket	John Gibbs & Hannah Haight
Feb 4?, 1831	York	George Morrison & Jane Duncan
Mar 20, 1831	Whitchurch	George Barclay & Jane Willson
Jun 13, 1831	York	James Morison & Jannet Gordon
Jun 15, 1831	York	Niel Dean & Hannah Smith

1 The following list of marriages has been compiled from Alexander Stewart, "Marriage register, 1830-1840." (Louis Melzack Collection, Thomas Fisher Rare Book Library, University of Toronto, Toronto).

Jun 17, 1831	York	Hugh McWilliams & Jane Ross
Jul 1, 1831	York	William Douglass & Jannet Butler
Jul 8, 1831	York	James Graham & Mary Stewart
Aug 11, 1831	York	Andrew McLean & Jane Wright
Oct 17, 1831	York	Archibald Jackson & Catharine McCorquadale
Dec 8, 1831	York	John Baker & Bridget Langren
Aug 8, 1832	York	Duncan McAlister & Catharine Graham
Aug 17, 1832	York	Archibald McIntyre & Mary Murray
Sep 4, 1832	York	Alexander Armstrong & Mary Cullen
Nov 15, 1832	York	Benjamin Bache & Mary Scantlebury
Nov 30, 1832	York	William Millard & Latitia Brooks
Dec 28, 1832	York	William Symes & Catharine McIntyre
Jan 21, 1833	York	Charles De Meriss & Amanda Emerson
Feb 14, 1833	York	James Killy & Johanne Martin
Feb 16, 1833	York	Isaac Rattenbury & Mary Anne Humphrey
Mar 15, 1833	York	Duncan McCall & Mary McCallum
Mar 22, 1833	York	James Bell & Jane McGill
Apr 13, 1833	York	John Gordon & Mary McIntosh
Oct 25, 1833	York	John Douglass & Eliza Kerr
Jan 3, 1834	Vaughan	Adam Kline & Christian Shaver
Feb 8, 1834	York	John Elliot & Mary Campbell
Mar 10, 1834	Toronto	James McIntosh & Elizabeth Butler
Mar 19, 1834	Toronto	William Ross & Elizabeth Mosley
Apr 9, 1834	Toronto	Isaac Vanderburgh & Eliza Dillon
Apr 19, 1834	Toronto	John Nield & Sarah Gilbraith

May 21, 1834	Toronto	William Campbell & Jane Murray
Jun 5, 1834	Toronto	Thomas McNicol & Elizabeth Campbell
Jul 7, 1834	Toronto	Jacob Wiart & Susannah Lake
Aug 28, 1834	Toronto	John Grant & Jannet Currie
Aug 29, 1834	Toronto	Michael Robinson & Elisabeth Curry
Oct 3, 1834	Toronto	Alexander McGregor & Catharine Morrison
Oct 11, 1834	Toronto	Robert Riddell & Elisabeth McConachy
Oct 16, 1834	Toronto	Peter Gaudy & Martha Ann Clinklord
Nov 5, 1834	Toronto	Charles Pumprey & Elisabeth Butler
Dec 4, 1834	Toronto	John McGill & Mary McCallam
Dec 19, 1834	Toronto	Hugh Hunter & Anne Reis
Dec 20, 1834	Toronto	John Blyth & Alea Smith
Dec 28, 1834	Toronto	John C Turpel & Mary Minis
Jan 8, 1835	Toronto	Alexander Gray & Marrian McLean
Jan 19, 1835	Toronto	Mark Hurd & Jean Shutter
Jan 27, 1835	Toronto	James Menzies & Ann Ferguson
Feb 3, 1835	Toronto	John McGilvray & Catharine Sinclair
Feb 5, 1835	Toronto	James Smith Amos & Sarah Blair
Feb 5, 1835	Toronto	Archibald Reid & Jannet McEachenie
Feb 7, 1835	Toronto	Edward Pottage & Elizabeth Beal
Feb 28, 1835	Toronto	Niel Ferguson & Catharine McDonald
Mar 21, 1835	Toronto	John Burnside & Catharine Cochrane
Mar 23, 1835	Toronto	Malcom McNeil & Flora McKinnon

Mar 23, 1835	Toronto	John McNiven & Mary Stewart
Apr 10, 1835	Toronto	James Kerr & Jannet Wilson
Apr 20, 1835	Toronto	John Currie & Christiana Reid
Apr 23, 1835	Toronto	James Low & Elisabeth Lawson
May 5, 1835	Toronto	Neil McDougal & Barbara Campbell
May 21, 1835	Toronto	John Sutherland & Isabella Fraser
Jun 5, 1835	Toronto	John Houston & Mariah Balantine
Jun 22, 1835	Toronto	James Barker & Jane Fields
Sep 12, 1835	Toronto	John Marr & Elisabeth Shuttleworth
Nov 27, 1835	Toronto	James Porter & Flora McKay
Dec 25, 1835	Esquesing	James Mitchell & Grace Robertson
Mar 18, 1836	Toronto	Donald Morrison & Mary Gilchrist
Mar 22, 1836	Toronto	John Eastwood & Jannet Graham
May 24, 1836	Toronto	George Graham & Jane Turo
Jul 12, 1836	Toronto	Thomas Whitham & Harriet Wilson
Jul 26, 1836	Toronto	Jacob Stover & Barbara Wideman
Aug 2, 1836	Toronto	James Russel & Charlotte Lee
Aug 24, 1836	Summerdale?	Duncan Gilchrist & Ann Shaw
Aug 25, 1836	Toronto	Thomas Harper & Catharine McBirnie
Sep 11, 1836	Toronto	John Ross & Emer Elson
Nov 4, 1836	Toronto	Reuben Jackson & Margret McCourt
Dec 2, 1836	Toronto	Samuel Lee & Jane Taylor
Dec 7, 1836	Chinguacousy	John Campbell & Margret Sinclair
Feb 7, 1837	Toronto	Joseph Collard & Jane Lee
Feb 9, 1837	Pickering	Benjamin Holmes & Phebe Shaw
Mar 11, 1837	Toronto	Peter Baxter & Ann McKichnie[2]

---

2 Note: William Lyon Mackenzie witnessed marriage.

Mar 18, 1837	Toronto	Thomas Francis (a man of colour) & Margret Jackson
Jul 4, 1837	Vaughan	William Nixon & Jane Chadwick
Jul 5, 1837	Toronto	John Calvert & Sarah Sanders
Aug 28, 1838	Caledon	Patrick Garity & Margaret McCabe
Dec 12, 1838	Markham	Randall Spencer Bentley & Hellen Scott
Dec 21, 1838	Scarborough	John Batty & Jane Scott
Dec 27, 1838	Toronto	Charles Johnson & Elizabeth Cain
Jan 1, 1839	Uxbridge	Joseph Gould & Mary James
Jan 10, 1839	Pickering	Squire Vanhorn & Elisabeth Beatty
Jul 23, 1839	Markham	Neil Patterson & Ann McLean
Nov 29, 1839	Toronto	George Simpson & Martha Elson
Nov 30, 1839	Thorold	Michael McDearmid & Margret McNab
n.d., 1839?	Thorold?	Robert Lieth & Moriagh Langren
Jan 13, 1840	Toronto	William Lang & Mary Stone
Feb 3, 1840	Toronto?	Edward Wyatt & Ann Fraser
Apr 4, 1840	Toronto	George Redrelle & Catharine Busby

Biographical glossary

Aikman, John (1770-1834)

John Aikman was born in 1770 in St. Cuthberts, Midlothian, Scotland. He was a friend and colleague of James Alexander Haldane and accompanied him as a "minister of the gospel" on his northern tour of Scotland in 1797. He served at Robert Haldane's Theological Seminary in Edinburgh from 1802 to 1803 and was Alexander Stewart's theology tutor.

Ballantine, William (d.1836)

William Ballantine studied at David Bogue's (1750-1825) Academy in Gosport, Hampshire, England and was ordained as an evangelist in that place on April 7, 1798. He was an itinerant preacher for the Society for Propagating the Gospel at Home from 1798 to 1799. On September 4, 1799 he accepted a call to the pastorate of the Thurso Congregational Church. He married Jean White on September 28, 1799, in Elgin. He later removed to Elgin, and accepted a call to the Free Presbyterian Congregation in Moss Street on May 26, 1801. He was dismissed from this charge in 1803, but continued to preach in Elgin, and presided over the Elgin Congregational Church beginning on January 4, 1804. In 1806, he invited Alexander Stewart to assume the pastoral charge in Elgin and maintained an intimate friendship with him until his death. He became a Baptist in 1806, and joined with the Scots Baptists at Redcross Street, London. He later emigrated to America and fellowshipped with the Baptists in Bank Street, Philadelphia. William Ballantine died in January 1836.

Barclay, George (1780-1857)

George Barclay was born in July 1780 in Cupar, Fifeshire, Scotland. He emigrated to Canada in 1816, and was a minister of the gospel at Cramahe, Upper Canada. He was the officiating minister at Alexander Stewart's ordination in 1828. He died at Claremont, Ontario in 1857.

Beaty, James (1798-1892)

James Beaty was born on October 2, 1798, in Killashandra, County Cavan, Ireland. He emigrated to Canada in 1818 and likely joined with the Baptists in York under the leadership of Alexander Stewart and John Menzies. He was baptized by immersion in Toronto Bay. He married Sarah Ann Armstrong on December 26, 1822. In 1836, he left the Baptists of March Street over a dispute on Calvinism and became prominent in founding the first Disciples of Christ congregation in the city. Beaty was a politician and founded a newspaper called the *Christian Leader*. He died on March 5, 1892, in Parkdale, Ontario and is buried in the Necropolis Cemetery, Toronto.

Birnie, John

John Birnie married Janet Carfrae, the daughter of Thomas Carfrae on September 27, 1813 at Saint Cuthberts, Edinburgh, Scotland. He was among the nine constituent members that formed the first Baptist church in York on October 25, 1818.

Black, James (1797-1886)

James Black was born in the parish of Kilmartin, Argyllshire, Scotland, on August 15, 1797. He emigrated to Canada in June 1820 and first settled in Aldborough, Elgin County, and lived there until 1825. He was an itinerant preacher in Nassagweya, Beamsville and Eramosa until 1830 and eventually settled in Eramosa. James Black and Alexander Stewart were prominent in founding the Scotch Baptist Church in Eramosa. He also assisted Stewart in the work of the York Auxiliary Bible Society and is listed as an agent of the Society in the townships north of Toronto in 1836. He became a member of the Disciples of Christ by 1840, after several years of reading Alexander Campbell's periodicals. He died April 21, 1886.

Bosworth, Newton (1776-1848)

Newton Bosworth served as pastor of the Baptist church in Montreal.

He moved to Toronto in 1839 and led the scattered Baptists in weekly prayer meetings. It was this work that led to a rebirth of Alexander Stewart's March Street Baptist Church. Subsequently, members desiring a formal Baptist assembly sent a letter to the Colonial Baptist Missionary in London, England, and engaged the services of Rev. William H. Coombs beginning in July 1840.

Caldicott, Thomas Ford (1803-1869)
Thomas Ford Caldicott was born in Northamptonshire, England. He came to Canada in 1824 as a tutor to the children of some military officers (79th Highlanders) and lived at the garrison in Quebec, Kingston and York. He established himself in York as a stationer, and in 1833 opened the York Commercial and Classical Academy on Colborne Street. He was active in the reorganized Baptist congregation in York and served as a deacon. He became celebrated as the "soldier preacher." He had a splendid, deep-toned musical voice, and he deliberately and distinctly pronounced every word he uttered. His services as a preacher were so much in demand, not only in March Street church, but also, in the country, that he was strongly urged by many friends to give himself wholly to the work of the ministry. Acquiescing, he relinquished his business and his academy and was ordained as a regular Baptist minister in Cheltenham, in the township of Chinguacousy in 1835. Long afterwards he returned to Toronto in 1860 as the minister of Bond Street Baptist Church.

Candie, William (b.1764?)
William Candie was likely christened October 29, 1764, at Kirriemuir, Angus, Scotland, the son of John Candie. He was a licentiate preacher in the Baptist church, Perth, Scotland, during the years of Alexander Stewart's eldership from 1812 to 1815.

Carfrae, Thomas (1766-1834)
Thomas Carfrae emigrated from Edinburgh, Scotland, to York,

Upper Canada and opened a general store on King Street in 1805. He and his wife Janet Muir Carfrae (1760-1832) were among the nine constituent members that formed the first Baptist church in York on October 25, 1818. His home was used for the first services of the Baptist church at York.

Cathcart, Robert (1799-1863)

Robert Cathcart was born in Ireland and opened a general dry goods store on King Street, York, Upper Canada, around 1828. He likely fellowshipped with Alexander Stewart and the Baptists of York the same year. Robert Cathcart was a model merchant, equity and fair dealing characterized his establishment. In the old March Street Baptist Church meeting house, Robert Cathcart occupied the large square pew to the east of the pulpit. Robert Cathcart was constant in attendance and Robert Alexander Fyfe testified that he found him a comfort and support in the struggles and difficulties he had to encounter.

Dewar, Alexander (1785-1849)

Alexander Dewar was born at the North Bank of Loch Tay, Scotland on May 13, 1785. He studied at Robert Haldane's Theological Seminary in 1803 or 1804, where he likely came into contact with Alexander Stewart. On completion of his studies in June 1805, Dewar was sent by the Society for Propagating the Gospel at Home to Inverness. He preached in Inverness and environs from July to October. By the end of October he arrived and settled at Avoch. Here he planted a church and received assistance from Alexander Stewart starting in the spring of 1807. He was the pastor of the Avoch Congregational Church until his death on August 30, 1849.

Fyfe (or Fife), Thomas (b.1774?)

Thomas Fyfe was likely christened April 5, 1774, at Glamis, Angus, Scotland, the son of Andrew Fyfe. He was a prominent member of the first Baptist church at York, Upper Canada, founded by Alexander Stewart and John Menzies. While in York, he resided with Stewart and his family. He moved to Esquesing Township around 1820, and was likely a member of the church at Norval, planted by Stewart and Menzies. Later, he assisted Stewart in the work of the York Auxiliary Bible Society as an agent for Esquesing Township. He was also the first Collector for the Township of Esquesing in 1821 and 1822.

Haldane, James Alexander (1768-1851)

James Alexander Haldane was born on July 14, 1768, in Dundee, Scotland. He served in the East India Merchant Service from 1785 to 1795. Through quiet meditation on the Word, James Haldane was converted. He subsequently surrendered his command and returned to Scotland. Thereafter, he devoted himself entirely to the ministry of the gospel. He was a major figure in the home missionary movement; a founder of the Society for Propagating the Gospel at Home; a preacher in the independent Congregational Church in Edinburgh starting in 1799; he made several important missionary tours of Scotland, mainly the north and the east; he became a Baptist in 1808; he maintained his missionary interest through his church in Edinburgh and the Baptist Home Missionary Society. He was Alexander Stewart's friend and mentor.

Haldane, Robert (1764-1842)

Robert Haldane was born on February 28, 1764, in London, England. After serving with the navy, Robert retired to the life of a country gentleman on his estate at Airthrey, near Stirling. As he observed William Carey's zeal to reach the lost of India, he studied Christian evidences and his soul was awakened from its spiritual slumber. After selling a major part of his lands in 1798, he was prevented by the British East India Company from proceeding with a mission to Bengal. Instead he gave himself up to the spread of the gospel in Scotland and Europe. He was the financer of "Tabernacle" churches in Scotland—meeting places which the poor could attend freely in order to hear a succession of evangelical preachers. He also financed and founded a seminary in Edinburgh to which Alexander Stewart owed his theological training. His remarkable visit to Geneva in 1816 led to a widespread awakening and ultimately to the publication of his *Exposition of the Epistle to the Romans*.

Harris, James (1793-1873)
The Rev. James Harris came to York, Upper Canada, in 1820 as a licentiate of the Presbytery of Monaghan, of the Secessionist Presbyterian Church in Ireland. He organized a Presbyterian congregation in York, retiring in 1844 when his congregation combined with those who "came out" from St. Andrew's Church of Scotland in the Great Disruption, to form Knox Presbyterian Church. He served with Alexander Stewart as one of the first secretaries of the York Auxiliary Bible Society, formed in 1828.

Hewitt, William (1794-1883)
William Hewitt was born at Hazelan, Essex, England, on July 21, 1794. He emigrated to Canada and settled first at Montreal in 1820, then relocated to Toronto in 1824. He was one of the earliest members of the reorganized Baptist church in York under the presidency of Alexander Stewart. Some years later Mr. Hewitt removed to the Credit, and afterwards settled in Charlotteville, Norfolk County, where he remained until his death on August 1, 1883.

Hutchison, William (1781-1850)
William Hutchison served as pastor of the independent Congregational church in Kingussie, Scotland, commencing in 1805. In 1806, he was assisted in the work by Alexander Stewart. The church was led to a Baptist position under Hutchison's leadership in 1808. He not only led the Baptist church of Kingussie until his death in 1850, but he was also used of God on missionary tours to the northern Highlands and the Hebrides.

Laidlaw, James (b.1763)

James Laidlaw was born at Ettrick, Selkirk, Scotland, and was a cousin of the famed Scottish poet James Hogg (1770-1835). He was a Scottish shepherd who became obsessed with North America and emigrated when he was almost fifty years old, although some of his sons refused to accompany him. He arrived in York on April 25, 1819, and attended the Baptist church in York under the leadership of Alexander Stewart and John Menzies. He removed to Esquesing in 1820 and was likely one of the members at the church at Norval, also under Stewart and Menzies.

Langley, William (b.1810)

William Langley was born in County Tipperary, Ireland, in 1810. He emigrated to York, Upper Canada, and joined with the Baptists in 1830. His sons Henry and Edward were architects in the firm Langley, Langley and Burke and designed the Jarvis Street Baptist Church building in 1875. This was the same congregation which resided in March Street (1832-1848) and Bond Street (1848-1875).

Lesslie, James (1802-1885)

James Lesslie was born in Dundee, Angus, Scotland, the son of Edward Lesslie (1764-1828). He and his family came to Canada around 1820. He established a drug and stationery shop in York in 1832. In the same year, he joined with the Baptists of March Street, led by Alexander Stewart, and became one of the first trustees of the church property. James was an alderman in Toronto in 1834, and later president of the People's Bank. In 1844 he bought the newspaper *Examiner* from Francis Hincks.

Lothian, John

John Lothian married Christian Mackenzie on July 15, 1799, in Perth, Scotland. He was a prominent member of the Baptist church in Perth, Perthshire, Scotland, under the leadership of Alexander Stewart, John McFarlane and John Stalker.

McCord, Andrew Taylor (1808-1881)

Andrew Taylor McCord was born in Cookstown in the north of Ireland, on July 12, 1808. He came to Canada with his father Andrew McCord (d.1851). He held the office of City Treasurer for forty-five years, having been appointed in 1834. He was president of the Irish Protestant Benevolent Society; he was one of the vice-presidents of the Tract and Bible Society for thirty-three years; he was connected with the Home of Incurables, House of Industry, Newsboys Home, as a director or otherwise; he was a Justice of the Peace; and in politics he was a stout Reformer. He was one of the earliest members of the reorganized Baptist church at York, joining their cause in 1829.

McFarlane, John

John McFarlane was one of the first ministers of the Baptist church in Perth, Scotland. He shared the eldership with Alexander Stewart and John Stalker from 1812 to 1815.

McIntosh, Catherine Oswald Stewart (1803-1832)

Catherine Oswald Stewart, the daughter of Alexander and Janet Stewart, was baptized on February 6, 1803, by James Alexander Haldane, minister of the Dissenting Congregation in Edinburgh. She was named for Robert Haldane's wife, Catharine Oswald. She married John McIntosh in 1824 and had five children, two of whom died in infancy. She died on February 10, 1832, and was buried in the Potter's Field, York (later moved to the Necropolis Cemetery, Toronto).

McIntosh, John (1796-1853)

John McIntosh was the eldest son of John McIntosh (1754-1830), a blacksmith who came to Canada from Scotland in 1801, and to York in 1803. The younger John was educated at the Home District School and served in the War of 1812 and was present at the capitulation of Detroit. He was also in the militia at the time York was taken by the Americans. After the war, he and his brothers owned a schooner called the *Brothers*. He was a Baldwin Reformer, and was chairman of the Reform Committee at the time when William Lyon Mackenzie went to England to lay the grievances of the people before the British Government. For eight years he represented the North Riding of York in the Parliament of Upper Canada (1834-1841). He was twice married. In 1824 he married Catherine Oswald Stewart (1803-1832), daughter of Alexander and Janet Stewart. By her, McIntosh had five children: Catherine, John, Ann Jane, James, and another, who died in infancy. In 1833 he married a widow, Ellen or Helen Ferguson (nee Baxter), by whom he had seven children: Isabel, Robert, Ellen, Eliza, James, Charles and Margaret. John McIntosh was a Protestant. He died in Toronto on July 3, 1853, aged fifty-seven.

Mackenzie, William Lyon (1795-1861)

William Lyon Mackenzie was born near Dundee, Scotland, and came to Canada in 1820. He established a book and drugstore in York, moving to Dundas at the end of 1821. Mackenzie then kept a shop himself in Dundas and in the autumn of 1823 moved to Queenston, opening another shop. In May 1824, he began the *Colonial Advocate*, moving with it to York in November. In June 1826, his types were thrown into the bay by a group of young Tories. Alexander Stewart warned Mackenzie and suggested that he even leave York. However, Mackenzie persisted, and he received £625 damages. In 1828 he was elected to the Assembly from York County, and again in 1830. In 1831 he was expelled from the House for libel against it; he was re-elected four times by York County in 1832-1833. He became the first mayor of Toronto in 1834 and was elected to the Assembly from York County later in the same year and allowed to take his seat. In December 1837, he led an unsuccessful armed rebellion and withdrew to the United States. In 1849 he was allowed to return to Canada.

McMaster, William (1811-1887)

William McMaster came to York in 1833 from County Tyrone, Ireland, and likely joined Alexander Stewart and the Baptists of March Street the same year. He was a faithful member and was loyal to Stewart during the difficulties the church experienced in 1836. In business, he entered Robert Cathcart's employment, becoming a partner in 1834. Cathcart retired about ten years later, but McMaster built up the business he had begun into a large wholesale firm. His masterful attitude and dominating character, carried him into wealth and fame. He was the driving force in founding the Canadian Bank of Commerce in 1867. He served in the Canadian Senate for twenty years until his death. His generosity led to the building of Jarvis Street Baptist Church in 1875 and the founding of McMaster University in 1887. As merchant, banker, senator and philanthropist, the name of William McMaster became a household word in his city, his country and his church.

McNaughton, Peter

Peter McNaughton married Betty MacPhearson on January 11, 1796, in Perth, Scotland. He was a prominent member of the Baptist church in Perth under the leadership of Alexander Stewart, John McFarlane and John Stalker.

McRobbie, John (b. 1762?)

In 1807, John McRobbie and John Stalker were ordained as elders of the Perth Congregational Church, Perthshire, Scotland. William Orme was added to the eldership in February 1808. Later that year, McRobbie and Stalker adopted Baptist sentiments, separated themselves from William Orme and formed the Baptist church in Perth. Alexander Stewart joined the Baptists of Perth in 1810, and thereafter McRobbie's influence in the church's leadership affairs diminished.

Maitland, Peregrine (1777-1854)

Sir Peregrine Maitland was born at Longparish Hall, Hampshire, England. He entered the British Army in 1792 and served through the Napoleonic Wars, commanding the 1st Brigade of the 1st Division at Waterloo. In 1815 he married Lady Sarah Lennox, the daughter of the Duke of Richmond, and in 1818 he was appointed Lieutenant Governor of Upper Canada. Alexander Stewart referred to him as a "friend of the gospel." He was transferred to the lieutenant-governorship of Nova Scotia in 1828. In 1832 he became Commander-in-Chief at Madras and in 1843 Governor of the Cape of Good Hope.

Maxwell, John Eglinton (b.1803)

John Eglinton Maxwell, the son of Eglinton and Elliot Maxwell, was a Baptist minister and teacher, who emigrated from Edinburgh to Toronto in the summer of 1834. He taught at Thomas Caldicott's Classical Academy until February 1835, when he opened a school of his own, first at 231 King Street, and later in Market Lane. He was the secretary of the Upper Canada Religious Tract and Book Society from 1834 to about 1837. Also in 1834, Maxwell joined the March Street Baptist Church, led by Alexander Stewart, and preached often at their services. He was at the centre of the schism that took place there in 1836 and consequently formed a second Baptist church in the city. He led this church until 1838 whereupon he accepted a call to the Baptist church in Clyde, New York. In 1852, after serving in the churches at Hartland, Pittsford and Bristol, New York, he settled on a farm near Nobleton, Ontario. He returned to Niagara County, New York, a few years later. While in Toronto, Maxwell married Johanna Carfrae Paterson (1795-1846), the daughter of Thomas Carfrae (1766-1834). On September 21, 1848, two years after the death of his wife Johanna, he married Diantha Brown of Jeddo, New York.

Menzies, John (1779-1859)

John Menzies was born in November 1779 at Kenmore, Perthshire, Scotland. He emigrated with his wife Isabella from Aberfeldy in 1817. In the fall of 1818, he met Alexander Stewart in Montreal and travelled with him to York where they co-founded the first Baptist work. In 1820, he and Stewart moved to Esquesing Township and planted the Baptist work at Norval. Though he later became a member of the Church of Christ Disciples, he never gave up some of his Baptist tendencies, as this description in 1843 attests:

> ...the old man (Menzies), though known as a disciple or reformer, held to some of his old Baptist usages in the examination of candidates for baptism. At a certain examination conducted by the old man, father modestly challenged the right and propriety to ask such questions and pleaded for the plain acknowledgement of Jesus Christ as the Son of God. The old man sat like an old judge, listening thoughtfully, at the same time was almost unconsciously cutting tobacco, and filling his pipe; when this was completed, and a coal placed upon it, he went out, saying, go on and have it your way. That was the last of any critical examination of baptismal candidates."[1]

He died on December 2, 1859, and is buried in Hillcrest Cemetery, Norval, Esquesing Township.

Mitchell, James (1783-1849)

James (or William) Mitchell was christened on February 2, 1783, in Montrose, Angus, Scotland, the son of David Mitchell and Jean Myer. He emigrated to Canada in 1827 and was a prominent member in the reorganized Baptist church at York under President Alexander Stewart. Along with Joseph Wenham, James Mitchell

---

1 W.H. Trout, *Trout family history* (Milwaukee: Meyer-Rotier Printing Co., 1916), 61-62.

was appointed to serve as deacon of the church in 1829. He also exercised his preaching gift in the church. On May 23, 1830, he organized a Baptist church at York Mills and moved his family into the country. He was ordained in December 1830. Under his direction, a church building was dedicated in 1833. Rev. James Mitchell served as pastor of York Mills Baptist Church until his death in 1849.

Mosley, Henry M.

Henry M. Mosley was the son of Thomas Mosley (1767-1827), a native of Kent, England. The Mosley family was in York as early as 1800. Like his father, Henry was an auctioneer and carried on the family business on King Street. Henry Mosley was a member of the reorganized Baptist church of York under Alexander Stewart. Mosley was so committed to the work that he purchased a building lot for the congregation and paid the first installment.

Orme, William (1787-1830)

William Orme was born in Falkirk, Scotland, on February 3, 1787. He was a member of James Haldane's Tabernacle Church, Leith Walk, Edinburgh, and attended Robert Haldane's Theological Seminary from October 1805 to 1807. In February 1808, John Stalker and John McRobbie presided over his ordination at the Perth Congregational Church. Later in the same year, Stalker and McRobbie adopted Baptist sentiments. Orme did not follow suit and thus, the three men parted ways, and Orme was left the sole elder of the Perth Congregational Church. In 1824, he was called to Mansion House Chapel, Camberwell, near London and served this fellowship until his death on May 8, 1830.

Orr, James

James Orr was a gardener in York, Upper Canada, and was one of the earliest members of the reorganized Baptist church under Alexander Stewart.

Parson, Timothy (b. 1808?)

Timothy Parson was among the first members of the reorganized Baptist church at York under the leadership of Alexander Stewart. In 1831, he was asked by the church to exercise his gift as a public preacher. Timothy Parson also operated a Straw-Bonnet & Drapery Warehouse. His residence was at 215 King Street.

Paterson, Peter (1780-1844)

Peter Paterson was born at Blantyre, Scotland, in 1780. In 1819, he emigrated to Upper Canada and made his home in York, where in 1821 he began a hardware store in the Market Square. In 1833 he moved to King Street and took his sons David (d.1856), John and Peter (1808-1883) into partnership. He became a magistrate in 1833. Peter Paterson likely identified himself with Alexander Stewart and the Baptists of York as early as 1819. He was the first deacon of the reorganized church and materially assisted in the erection of the first Baptist church edifice in York, in 1832 on March Street. The pew he occupied was the second from the front on the west side of the church, a large square pew jointly occupied by the Hewitts. He died on March 30, 1844, and was buried in the Potter's Field, Toronto.

Pullar, Robert (b. 1782)

Robert Pullar was born on January 3, 1782, in Perth, Scotland, the son of John Pullar and Isolbel Ower. He married Elizabeth Black on October 6, 1801, in Perth. He was a licentiate preacher in the Baptist church in Perth during the years of Alexander Stewart's eldership from 1812 to 1815.

Roaf, John (1801-1862)

John Roaf went from his native Kent to London, England, to learn printing. He was converted, however, by an evangelical preacher and in 1819 began studying for the ministry. From 1823 to 1837 he was a minister in Wolverhampton, coming in the latter year to

Upper Canada to manage the finances of the Congregationalist Missionary Society. In 1838 he became minister of a small Congregationalist body in Toronto. This grew into the mother church for other Upper Canada congregations. Roaf was very active in organizations opposed to state-church connections and in the temperance movement. He retired in 1856. Subsequent to the March Street Baptist Church schism of 1836, many of the dispersed Baptists would attend his congregation — including Alexander Stewart. In 1840, John Roaf served as the officiating minister at the funeral service for Alexander Stewart.

Stalker, John (b.1775)

John Stalker was born on April 3, 1775, in Perth, Scotland, the son of Laurence Stalker and Helen Niven. He married Ann McLaren on June 8, 1804, in Perth. In 1807, John Stalker and John McRobbie were ordained as elders of the Perth Congregational Church, Perthshire, Scotland. William Orme was added to the eldership in February 1808. Later that year, Stalker and McRobbie adopted Baptist sentiments, separated themselves from William Orme and formed the Baptist church in Perth. Alexander Stewart joined the Baptists of Perth in 1810, and shared the eldership responsibilities with John Stalker and John McFarlane.

Stephens, Thomas (1771-1833)

Thomas Stephens was born in Belfast, Ireland, in 1771. He attended Robert Haldane's Theological Seminary in Edinburgh after which he was a preacher in Scotland and then in Ireland. He and his wife Eleanor Newburn immigrated to New York in 1811 on the *Jupiter*. He became a member of the Haldane Church under Elders William Ovington and Henry Errett. He gave the exhortation at the opening services of the Baptist church at York in 1818. Along with Alexander Stewart, John Menzies and several others he moved to the Township of Esquesing and was likely the other preacher who disagreed with Stewart in Norval, which split the church in 1821.

He died on February 8, 1833, and is buried in Hillcrest Cemetery, Norval, Esquesing Township.

Stewart, Alexander (1764-1821)

Alexander Stewart commenced his ministerial labours in Moulin, Perthshire, Scotland in 1786. Through the influence of Charles Simeon and James Haldane, he was converted by God's grace in June 1796. Following that, his preaching was used of God to bring about a revival in the village. Alexander Stewart and Janet Douglass were converted during this awakening in the spring of 1799. In 1805, Mr. Stewart moved to Dingwall and then in 1809 he moved to Edinburgh, to be near the best medical help for a serious malady under which he suffered. About that time King's College, Aberdeen, honoured itself by conferring on him the degree of Doctor of Divinity. He was only in Edinburgh for a few months when the first charge of the parish of Canongate fell vacant through the death of its occupant. The Crown presented Dr. Stewart to the charge and he filled it till his death on May 27, 1821.

Stewart, Alexander, Jr. (1811-1885)

Alexander Stewart Jr. was born on July 30, 1811, in Perth, Scotland, the second son of Alexander and Janet Stewart. He died on March 26, 1885 at Toronto, York County, Ontario, and is buried in the Necropolis Cemetery. The circumstances of his life are not known.

Stewart, James (1807-1822)

James Stewart was born at Avoch, Scotland, in 1807, the first son of Alexander and Janet Stewart. Alexander Dewar, Minister of the Dissenting Congregation in Avoch, baptized him on May 7, 1807. He died in 1822 in Esquesing Township, Upper Canada. His remains were reburied in the Potter's Field in 1832.

Stewart, Janet Douglass (1770-1848)

Janet Douglass was baptized in the parish of Logierait, Perthshire,

Scotland, on June 10, 1770, the daughter of James Douglass. She was converted under the instrumentality of Rev. Alexander Stewart, the parish minister of Moulin, during a revival in the spring of 1799. On November 16, 1800, she married Alexander Stewart (the subject of this book) in Logierait. She was Alexander's constant and faithful companion throughout their many trials. Robert Alexander Fyfe referred to her as a "mother in Israel." Janet Stewart died in July 1848, in Toronto.

Strachan, John (1778-1867)

John Strachan was born in Aberdeen, Scotland, and educated at the universities of Aberdeen and St. Andrews. He came to Upper Canada in 1799 and taught at Kingston. In 1803 he was ordained priest in the Church of England and was appointed to Cornwall. While there he also ran a school, which many boys from York attended. In 1812 he moved to York as minister of St. James' and master of the Home District Grammar School, giving up the latter post in 1823 when he was appointed General Superintendent of Education in Upper Canada. In 1827 he became Archdeacon of York and first president of King's College, and in 1839 first Bishop of Toronto. He was a member of the Executive Council (1817-1836) and the Legislative Council (1820-1841). During the Maitland regime, Alexander Stewart discovered that Strachan was one of the most powerful men in Upper Canada.

Tapscott, Samuel (1804-1888)

Samuel Tapscott was born on December 27, 1804, in the parish of Culmstock, Devonshire, England. Recognizing the call of God to share the gospel with the lost in Canada, he emigrated and reached Quebec City on June 17, 1836. He became an agent for the *Canadian Baptist Magazine & Missionary Register* and was engaged by the trustees of the March Street church to fill the pulpit in 1837—he likely ministered to Alexander Stewart and his family during that year. Subsequent to this, he engaged in farming operations and held pastoral charges in Haldimand, Cramahe, Whitby, Pickering, Markham, Fenelon Falls, Teeswater, Stouffville and Whitevale. He moved to Brampton in 1883 and resided there until his death on October 4, 1888.

Thomson, Alexander
Alexander Thomson was a mason in York, Upper Canada, and was one of the earliest members of the reorganized Baptist church under Alexander Stewart.

Tost, Henry
Henry Tost (or Toast) was a blacksmith who came into the membership of the March Street Baptist Church with his wife in 1831. He broke fellowship with Alexander Stewart and left with John Eglinton Maxwell in 1836. Together, they formed a new church and he served as its first deacon. Henry Tost's wife, Jane died in 1840 at the age of sixty-six and is buried in the Potter's Field, Toronto.

Wemyss, Thomas
Thomas Wemyss served at Robert Haldane's Theological Seminary in Edinburgh from 1802 to 1804. He was Alexander Stewart's tutor in classical studies.

Wenham, Joseph (b.1795?)
Joseph Wenham, an Englishman, was bookkeeper in the Bank of Upper Canada from 1822. He was prominent in the founding of the Baptist congregation in York and was elected a deacon in 1829. In 1832 he left York to become cashier of the Bank in Brockville.

Yorston, Robert (1802-1892)
Robert Yorston was born on October 27, 1802, in Corse Fluflets, Rousay, Orkney, Scotland, the son of Alexander Yorston and Janet Marwick. He emigrated to Upper Canada and was a labourer in York. He was also one of the first members of the reorganized Baptist

church under Elder Alexander Stewart. He died on January 19, 1892, and is buried in the Necropolis Cemetery, Toronto.

Bibliography

Manuscript records

Canadian Baptist Archives, McMaster University, Hamilton, Ontario
  John Menzies Papers.
Congregational Union of Scotland Archives, Glasgow
  General account of Congregationalism in Scotland from 1798 to 1848 and particular accounts referring to separate counties.
Dundas Historical Society Museum, Dundas, Ontario
  James Lesslie Diaries.
Jarvis Street Baptist Church Archives, Toronto, Ontario
  Finances in Sterling of Bond Street Baptist Church, 1840-1846.
  Minutes of the Baptist church at York, Upper Canada, 1829-1833.
Public Archives of Ontario, Toronto, Ontario
  Court of Probate Estate Files.
  Crown Land Records.
  Deeds of Esquesing Township, Halton County, Vol. A-B, 1847-1855.

Minute Book, Township of Esquesing, Halton County 1821-1891.
Upper Canada Land Petitions
William Lyon Mackenzie Correspondence.
Toronto Reference Library, Baldwin Room, Toronto, Ontario
Alexander Stewart Papers.
John Eglinton Maxwell Diaries.
John Eglinton Maxwell Letterbooks.
York Auxiliary Bible Society Papers.
University of Toronto, E.J. Pratt Library, Toronto, Ontario
Historical collection on the Disciples of Christ.
University of Toronto, Thomas Fisher Rare Book Library, Toronto, Ontario
Alexander Stewart "Journal & Register" in the Louis Melzack Collection (Includes: "Sermon notes, 1810"; "Notes on the Baptist church at Perth, Scotland, 1812-1815"; "Register of sermons preached chiefly at York, Upper Canada, 1827-1833"; "Marriage register, 1830-1840"; "Returns of subscribers for *Essays on the gospel and the kingdom of Christ*.")
University of Western Ontario, Lawson Memorial Library, London, Ontario
Rev. William Proudfoot Diaries.

Newspaper & periodical records
Aberdeen Chronicle, 1818-1820.
Canadian Baptist Magazine & Missionary Register, 1837-1840.
The Christian Guardian, Toronto, 1832, 1840.
The Colonial Advocate, York, Upper Canada, 1824-1834.
The Examiner, Toronto, 1840, 1848.

Published records
History of Toronto and County of York, Vol. II. Toronto: C. Blackett Robinson, 1885.
Jarvis Street Baptist Church: directory and historical sketch. Toronto: Dudley & Burns, 1897
Rebels arrested in Upper Canada 1837-1838. Toronto: Ontario Gene-

alogical Society, 1987.
The City of Toronto and the Home District commercial directory and register with almanack and calendar for 1837. Toronto: Thomas Dalton, Printer.
The eighth report of The City of Toronto Auxiliary Bible Society; for 1836. Toronto: Guardian Office, 1837.
The eleventh report of The City of Toronto Auxillary Bible Society; for the year ending April 30, 1840. Toronto: Upper Canada Bible Society, 1840.
The fifth report of The City of Toronto Auxillary Bible Society; for 1833. Toronto: W. J. Coates, 1834.
The first report of The York Auxillary Bible Society. York: Christian Guardian, 1830.
The first report of The Upper Canada Bible Society and twelfth of the Society's operations; for the year ending April 30, 1841. Toronto: Upper Canada Bible Society, 1841.
The fourth report of The York Auxillary Bible Society for the Year 1832. York: Colonial Advocate, 1833.
The ninth report of The City of Toronto Auxillary Bible Society; for 1837. Toronto: Guardian Office, 1838.
The second report of The York Auxillary Bible Society. York: Christian Guardian, 1831.
The seventh report of The City of Toronto Auxiliary Bible Society; for 1835. Toronto: Guardian Office, 1836.
The sixth report of The City of Toronto Auxillary Bible Society; for 1834. Toronto: W J Coates , 1835.
The tenth report of The City of Toronto Auxillary Bible Society; for the year ending April 30, 1839. Toronto: Guardian Office, 1839.
The third report of The York Auxiliary Bible Society: 1832. York: Christian Guardian, 1832.
York commercial directory, street guide and register 1833-4, with almanack and calendar for 1834. York, UC: Thomas Dalton, Printer.
Ash, Joseph. "History of the rise and progress of our cause in Canada." *Christian Worker*. Meaford: 21 "Reminiscences" starting

November 1882 to February 1884.

Ballantine, William. *treatise on the elder's office shewing the qualifications of elders, and how the first churches obtained them; also their appointment, duties & maintenance; the necessity of a presbytery in every church; and exhortation, and the observance of every church ordinance on the Lord's Day, in order, amongst other ends, to the obtaining of elders.* Edinburgh: J Ritchie, 1807. (Reprint. Dundee: E. Lesslie, 1807.)

Butchart, Reuben. *Old Everton and the pioneer movement amongst the Disciples of Christ in Eramosa Township, Upper Canada, from 1830.* Toronto: Church of Christ Disciples, 1941.

Butchart, Reuben. *The Disciples of Christ in Canada since 1830.* Toronto: Churches of Christ Disciples, 1949.

Carter, John. "Reminiscences of the Baptists of Toronto." *The Canadian Baptist,* April 22, 29; May 6, 13, 1885.

Coupland, R., ed. *The Durham Report.* Oxford: Oxford University Press, 1946.

Cox, Claude, ed. *The Campbell-Stone Movement in Ontario.* Queenston: Edwin Mellen Press, 1995.

Edwards, Jonathan. "Thoughts on the revival." *The works of President Edwards.* Vol. 6. London: Hughes & Baynes, 1817.

Firth, Edith, ed. *The town of York, 1793-1815.* Toronto: Champlain Society, 1966.

Firth, Edith, ed. *The town of York, 1815-1834.* Toronto: Champlain Society, 1966.

Fyfe, Robert Alexander. *A forty years survey from the Bond Street pulpit.* Toronto: Dudley & Burns, Printers, 1876.

Gibson, Theo T. *Robert Alexander Fyfe; his contemporaries and his influence.* Burlington: Welch Publishing Co., 1988.

Goodwin, Daniel C. "'The Footprints of Zion's King': Baptists in Canada to 1880." In G.A. Rawlyk, ed. *Aspects of the Canadian evangelical experience,* 1997.

Haldane, Alexander. *The lives of Robert Haldane of Airthrey, and of his brother, James Alexander Haldane.* London: Hamilton, Adams & Co, 1852. (Reprint. Edinburgh: The Banner of Truth Trust, 1990.)

Haldane, James Alexander. *Reasons for a change of sentiment on the subject of baptism*. (Two editions, 1808 & 1809.)

Hancocks, Elizabeth, ed. *Potter's Field Cemetary 1826-1855; otherwise called the Stranger's Burying Ground*. Agincourt: Generation Press, 1983.

Hodgins, J.G., ed. *Documentary History of Education in Upper Canada, 1790-1840*. Vol. 1. Toronto: Warwick Bros. & Rutter, 1894.

Ivison, Stuart & Rosser, Fred, eds. *The Baptists in Upper and Lower Canada before 1820*. Toronto: University of Toronto Press, 1956.

Kinniburgh, Robert, ed. *Fathers of Independency in Scotland; or, Biographical sketches of early Scottish Congregational ministers. A.D. 1798-1851*. Edinburgh: A Fullarton & Co., 1851.

Lovegrove, Deryck W. "James Alexander Haldane." In Donald M. Lewis, ed., *The Blackwell dictionary of evangelical biography 1730-1860*. Oxford, Massachusetts: Blackwell Publishers Ltd., 1995.

Lovegrove, Deryck W. "Unity and separation: contrasting elements in the thought and practice of Robert and James Alexander Haldane." In Keith Robbins, ed. *Protestant Evangelicalism: Britain, Ireland, Germany and America c.1750-c.1950. Essays in honour of W.R. Ward*. Oxford: Basil Blackwell, 1990.

MacInnes, John. *The Evangelical Movement in the Highlands of Scotland*. Aberdeen: University of Aberdeen Press, 1951.

Marshall, William. *Historic scenes in Perthshire*. Edinburgh: Wm. Oliphant & Co., 1879.

McNaughton, William D., ed. *The Scottish Congregational ministry, 1794-1993*. Glasgow: The Congregational Union of Scotland, 1993.

McLean, Marianne. *The people of Glengarry: Highlanders in transition 1745-1820*. Ottawa: McGill/Queen's University Press, 1991.

Meek, Donald E. "Evangelical Missionaries in the Early Nineteenth-Century Highlands" in *Scottish Studies*, Vol. 28, 1987.

Meek, Donald E. "Evangelicalism and emigration: aspects of the role of dissenting evangelicalism in Highland emigration to Canada." In Gordon MacLennan, ed. *Proceedings of the first North*

American Congress of Celtic studies. Ottawa: 1986.

Meek, Donald E. "'The fellowship of kindred minds': some religious aspects of kinship and emigration from the Scottish Highlands in the nineteenth century." In *Hands across the water: emigration from Northern Scotland to North America.* Aberdeen: Aberdeen and North East Scotland Family Historical Society, 1995.

Meek, Donald E. "The Independent and Baptist churches of Highland Perthshire and Strathspey." *Transactions of the Gaelic Society of Inverness,* Vol. LVI, 1991.

Mosser, Christine, ed. *York, Upper Canada: Minutes of town meetings and lists of inhabitants, 1793-1823.* Toronto: Metropolitan Library Board, 1984.

Newman, Albert Henry. "Sketch of the Baptists of Ontario and Quebec to 1851." In *The Baptist Year Book for Ontario and Quebec,* 1900, 73-91.

Pope, J.H. *Illustrated historical atlas of the County of Halton Ontario.* Toronto: Walker & Miles, 1877.

Raible, Chris. *Muddy York mud: scandal & scurrility in Upper Canada.* Creemore: Curiosity House, 1992.

Rawlyk, George A. *The Canada fire: radical evangelicalism in British North America 1775-1812.* Montreal: McGill/Queen's University Press, 1994.

Reid, W. Stanford, ed. *The Scottish tradition in Canada.* Toronto: McClelland and Stewart, 1988.

Robertson, John Ross. *Landmarks of Toronto.* Toronto: Telegram, 1914.

Ruggle, Richard. *Norval on the Credit River.* Erin: Press Porcepic, 1973.

Romney, Paul. "A struggle for authority: Toronto society and politics in 1834." In Victor Russell, ed. *Forging a Consensus: Historical Essays on Toronto.* Toronto: University of Toronto Press, 1984.

Stagg, Ronald, ed. *The Rebellion of 1837 in Upper Canada: a collection of documents.* Toronto: Champlain Society, 1985.

Stewart, Alexander [1764-1821]. *Memoirs of the late Rev. Alexander*

Stewart, D.D. One of the ministers of Canongate, Edinburgh; to which are subjoined, a few of his sermons. Edinburgh: Wm. Oliphant & Co., 1822. Authored anonymously by James Sievewright.

Stewart, Alexander [1764-1821]. *An account of the late revival of religion in a part of the Highlands of Scotland.* Edinburgh: J. Ritchie, Printer, 1800.

Stewart, Alexander [1774-1840]. "Letter from Alexander Stewart, Canada." *New Evangelical Magazine and Theological Review*, Vol. V. London: 1819.

Stewart, Alexander [1774-1840]. "Letter from Alexander Stewart, Canada." *New Evangelical Magazine and Theological Review*, Vol. VI. London: 1820.

Stewart, Alexander [1774-1840]. *Two essays: the first, on the gospel; the second, on the kingdom of Christ; and a sermon on baptism.* York: Colonial Advocate, Wm. Lyon Mackenzie, Printer, 1827.

Stewart, Kenneth J. "Robert Haldane." Donald M. Lewis, ed. *The Blackwell dictionary of evangelical biography 1730-1860.* Oxford, Massachusetts: Blackwell Publishers Ltd., 1995.

Tracy, Frederick. "Samuel Tapscott." *McMaster University Monthly.* Toronto: Dudley & Burns Printers, 1897.

Trout, W.H. *Trout family history.* Milwaukee: Meyer-Rotier Printing Co., 1916.

Wells, J. E. *Life and labors of Robert Alex. Fyfe, D.D., Founder and for many years principal of the Canadian Literary Institute.* Toronto: W.J. Gage & Co., 1885.

Westfall, William. *Two worlds: the Protestant culture of nineteenth century Ontario.* Montreal: McGill University Press, 1989.

White, E.O. "The first Baptist church in Toronto." *The Canadian Baptist.* August 16, 1906.

Whyte, Donald. *A dictionary of Scottish emigrants to Canada before Confederation.* Vol. 1 & 2. Toronto: Ontario Genealogical Society, 1986.

Yuille, George, ed. *History of the Baptists in Scotland, from pre-Reformation times.* Glasgow: Baptist Union Publications, c.1926.

Vital records

Marriage registers of St. James Anglican Church, Toronto, Ontario.
Parish registers of Logierait & Moulin, Perthshire, Scotland.
Parochial registers, County Perth, Parish Perth, Scotland.

Credits

Maps and documents

Maps (26, 58, 82, 133) by Janice Van Eck.
Map of "Upper Canada" (94) by David William Smith, Esq.
Alexander Stewart's "Certificate of ordination" (166). Courtesy of the Baldwin Room, Toronto Reference Library, Toronto, Ontario.
"The first page of minutes of the Baptist church at York, Upper Canada" (168). Courtesy of Jarvis Street Baptist Church Archives, Toronto, Ontario.
"Rev. W.H. Coombs subscription list" (233). Courtesy of Jarvis Street Baptist Church Archives, Toronto, Ontario.

Photographs, sketches and engravings

Portraits of "Charles Simeon" (33), "David Black" (34) and "James Alexander Haldane" (45). From John Kay, *A series of original portraits, with biographical sketches and illustrative anecdotes* (Edinburgh: A & C Black, 1877).

Engraving of "John McIntosh House" (162). From John Ross Robertson, *Landmarks of Toronto* (Toronto: Telegram, 1914).

Sketch of "Market Lane Hall" (165) by Henry Scadding. Courtesy of the Baldwin Room, Toronto Reference Library, Toronto, Ontario.

Photograph of "Thomas Ford Caldicott" (183). Courtesy of Jarvis Street Baptist Church Archives, Toronto, Ontario.

Sketch of "March Street Baptist Church" (187) by Owen Staples. Courtesy of the Baldwin Room, Toronto Reference Library, Toronto, Ontario.

Photograph of "William Lyon Mackenzie" (199) [c.1851–1861]. Library and Archives Canada/C-001993.

Photograph of "Samuel Tapscott" (223). Courtesy of Jarvis Street Baptist Church Archives, Toronto, Ontario.

"Alexander Stewart's grave" (231). Photograph by the author.

Index

Aberdeen, Scotland, 88, 261, 313, 314
Aberfeldy, Scotland, 26, 51, 82, 93, 309
Aikman, John, 52-53, 298
Anderson, Christopher, 81
Appleton, Thomas, 143-144
Armstrong, George, 204, 214
Ash, Joseph, 93, 201-203, 214

Ballantine, William, 48-49, 61-62, 64-66, 90, 92-93, 114-117, 126-129, 181-182, 298
Bangs, Nathan, 109
Barclay, George [d.1838], 81
Barclay, George [1780-1857], 110-111, 164, 291, 298
Battle of York, 102, 109
Beddome, Benjamin, 280
Beaty, James, 16, 201-203, 214, 283, 299
Bentley, Elijah, 178, 229
Bentley, William, 229
Birnie, John, 245, 299
Black, David, 31-32, 34, 38
Black, James, 134, 178, 228, 299
Blantyre, Scotland, 163, 311
Blood, Caleb, 111
Bond Street Baptist Church, 18, 145, 203, 234, 237, 300, 304
Bosworth, Newton, 221-224, 299
British East India Company, 51, 302
Buchanan, James, 251

Caldicott, Thomas Ford, 179-180, 182-184, 205-212, 282, 300, 308
Camilla, 87, 92-93
Campbell, Ann, 81-82, 243
Campbell, Alexander, 156, 204, 299
Campbell, Thomas, 156
Candie, William, 79, 243, 300
Canongate, Edinburgh, 29, 313
Carey, William, 51, 302
Carfrae, Thomas, 114-115, 211, 246, 249, 251, 299, 300, 301, 308
Carter, John, 164, 186, 188, 194, 213-214, 220-222, 224, 234, 284
Cathcart, Robert, 214, 284, 301, 307
Chalmers, Thomas, 208-209
Chinguacousy Township, Upper Canada, 132, 133, 169, 212, 259, 294, 300
cholera epidemic of 1832, 188-190
Christian, Washington, 17, 222
church—Canada—Anglican, 102, 107-109, 136, 139, 145, 178
church—Canada—Baptist, 10, 15-17, 116, 124, 153-155, 181, 194, 198, 206, 210, 239
church—Canada—Church of Christ Disciples, 10, 93, 134, 156, 201, 203, 214, 299, 309
church—Canada—Methodist, 90, 109, 115, 145
church—Canada—Scottish Kirk, 195

church—Scotland—Baptist, 9, 11, 16, 80-81, 116, 153-155, 181, 210
church—Scotland—Scottish Kirk, 23, 28, 140
Colonial Advocate, 134-135, 141-143, 148, 161, 167, 180, 198, 259, 306
Colonial Baptist Missionary Society, 224, 234, 300
Common Schools, 118, 119, 143-145
Coombs, William H., 233, 234, 300

Dearborn, Henry, 109
Dewar, Alexander, 60-61, 301, 313
Dewar, John, 194
Duncan, John, 102-103

Edwards, Jonathan, 37, 159-160
emigration to Canada, 88-90, 106, 189
Eramosa Township, Upper Canada, 132, 133-135, 299
Errett, Henry, 251, 258, 312
Esquesing Township, Upper Canada, 123, 124, 125, 127, 133, 134-135, 169, 173, 180, 194, 230, 294, 302, 304, 309, 312

Family Compact, 107, 141, 222
First Nation peoples of Upper Canada, 123, 173
FitzGibbon, Colonel James, 142
Fort York, 102
Fyfe, Robert Alexander, 18, 145, 198, 201, 212-213, 214, 230, 236, 239, 301, 314
Fyfe, Thomas, 125, 173, 194, 245, 301

Garie, James, 76
General Assembly of the Church of Scotland, 49, 139
George, Samuel, 221
Glas, John, 67
Great Awakening, 37, 159-160

Haldane, James Alexander
  baptism, 66-68, 305
  influence in Alexander Stewart's (minister at Moulin) conversion, 31-33
  ministry of, 9, 44-50, 55, 57, 62, 63, 71, 76, 80, 81, 95, 114, 147, 157, 235, 302, 311, 312, 313
  Society for Propagating the Gospel, 48-50
Haldane, Robert
  ministry of, 51, 67, 71, 80, 81, 84, 147, 235-236, 298, 302
  Theological Seminary, 9, 19, 51-55, 57, 60, 61, 76-77, 298 301, 302, 310, 312, 315
Harris, James, 173, 195, 198, 303
Hewitt, William, 170, 178-179, 284, 303
Hogg, James, 117
Hogg, Thomas, 116-117
Hume, David, 46
Humphrey, Caleb, 186
Hutchison, William, 59, 303

Inverness, Scotland, 49, 58, 60, 301
Jacobite Rebellion, 25
Jarvis Street Baptist Church, 10, 13, 15, 17, 18, 24, 237, 239, 240, 304, 307

Kendrick, Nathaniel, 111
Ketchum, Jesse, 142
Killiecrankie, Scotland, 25, 26, 27
King's College (University of Toronto), 145, 314
Knox Presbyterian Church, York, 219, 303

Laidlaw, James, 103-104, 116, 125, 134-135, 245, 304
Langley, William, 284, 304
Lesslie, Edward, 64, 304
Lesslie, James, 64, 179, 189-190, 284, 304

Lambton, John George (Lord Durham), 107-108
Logierait, Scotland, 23-25, 26, 28, 43, 87, 313, 314
London, Upper Canada, 133, 196
Long Point, Upper Canada, 111
Lothian, John, 83, 244, 304

MacGregor, Rob Roy, 25
Mackenzie, Hon. Alexander, 24
Mackenzie, William Lyon, 134-135, 141-143, 148, 198, 199, 222, 294, 306
Maitland, Sir Peregrine, 107, 116, 123, 124, 143, 247, 249, 308, 314
March Street Baptist Church, 64, 145, 177, 186-188, 190, 193-194, 195, 197, 198, 201-204, 205-206, 210-215, 219-225, 233, 234, 236-237, 283, 299, 300, 301, 304, 307, 308, 311, 312, 314, 315
Maxwell, John Eglinton, 13, 186, 205-215, 220-222, 284, 308, 315
McCord, Andrew Taylor, 284, 305
McDearmid, Allan, 96
McDougal, Peter, 96
McFarlane, John, 79, 80, 83, 244, 304, 305, 307, 312
McIntosh, Ann Jane, 179, 230, 306
McIntosh Catherine, 179, 230, 306
McIntosh, Catherine Oswald Stewart
 birth, 53-54
 children, 179, 230, 306
 death, 179-180, 231, 232
 life, 61, 87, 180, 305
 marriage, 136, 306
McIntosh, Ellen or Helen Baxter Ferguson, 231, 306
McIntosh, John, 136, 162, 180, 230, 231, 305-306
McIntosh, John Jr., 19, 230, 306
McKillican, William, 90, 96
McLean, Donald, 134
McMaster, William, 16, 203-204, 214, 234, 284, 307
McNaughton, Peter, 83, 151, 244, 307
McRobbie, John, 76-79, 244, 307, 310, 312
Menzies, John, 13, 93, 95, 113-116, 118, 119, 123-125, 127-129, 131, 134, 134, 136, 173, 230, 244, 249, 252, 299, 302, 304, 309, 312
Mitchell, James "William", 170, 178-179, 284, 309-310
Montreal, Lower Canada, 92-93, 97, 101, 113-114, 222, 287, 299, 303, 309
Mosley, Henry, 171-172, 177, 179, 284, 310
Moulin, Scotland, 9, 23-39, 43-44, 57, 59, 71, 82, 87, 195-196, 313, 314

Necropolis Cemetary, Toronto, 180, 231, 232, 299, 305, 313, 316
New York, 251, 252, 312
New York State, 111, 221, 308
Norval, Upper Canada, 123-129, 131, 133, 134, 136, 153, 302, 304, 309, 312-313

Oliphant, David Sr., 134
Orme, William, 52, 76-77, 307, 310, 312
Orr, James, 284, 310
Ovington, William, 251, 258, 312

Parson, Timothy, 182, 206, 209, 211, 284, 311
Paterson, David, 163, 164, 285, 311
Paterson, Johanna Carfrae, 210-212, 220, 308
Paterson, John, 163, 311
Paterson, Peter Jr., 163, 311
Paterson, Peter, 163, 170, 171, 178-179, 182, 186, 206, 209, 214, 230, 284, 311
Perth Baptist Church, 75-85, 87-90, 97, 150, 151, 153, 243-244, 300, 304, 305, 307, 311, 312

Potter's Field Cemetary, York, 180, 232, 305, 311, 313, 315
Proudfoot, William, 178, 195-197
Pullar, Robert, 79, 244, 311

Rebellion of 1837, 222, 229, 306
Reid, Hugh, 211, 285
Rintoul, William, 195-196
Roaf, John, 222, 232, 311-312
Robert III, 25
Robinson, John Beverley, 104
Roots, Peter P., 111
Rose, Walter, 163-164
Rutherford, Peter, 16, 203, 214, 285

St. George's Masonic Lodge (Market Lane Hall), 163-164, 165, 171, 213, 220
St. James Anglican Church, York, 109, 136, 314
Sandeman, Robert, 67
Scott, Mr., 179
Scott, Margaret, 23
Simcoe, John Graves, 102
Simeon, Charles, 31-33, 313
Smith, Adam, 46
Smith, James, 246, 247-258
Stalker, John, 76-80, 151, 244, 304, 305, 307, 310, 312
Stephens, Thomas, 110, 114, 125, 128, 134, 246, 247-258, 312
Stewart, Alexander [1764-1821]
  conversion, 29-32
  Moulin revival, 32-39, 44

Stewart, Alexander [1774-1840]
  baptism, 68
  Baptist church at Perth, 75-85, 87-90, 97, 150, 151, 153, 243-244, 300, 304, 305, 307, 311, 312
  Baptist church at Norval, 127-129, 134-136
  Baptist church at York (1818-1820), 114-120
  Baptist church at York (1826-1840), 161-214
  Bible Society (Perth), 81
  Bible Society (York), 172-173, 227-229, 287-289
  birth, 23-25
  call to the ministry, 39, 43-44, 50, 90, 97
  Campbellism, 203-204
  character, 71, 81, 85, 90, 131, 167, 174, 181, 194-197, 207-209, 227, 232
  conversion, 36-39
  death, 230-234
  emigration to Canada, 87-93
  hymns, 158-159, 235, 279-282
  itinerant ministry Upper Canada, 90-92, 125-127, 131
  license to marry & register, 167, 178-179
  marriage, 43
  missionary station—Avoch, 59-61
  missionary station—Elgin, 61-62
  missionary station—Kingussie, 59
  missionary tour 1812, 80-85
  resignation, 214-215
  secular employment, 106, 118, 124-125, 161
  theological training, 43, 51-55
  views on baptism, 63, 68-72, 119, 132, 141, 156, 236-237, 259-278
  views on bibliology, 53, 72, 148-149
  views on Canada as a mission field, 90-92, 96, 102, 110-111
  views on ecclesiology, 54, 66, 79-80, 108, 116-117, 127-128, 139-141, 153-158
  views on eschatology, 158-160
  views on itinerant ministry, 57, 75, 85, 118-119
  views on missions, 50, 80-81, 90-92, 126, 237-238
  views on politics, 106-108, 140,

142-143, 174
views on revival, 37-38
views on soteriology (salvation), 50, 54, 61, 79, 146, 149-153
views on theological training, 53-54

Stewart, Alexander Jr., 87, 313
Stewart, Anabil, 23
Stewart, Hellen, 23
Stewart, James [b.1764], 23
Stewart, James Jr.
  birth, 60-61
  death, 136, 232, 313
Stewart, James Sr., 23
Stewart, Janet, 23
Stewart, Janet Douglass
  birth, 43, 313
  conversion, 43, 313
  death, 44, 313
Stewart, John, 23
Stewart, Margaret, 23
Strachan, John, 102, 109, 136, 143, 144, 186, 314

Tapscott, Samuel, 221-223, 314
The Great Disruption, 303
The Society for Propogating the Gospel at Home, 48-49, 298, 301, 302
Thomson, Alexander, 179, 285, 315
Tost, Henry, 184-185, 186, 213, 221, 234, 285, 315
Turner, James, 186
Types Riot, 141-142

War of 1812, 102, 104, 109, 110, 142, 197, 305
Watson, Richard, 163, 164
Wemyss, Thomas, 52, 315
Wenham, Joseph, 16, 169, 170, 178-179, 182, 184, 186, 206, 285, 309, 315
Wooster, Hezekiah Calvin, 109

York (Toronto), Upper Canada, 11, 97, 101-112, 113-120, 123, 124, 133, 136, 139, 141-146, 148, 153, 154, 155, 160, 163, 167-174, 177-179, 182, 188-190, 193, 195-196, 197, 230, 245, 249, 252, 283, 300-315
York Auxiliary Bible Society, 172-174, 215, 227, 229, 232, 287-289, 299, 302, 303, 305
York Commercial and Classical Academy, 206, 300, 308
York Mills Baptist Church, 170, 310
Yorston, Robert, 170, 179, 285, 315

Other titles available from Joshua Press...

When God walked on campus
A brief history of evangelical awakenings at American colleges and universities
By Michael F. Gleason

HERE ARE SOME accounts of revivals in the past two centuries that will whet your appetite for the transforming work of God's Spirit on campuses today. From the halls of Princeton, Yale, Harvard, Dartmouth, Bethel, Wheaton, Trinity, Ashland, and many others, comes stories of awakening and revival. On both secular and Christian campuses, the moving of God was evident as men and women were converted and stirred to ministry and foreign service. Out of these awakenings came the formation of many of the student and campus fellowships still at work today.

JOSHUA PRESS / ISBN 1-894400-16-X

Friendship
By Hugh Black

THE HIGH IDEAL to which friendship was held by the ancient writers seems to be an obsolete sentiment today. Western society, with its busyness and self-centredness, to many people, feels like a cold and lonely place. In this culture of cynicism and malaise Hugh Black directs our attention to the importance of friendship and the blessing that it can be. He addresses the challenges and responsibilities associated with friendship including the tragic consequences of wrecked friendships. He defines the limitations of friendship but also highlights the blessings it can bring. In true friendship, accountability and love inspire us to live with more honour, integrity and grace. Ultimately, we see that in Jesus Christ we can have that "higher friendship," which revolutionizes the way we live, the way we think and the things we value.

JOSHUA PRESS
ISBN 978-1-894400-28-2 (HDBK) / ISBN 978-1-894400-27-5 (PBK)

Deo Optimo et Maximo Gloria
To God, best and greatest, be glory

www.joshuapress.com

www.ingramcontent.com/pod-product-compliance
Lightning Source LLC
Chambersburg PA
CBHW032033150426
43194CB00006B/255